The Essential
BICYCLE
COMMUTER

Trudy E. Bell

RAGGED MOUNTAIN PRESS • CAMDEN, MAINE

NEW YORK • SAN FRANCISCO • WASHINGTON, D.C. • AUCKLAND • BOGOTÁ • CARACAS • LISBON
LONDON • MADRID • MEXICO CITY • MILAN • MONTREAL • NEW DELHI • SAN JUAN
SINGAPORE • SYDNEY • TOKYO • TORONTO

To Jerry Schad and David Pope,
mentors in inspiration for both writing and life,
and—ever—to Roxana

International Marine/
Ragged Mountain Press

A Division of The McGraw·Hill Companies

2 4 6 8 10 9 7 5 3 1

Copyright © 1998 by Trudy E. Bell.

Library of Congress Cataloging-in-Publication Data

Bell, Trudy E.
The essential bicycle commuter / by Trudy E. Bell
p. cm.
Includes bibliographical references and index.
ISBN 0-07-005503-3 (pbk.)
1. Bicycle commuting.   2. Bicycles—Maintenance and repair.   I. Title.
HE5736.B45   1998
388.3'472—dc21   97-37886
CIP

Questions regarding the content of this book should be addressed to:
Ragged Mountain Press, P.O. Box 220, Camden, ME 04843
www.books.mcgraw-hill.com

Questions regarding the ordering of this book should be addressed to:
The McGraw-Hill Companies, Customer Service Department, P.O. Box 547, Blacklick, OH 43004
Retail customers: 1-800-262-4729, Bookstores: 1-800-722-4726

Printed by Quebecor Printing, Fairfield, PA
Edited by John Kettlewell, Tom McCarthy, Larry Floersch
Technical review by James Ostergard
Design by John Reinhardt
Illustrated by Brad Ford
Photographs by Trudy E. Bell, unless otherwise specified
Production by Dan Kirchoff, Deborah Krampf, and Shannon Thomas

CONTENTS

Dennis Coello

With a Little Help from My Friends

The United States is a big country and the challenges faced by bicycle commuters in terms of terrain, traffic patterns, attitudes of motorists, weather, and other conditions differ enormously and surprisingly. Thus, this book relies heavily on long interviews with seasoned bicycle commuters —some of whom are well-known in bicycling circles from other regions of the country: Jim Arth (who has bicycle commuted in Illinois, New York City, and Florida); my brother, John K. Bell (northern and southern California); Dennis Coello (Utah and Missouri); Michael Leccese (Washington, D.C. and Colorado); and Jerry Schad (northern and southern California).

Many other bicycle commuters unwittingly contributed to this book as well, through my recollections of informal conversations with them— some of them years before I knew I was even going to write a book. Notable among them are a former Ragged Mountain Press editor John Kettlewell (Maine), John King (New Jersey), Arlene Plevin (Washington, D.C. and Baltimore), Richard Shuldiner (New York City), and Elly Spangenberg (New York City). Two professional bicycle mechanics who taught me a great deal, some of which is in this book, are Brad Ford (New Jersey)—who is also this book's illustrator—and Les Welch (Virginia). And for both mechanical advice and eye-opening commuting tips (especially from people

commuting on recumbents or in Alaskan and Canadian winters), I wish to thank the scores of participants in the VeloNet list servers commute-logistics, safety-n-education, and facilities-n-planning@cycling.org. There is a tremendous wealth of wisdom and good-hearted sharing of it out there on the Internet: All you have to do to learn is just read ("lurk").

For tips on photography, I wish to thank professional photographers Dennis Coello and Karl Esch; whatever I've done right in the pictures, I owe to them, but all mistakes are my own. For hands-on help in photography—including some uncomfortable hours in snow and slush, I thank Craig B. Waff. For development of film and prints, I thank Eddie and his crew at Graphic Labs in New York City and Kevin Lytle and Margaleet Sweeney at Ritz Camera in Cleveland.

For being a child model (as well as a model child), I wish to thank my daughter Roxana K. Bell. For her listening ear and occasional child care, I thank my mother, Arabella J. Bell. For allowing me so much writer's seclusion in guest rooms, I thank Copeland Oaks.

I wish also to thank the editors at Ragged Mountain Press for their patience in waiting for the manuscript and their faith that it would be worth the wait.

—Trudy E. Bell

Introduction: Why Commute by Bicycle?

It started with true love. In 1983, a man I was dating helped me buy a second-hand bicycle so we could go riding on weekends like a couple of kids. I hadn't been astride a bicycle since 1971, when I had moved from California to New York City, but to my surprise the old adage was true: Once you've learned to ride, you never forget how. Soon we were taking day-long tours.

And as much as I shuddered when watching bicycle commuters brave the traffic in midtown Manhattan, I found myself wondering whether I could pedal to work instead of squeezing onto the bus or subway. After all, it was only three miles.

The first time I tried riding down Second Avenue in rush-hour gridlock, I was so unnerved I had to rest for a couple of days before trying it again. And a low-speed crash into an iron fence suggested that maybe a helmet would be a smart idea. Eventually I learned all kinds of tricks for urban riding—some helpful tips from seasoned commuters and much from my own experiences.

Within a couple of years, my bicycle had become my sole mode of transportation in New York City. I even rode it to press conferences, church, and parties. I absolutely loved it. Riding to work woke me up in the morning and turned the daily chore of commuting into a joy. Only ice and snow could make me leave my bike at home. How much a part of my life the bicycle had become was driven home once by a colleague. When we encountered a friend of hers on the sidewalk, she introduced me by saying: "This is Trudy Bell, and this is Trudy's bicycle. It follows her everywhere."

Later I lived in a New Jersey suburb and telecommuted three days a week. But the bicycle was still my workhorse for grocery shopping, lunchtime errands, and conveying my daughter to and from school. Now that I am again commuting to an office (in Cleveland, Ohio), the bicycle is once again my weekday transportation.

It can be yours, too.

According to a 1990 Harris survey conducted for *Bicycling* magazine, there are some three million Americans who commute to and from work by bicycle. And they have many tangible reasons.

Saves Big Money

Bicycle commuting can save you remarkably large sums of money, depending on the local cost of car insurance, tolls, gasoline, parking fees, or public transportation fares. In a high-cost area such as New York City, where the average monthly parking fee is $250 to $400 and car insurance runs upward of $2,000 per year, a car can set you back $5,000 per year, even before you pay for a car loan, gasoline, and maintenance. (That's why most New York City residents don't own cars.)

Even commuting by bus or subway runs $1.50 per trip, or $750 per year if done round-trip five days a week. That's the one-time cost of a decent bicycle with all the accessories. Even in lower-cost suburbs, regular bicycle commuting can allow a two-car family to become a one-car family, with attendant savings in upkeep and insurance—not to mention the freeing up of garage space.

Reduces Parking Problems

Commuting by bicycle reduces parking problems. In fact, you might be able to lock your bike closer to a building than you could park a car or get off of public transportation. At work, you might even be able to keep the bicycle in your office or in some designated bicycle parking area.

Can Be Faster

In certain circumstances, bicycle commuting may be more direct and possibly even faster than commuting by automobile or public transportation. If your bicycle commuting route takes you on little-traveled suburban roads or cuts through a park, you may be able to bypass all the busy thoroughfares with their tailgating rush-hour motorists trying to beat red lights.

Can Be Safer

For people with certain handicaps, bicycle commuting may be safer than driving. One bicycle commuter of my acquaintance rides because he suffers from narcolepsy—a neurological condition that overwhelms him with uncontrollable sleep when his body is relatively immobile, as in a car. With the constant activity of pedaling and the fresh air in his face, he feels safer in traffic on a bicycle than behind the wheel.

Improves Car-Driving Skills

One little-known benefit of bicycle commuting is that it actually improves your defensive alertness and skills when driving a car. On a bicycle, you have to be aware of so much: whether a driver coming up behind you intends to turn right at the

In some places, such as Southern California, bicycle commuters can ride on the marked shoulder of an interstate highway.

next corner in front of you; whether an oncoming car with its left turn signal blinking intends to cut in front of oncoming traffic (including you); whether some car on a cross street may try to race through the intersection even though the light for you has just turned green; whether pedestrians are aware of your presence; whether a child or a dog might dart from between parked cars . . . the list goes on. If you ride a lot, the anticipatory awareness needed makes you a more defensive and considerate driver as well as a safer cyclist.

Reduces Pollution

Bicycle commuting reduces air pollution. Among other things, that can help your employer meet new state and federal regulations about encouraging employees in carpooling and alternative transportation. It might even earn you a free bicycle. In southern California, for example, some companies buy bicycles for their employees to use for commuting; if the employees ride to and from work for at least several months, the bike is theirs.

Not only that, bicycle commuting can reduce *your* exposure to pollutants, especially in bumper-to-bumper traffic when each motorist is right up next to the exhaust pipe in front.

Increases Fitness

Bicycle commuting is a natural and time-efficient way to squeeze fitness into a busy schedule. A commute as short as three miles each way amounts to more than 1,000 miles per year, even if done only eight months out of the year. A commute of ten miles each way, if ridden ten months out of the year, totals 4,000 miles in the saddle.

To be sure, it may take you one to two hours each day to pedal a twenty-mile round-trip, depending on the terrain, the traffic, your physical condition, and your riding style. But during an average twenty-mile round-trip commute in rush-hour traffic, you might be sitting behind the wheel for an hour anyway. According to Doug Foy, Director of the Conservation Law Foundation, in a forty-year career, the average auto commuter spends about four years sitting in traffic. With an hour or so bicycle ride to work and back, you can arrive home with a fairly good workout already under your belt.

If family responsibilities eliminate dedicated workout time after work or long rides on the weekend, the problem of squeezing exercise into a day is even more pressing. Here again, you can get creative about substituting bicycling for driving as much as possible. Need to go grocery shopping, stop at the post office and bank, or pick up your kid at the sitter? Those errands are easily done on a bike. In fact, in a standard 25-mph suburban community, you'll spend little more time using a bicycle than you would taking a car, and you may get five to twenty miles of pedaling exercise.

Relaxes Job Tensions

Bicycling at the end of the work day helps you to relax from a demanding job so you don't take your problems home. In the words of Dennis Coello, who commuted by bicycle to and from the junior high school in Missouri at which he taught, "I found I needed that fifteen miles home on the bike as a physical release of dealing with seventh- and eighth-graders each day."

It's Fun!

Most of all, bicycle commuting is a blast! As aptly put by Florida commuter Jim Arth, "The worst day on a bike is better than the best day in a car."

Part One

EQUIPMENT

Chapter One
CHOOSING A COMMUTER BICYCLE

*Bicycle commuters ride everything from 30-year-old clunkers to the latest models,
as evidenced by this commuter rack in Urbana, Illinois.*

What You *Don't* Need

Contrary to the advertising hype that suggests you need a specialized bike for every purpose, the best bicycle for commuting is likely to be the one you already have. It could be a 1960-vintage three-speed English racer or this year's carbon fiber and epoxy twenty-one-speed road racer. Commuters have used them all. So try using whatever bike you already have to see what you like and don't like about it for commuting.

After several months of daily commuting, you'll either be happy with what you own or you'll know specifically what you'd like to change. If its gearing, tires, handling, or load-carrying capability don't meet your needs, try modifying them as suggested here. Alternatively, go shopping for a new bike and customize it to be exactly what you want.

If your needs and preferences guide you to an unorthodox solution—even one against common practice—more power to you. Stick to your guns even if the pros at your favorite bike shop express doubts about your specifications. After all, you are the one who will be riding it every day.

If storage space is at a premium or if your bike must meet certain size regulations to travel with you on public transportation during rush hour, you might want to consider a folding bicycle. Several bikes of ingenious design not only fold but also have a ride that feels like that of a standard bike (see page 8).

No matter what type of bike you use, it must be sturdy, durable, and reliable. On a daily basis this machine will face a number of hazards: being ridden over broken glass that works its way into the tires, into potholes that challenge the truing of the wheels, in rain that sprays grit onto the chain and between the brake pads and rims, and through corrosive slush on roads salted in the winter to melt snow and ice. It may also be locked up outside and thus exposed to hours of the sun's ultraviolet radiation, which will age the saddle's leather and the frame's paint.

Types of Standard Bicycles

Time was, the biggest choice in buying a two-wheeler was the color. No more. Bicycles now have highly specific designs depending on what kind of riding people enjoy.

Don't think that the distinctions are so subtle that only an expert could tell. Once for a forty-mile ride I traded bicycles with a strong rider. He used my mid-range sport-touring bicycle so I could try out his high-end ultralight Masi road racer with sew-up tires. At the end of the day, I was charging up hills at 15 mph and ready for another forty miles, while my well-muscled, well-conditioned companion couldn't understand why after such a short ride he was lagging behind and feeling like road kill. That's the dramatic difference equipment can make.

It's because of this specialization that avid cyclists who enjoy different types of riding often own two or more bicycles. (There are even gearheads who own a dozen or more and who joke about being members of the Bike of the Month Club or Bike-Buyers Anonymous.)

If you haven't owned a bike since you were a kid and thus have no clue what kind of recreational riding you like, start out with an all purpose steed that will serve you well on your commute. For most first-time buyers who will be commuting over average roads in average weather, a safe and relatively inexpensive choice would be a hybrid (a cross between a touring bike and a mountain bike). Even if later you decide to upgrade to a different machine for weekend recreational riding, you'll still have your serviceable standby for getting to and from work.

If you have special conditions on the commute, you might want to consider one of the more specialized bicycles. For example, if you regularly need to carry heavy loads up hills, consider a dedicated touring bike with its super-low gearing. If your area has exceptionally rough roads or year-round rainfall, consider a mountain bike with its fat, knobby tires. If you don't need to carry much, the roads are well-maintained, and you have congenial weather year-round, consider a sport or racing bike for minimum rolling resistance and maximum speed.

Racing/Triathlon Bicycles

If road racing or triathlons are your pastime and you're commuting partly to keep in condition, then maintaining a consistent riding position on one bicycle whether training or commuting may be of paramount importance. Commute then on the lightest, most responsive, drop-handlebar road racing or triathlon bike you can find. The narrow, high-pressure tires offer minimum rolling resistance and make your commute effortless fun.

The fun on a racing bike can stop, though, if you must carry heavy items (laptop computer, publications, tools) to and from work. Many racing frames do not have the necessary threaded eyelets (drilled metal projections from the front fork and rear triangle) for attaching racks, so you must plan to carry stuff some other way.

If you can attach racks and panniers to the frame, keep in mind that the short wheelbase and upright angles of the seat tube (where the seat attaches) and head tube (where the front fork and handlebars attach), which give a racing bike its nimble handling, can make the thing feel skittish and bad-tempered when under load. Moreover, you may find that even the lowest gears are too high to carry the weight comfortably up hills. Also, road racers and triathlon bikes do not have enough clearance around the brakes to allow for fenders in wet weather.

Road Touring Bicycles

If your idea of a great vacation is long-distance, multiday, independent touring complete with tent and sleeping bag, you already have a great commuter bike. A genuine touring bicycle has a frame whose geometry is designed to be stable and comfortable while carrying significant weight at any speed: This means a longer wheelbase and more laid-back angles for the seat tube and head tube.

A touring bike is equipped with all kinds of threaded eyelets and other conveniences for mounting front and rear racks and panniers. It has a triple chainring that offers low gears for climbing hills. It may have drop handlebars to allow your hands to rest in many positions and to allow you to bend forward to reduce your resistance in a headwind. It has sturdy wheels with spokes that resist breaking when ridden over rough roads under a load, and middle-width, moderate-pressure tires that offer a good balance between low rolling resistance and adequate

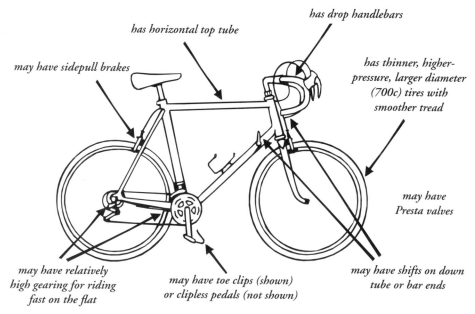

has drop handlebars

has horizontal top tube

may have sidepull brakes

has thinner, higher-pressure, larger diameter (700c) tires with smoother tread

may have Presta valves

may have relatively high gearing for riding fast on the flat

may have toe clips (shown) or clipless pedals (not shown)

may have shifts on down tube or bar ends

A typical road bicycle can offer fast, efficient commuting in dry conditions.

security over gravel and dirt. It usually has enough clearance around the brakes for lightweight plastic fenders, if desired.

Road Sport Bicycles

If you enjoy day or "credit card" touring with light loads and want maximum comfort for the long haul with a bit of the thrill of riding a racing bike, try a road sport or sport-touring bicycle. Road sport bikes combine certain features of a racing bike with those of a touring bike. Like a racing bike, a road sport bike has lightweight wheels and narrow tires for minimum rolling resistance. Like a touring bike, it has a slightly longer wheelbase and more relaxed angles for comfort and stable handling, a triple chainring that offers low gears, and, possibly, threaded dropouts for front and rear racks.

Be aware, though, that like a racing bike, a road sport or sport-touring bicycle is not designed for carrying full panniers. Get out on the road to test how the one you like handles under a heavy load at high speed. For example, my sport-touring bike, when fully loaded, develops a wicked shimmy at precisely 34 mph.

Mountain Bicycles

If off-road riding is your love, a mountain bike makes an excellent commuting bike. It's especially advisable if your commute takes you along dirt trails, gravel or severely rutted roads, or sandy beach fronts where narrow road tires would be skittish or bog down altogether.

The lower-pressure tires on mountain bikes are more resistant to flats than higher-pressure road tires. The wider tires, which also are made of thicker rubber, tend to wrap around a sharp object rather than presenting a drum-tight surface that is easily punctured; their deeper tread also increases their surface area for aggressive grip. These very characteristics, however, increase the tires' rolling resistance, so a mountain bike demands noticeably greater pedaling effort than a road bike on smooth roads. Thus, don't go for the fattest tires just for the knobby look. You could explore the possibility of two sets of wheels with quick-release hubs for easy changes—smoother, narrower tires for your commuting and an off-road set.

The high-leverage cantilever or cam brakes on mountain bikes afford reliable stopping power even in rain or slush, which is important if you want a bike suitable for all-weather riding or if you live in an area (such as the Pacific Northwest) where rainfall is high year-round. Mountain bikes can be equipped with fenders, splash guards, or mud guards.

Older mountain bikes had roadbike-sized frames with a touring geometry; most mountain bikes today have

may have slanted top tube and smaller frame than road bike for same rider

has upright handlebars

has high-leverage brakes

has extra-long seat post

has fatter, lower-pressure 26-inch diameter tires with deeper tread

has lower gearing (smaller chain wheels) and may have an alpine (granny) gear for hill-climbing

may have platform pedals

has Schrader valves

A typical mountain bicycle can allow for secure traction, even in rain and snow.

small frames with slanted top tubes and a racing or BMX-style geometry for a sprightly ride and quick handling.

A wide selection of lower-cost mountain bikes do not have suspension systems; like most other bicycles, they rely on the air in the tires and the rider's knees for cushioning bumps. Higher-end mountain bikes come equipped with front or dual suspension systems (oil-damped elastomer springs or some other system on the front fork and possibly the rear triangle). For commuting, a suspension system is overkill unless you really do ford rivers or crawl over rocks and logs on your way to work.

Hybrid Bicycles

The closest thing to an all-purpose bicycle is a cross or hybrid bicycle, so named because it combines features from a touring bike and a mountain bike.

A hybrid bicycle's frame, like that of a touring bicycle, is larger than a mountain bike's and it has no suspension. It may be fitted with either drop or straight handlebars, depending on whether you prefer to ride in an aerodynamic tuck (as do some touring cyclists) or sitting upright (as do most mountain bikers). Its handling remains stable while carrying loads, it has a good range of low gears, and it has the stopping power of the cantilever brakes found on mountain bikes. It has a touring bike's somewhat narrower wheels and tires for lighter weight and lower rolling resistance, so it's less work to ride on pavement than the average mountain bike, but it still won't flinch at gravel, potholes, or the occasional curb.

Note that a so-called "commuter" or "city" bike is usually no more than a regular cross or hybrid bike marketed with accessories useful for commuting, such as fenders, lights, and racks. But such accessories can be installed on many other bicycles, so don't feel you need to have a "commuter" or "city" bike for commuting. Indeed, you will have more choice for custom-

izing a bike to your taste if you buy the bike first and then choose the accessories separately.

Cruisers

The cruiser, the one-speed clunker of the 1950s that kids traded in when they upgraded to a ten-speed in the 1960s, is enjoying a resurgence of nostalgic popularity. Cruiser replicas come already outfitted with a rear rack, fenders, and a chain guard, which is a nice feature for keeping chain grease off your lower leg or long pants. Dozens of models are inexpensive: $160 to $300.

Be forewarned, however: There's a good reason kids of yore traded up to derailleur bikes for riding any kind of distance. The high-tensile-steel frame of a cruiser—especially of the cheaper models—is heavy, the low-pressure balloon tires offer a lot of rolling resistance; the fixed gear is high and can be hard on the knees on even a modest incline; the wide, upright handlebars cause the wind to catch you right in the chest; and the wide, spring-suspended saddle does not afford full leg extension. More serious are problems inherent with the coaster brake. It does not stop the bike as quickly as hand brakes; when you step off the pedals at a stop, the coaster brake is instantly disengaged and the bicycle can start to roll; and if the chain should fall off, you have no brake at all. Higher-end models may come with caliper brakes, an internal, multispeed rear wheel hub, or even a six-speed freewheel (sprocket assembly) with derailleur. But now you're talking a $500 model, and you're still getting a heavy bike with low gears that are inadequate for real hills.

Unless looking cool in a retro kind of way is a high priority while commuting, stick with a hybrid, mountain, or touring bike for greater functionality at the same price. If you really long to relive your childhood, rent a cruiser for a week at a resort and do some five- to ten-mile rides to see what your knees think before buying one for daily transportation.

Accessories can be installed on many types of bicycles, so don't feel you need to have a "commuter" or "city" bike for commuting.

Recumbents

A recumbent is a bicycle on which you sit upright or even lie back, as in an easy chair, and pedal with your legs stretched out in front of you. The handlebars may be above the seat (giving you, in some models, the feel of steering a Harley-Davidson motorcycle) or below the seat (where your arms come to rest naturally).

You might want to consider a recumbent bicycle if you just can't be comfortable on any standard bicycle. They have been known to give relief to people with lower-back, shoulder, or neck ailments that make it painful to ride with the body forward and the head bent back, and to people with carpal tunnel syndrome who cannot support their weight on the heels of their hands as they must on the handlebars of a standard bicycle.

Recumbent tricycles offer particular advantages in slippery conditions as well as for riders with balance problems or for those who like very low gears (where the riding pace is exceptionally slow).

On a recumbent, the rider's head position is slightly lower than where it is on a standard bicycle—roughly at the same level as that of a driver of an average compact car. Commuters with recumbent bicycles report, however, that the ability to see and be seen is actually enhanced, though it's more difficult to look to the rear on a recumbent. First, the upright sitting position gives you a completely unobstructed and panoramic view of the road and landscape, as if you were piloting a motorcycle or sportscar with the top down. Second, there's the "funny bike" factor: Motorists tend to slow down and gawk at the unusual machine, giving you a wider berth and passing with greater care.

There is such an astonishing variety of recumbent designs that some are almost unrecognizable as bicycles. In general, their wheels are smaller in diameter than those of a standard bicycle so your feet can rest flat on the ground when you stop. Some designs have two 20-inch or two 16-inch wheels while others have a 27-inch, 700 C, 26-inch, 24-inch, or 20-inch wheel in the rear and a smaller wheel in the front. Most are road bikes, but some are designed for racing (one model won the DuPont prize for breaking 65 mph and another set a Race Across America speed record of five days and one hour).

Recumbents are classed according to their wheelbase measurement: short wheelbase (33 to 39

Short-wheelbase recumbent with under-seat steering and wheels 26" and 20"

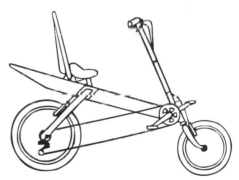

Compact long-wheelbase recumbent with above-seat steering and wheels 20" and 16"

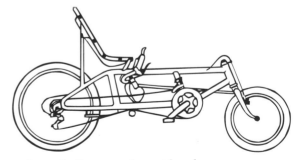

Long-wheelbase recumbent with under-seat steering and wheels 26" and 20"

Recumbent bicycles may offer comfortable commuting to people who just can't be comfortable on any standard upright bicycle.

inches), where the crankset is in front of the head tube and the front wheel is under the legs of the rider; medium wheelbase (40 to 46 inches); long wheelbase (60 to 72 inches or more), where the front wheel is in front of the crankset; and compact long wheelbase (50 to 59 inches), which has a higher seat and smaller wheels.

The short-wheelbase models are very compact, fitting most bike racks, elevators, and small cars, but their quick, unpredictable handling makes riding them somewhat tricky. Medium-wheelbase recumbents are nearly as compact and are more stable at high speed, and most have excellent weight distribution. Long-wheelbase models are extremely stable and do especially well for long-distance touring, but they are fairly heavy and will not fit in tight spaces or on standard car racks. Compact long-wheelbase models, although the rear wheel bears three-quarters of the rider's weight, are the easiest to ride and the most affordable—the "ultimate urban assault vehicle" for city commuting, according to Robert J. Bryant, editor of *Recumbent Cycling News*.

Few standard bicycle shops offer recumbents, especially with any variety. Instead, you'll probably have to travel to one of the specialty shops that will allow you to test-ride many models before you decide. (See Appendix II, page 162.)

Collapsible or Portable Bicycles

If your bicycle commuting is complicated by the need to carry your bike on public transportation during rush hour or up an elevator to your office, or if you want to beat the stiff airline surcharges for oversize baggage if your job calls for travel, you might want to consider a collapsible bike: one that folds or comes apart. Some collapsible bicycles have small wheels and look strange; others look like standard uprights or recumbents. Many work very well indeed.

You have quite a choice of characteristics, because the individual designers worked toward different goals and with different constraints. Note: If your commuting calls for appreciable riding over really rough roads or cobblestones, which are common in Europe as well as in older cities in the United States, you will likely prefer one of the bicycles with full-sized wheels; larger wheels can bridge the space between two cobbles, whereas smaller wheels tend to slide down between cobbles, making for a more difficult ride.

There is a wide variety of collapsible bicycles, including ones that are marketed in England and Germany. In addition to specialized bike shops, look for collapsibles in recreational vehicle (RV) stores, camping mail-order catalogs, and sites on the World Wide Web.

Green Gear Cycling

A collapsible bicycle, such as the Bike Friday, may allow you to take your bike on public transportation.

Well-known manufacturers include Bromption, C-Motion Cycles (high-end "no compromise" disassembling road racers, touring models, and off-road machines with standard-sized wheels), Dahon (entry-level three-speed or five-speed folders with 16-inch or 20-inch wheels), Nexus Bicycle Company (three-speed, five-speed, or seven-speed folders), Green Gear Cycling (semi-custom racers, tourers, and mountain bikes with 20-inch wheels and triple-crank low gearing), Montague (middle-range hybrid folders with standard 26-inch wheels), Moulton (high-end dissassemblers with 17-inch wheels), and Linear (folding recumbents).

Electric Bicycles

I know—we're supposed to be pedaling to work. But some people may feel their knees or heart need a little helpful "oomph" up a hill or into a headwind, especially on an exceptionally long commute. Or they may prefer to arrive at work without breaking a sweat, and pedal only on the way home.

Enter the—yes—electric bicycle. Since about 1994, sales of these vehicles have taken off. These are *not* the mopeds that older cyclists may recall from the 1970s, which were powered by internal combustion engines. (By the way, you can still get two-stroke and four-stroke engines for powering your bicycle—but that truly is turning a bicycle into a motorcycle and is thus outside the purview of this book.) Electric bicycles are available as upright road and mountain bicycles and as recumbents.

The designs of electric bicycles are rapidly changing as battery technology evolves. But here are some general observations that should remain useful for some time.

Electric bicycles seem to fall into two distinct camps. One camp comprises two-wheeled electric vehicles that—assuming the motor could be removed—may not ride like a real bicycle because the design was optimized for the placement of the electric motor. Many motorcycle makers and other high-tech companies—including Honda, Panasonic, Saigun, Sanyo, Suzuki, and Yamaha—have entered the market with at least one version of an electric bicycle. Many of these are intended for Asian markets, where the pollution from gas scooters is choking city air. Another primary market seems to be the over-50 crowd.

The other camp comprises genuine, preexisting bicycles equipped with an electric motor (which can be removed if desired). These latter bicycles are the only ones I will discuss.

The electrified real bicycles include the ElectriCruiser, an upright cruiser offered by ZAP (Zero Air Pollution) Power Systems of Sebastopol, California, and introduced through the Sharper Image catalog in 1996. Slung from the top tube near the saddle is a 12-volt, sealed, lead-acid battery that powers twin electric motors behind the seat tube. The motors, in turn, are joined by a knurled knob that presses down onto the rear tire to drive the bike; on downhills, the tire drives the knurled knob to recharge the battery through regenerative braking. There are two power settings: low (which will power the average rider along a flat road at about 11 mph with no pedaling) and high (19 mph under the same conditions). The motors are activated only as long as the rider holds down the thumb toggle. The bike's range is up to twenty miles, depending on the terrain, the rider, and the amount of pedaling. The battery can be recharged from an ordinary electric outlet in under three hours some 300 to 1,000 times, depending on the depth of the discharge. Replacement batteries are inexpensive (around $60). The company offers a quick-release battery system, which allows a rider to remove the battery and install a fresh one in a few seconds.

Zap ElectriCruiser hangs the battery from the top tube and anchors the motor in front of the rear wheel.

The battery (left) drives the motor (right), which has a knurled knob that presses on the rear tire.

The power system adds more than 20 pounds to the bike (for a total of 52 pounds for the Electri-Cruiser), but because of its position on the bike, that weight is less noticeable than you might expect. They're also working on developing a more efficient battery to reduce the weight or to get more juice from one of the same size. The power system delivers quite a kick (I tried it at a press conference). The big battery also allows the ElectriCruiser to be outfitted with a motorcycle-style headlight.

ZAP's ElectriCruiser comes standard with a rear rack, chain guard, and fenders, but with only six speeds: there's a rear derailleur but only a single large front chainwheel. If a person needs an electric motor for a bike, it seems to me the person could also benefit from lower gears. In my opinion, you would do better buying a twenty-one-speed bike of your choice from a bike shop and then retrofitting it with an electric motor, which ZAP also sells by itself.

The ZAP bicycles can be mail-ordered from their manufacturer, through Sharper Image, or purchased through—yes—*car* dealers, not bicycle shops.

In cooperation with the manufacturer of the BikeE recumbent, ZAP also offers an electric recumbent bicycle, predictably enough called the BikeE-lectric. It is available from Alternative Pedal Sports in Rancho Cucamonga, California.

Note: If you insist on feeling the wind through your hair, forget getting an electric bicycle—at least if you live in California. Effective January 1996, any rider of an electric bicycle "must wear a properly fitted and fastened helmet," and mandatory helmet laws for adult riders of electric bicycles are pending in other states.

For comprehensive, regularly updated, reports about electric bicycles, see *Bike Culture Quarterly*—a British publication that does comparative performance tests that cut through the hype. (See Appendix II, "Additional Resources," page 162.).

How Much Will It Cost?

There is a bicycle for every budget. High-end custom machines made of titanium can set a person back $5,000 to $8,000—and I'm sure you could spend more. The average decent bicycle, however, typically ranges from $500 to $800. Entry-level hybrids, mountain bikes, sport bikes, and cruisers can be had for under $300, with a few under $200. Accessories such as a helmet, gloves, and a rear rack will add at least another $100 to any purchase (see "Accessories for Safety and Comfort," page 35).

Recumbent bicycles are not inexpensive, primarily because they are such a small part of bicycle retailing. Most are still manufactured semi-custom by hand. Some may even be individually road tested before being shipped. Prices range from about $750 for a rock-bottom entry to more than $5,500, with the average being $1,000 to $2,500. But as recumbents become more popular, their prices are dropping. The BikeE-lectric recumbent runs around $1,250. The twenty-one-speed Vision VR30 folding recumbent can be had for under $900.

With collapsible bicycles you'll usually pay a premium for a bicycle that both rides well and collapses into a small volume. Nonetheless, if a folding bicycle is the only way that you will be able to ride to and from work, and if bicycle commuting will save you money over driving or taking public transportation (which it almost always will), you may well get back the extra expense within the first year. Prices range from under $300 for an entry-level model for a casual commuter to about $2,000 for a high-performance collapsible.

Electric bicycles are pricey. The cost of the complete ZAP ElectriCruiser—that is, the bike and the power system—is around $1,000. To retrofit any other bike, the power system alone can be purchased for half that.

A Word to People on a Tight Budget

Even if money is tight, don't go for the very bottom of the line. There is a tremendous difference in quality of manufacture, internal friction, and durability between a bicycle retailing for under $200 and one selling for $500. In contrast, the difference between a $500 bike and a $1,000 bike is less one of basic quality than of optimizing performance.

Whatever you do, *please do not make the mistake of buying a bicycle from a toy or department store—*buy only from a real bike shop. A much better value for your money is rehabilitating a second-hand bicycle (see "Rehabilitating a Second-Hand Bicycle," page 23).

You may be able to afford a better bike than you think. By pedaling to work many days, you'll be freeing up money you'd otherwise spend on transit fares, tolls, parking fees, or gasoline. You may also be able to get a break on your car insurance if you convincingly demonstrate to your insurance company you're no longer using your car for going to work. In fact, you may not even need a car, which is the biggest savings of all.

The amount of cash this means can be surprising. In the 1980s, when the New York City subway and bus fare was $1.00 each way, I was pedaling to and from work plus to and from my weekly adjunct teaching position and to and from church. Because I rode to work nine or ten months of the year (every day except during vacation or when there was snow or ice), I was saving $14 per week in tokens. That meant I was saving $500 to $600 per year, that is, *enough money for a new bike each year.* Since then, the bargain has gotten better—prices of bicycles have risen significantly less than the 50 percent rise in New York City transit fares over the same time. And if you can eliminate the need for a car and its expenses, especially if you live in a state (such as New Jersey) where auto insurance premiums even for low-risk drivers are well over $1,000 per year, the savings are even more dramatic.

Thus, even if you have no disposable income for luxuries, you probably can afford a decent new bicycle for commuting—*if* you discipline yourself to set aside the cash each day that you would otherwise have laid out for your commute by car or mass transit. Indeed, after a year or so, as the payoff continues, you'll have the savings to devote to other needs.

Because of these powerful economics—and because of the thousands of problem-free miles a year this machine will need to take you—I recommend starting out with a good-quality bicycle. It's not a luxury—it's your ticket to economic as well as physical freedom.

Chapter Two

SELECTING BICYCLE COMPONENTS

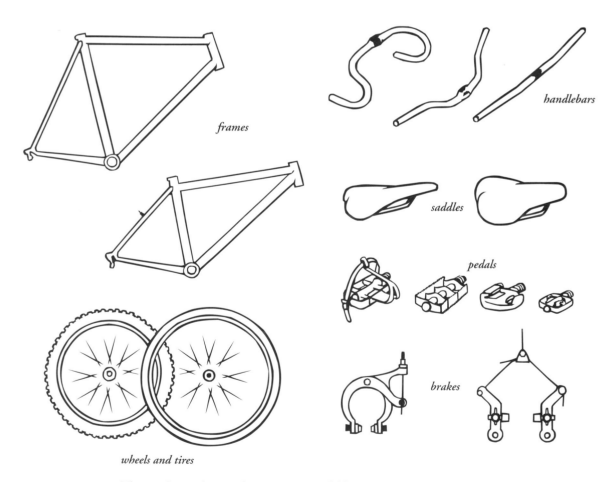

frames

handlebars

saddles

pedals

brakes

wheels and tires

The number and types of components available to a commuter are staggering.
Some careful thought will help assemble the right ones for you.

Your Commute Should Determine Your Needs

If you wish or need to buy a new bicycle, how can you make a wise selection from the vast choice of available features? If this bike is to be used primarily for commuting, make your decision based on the conditions of your commute:

- Is your commute flat or hilly? Long or short? (Affects your choice of gearing.)
- Is the pavement generally smooth or is it riddled with potholes? Are broken glass, thorns, and other debris that can cause punctures prevalent? What about sand, ice, gravel, oil, or other slippery conditions? How often will you be riding in snow or through dirt or sand? (Affects your choice of tires and brakes.)
- Will you regularly be bucking a headwind or crosswind? (Affects your gearing and perhaps your choice of wheels.)
- Do you weigh more than 200 pounds? Will you be carrying a lot of stuff to and from your job? Will the bicycle be a workhorse for other errands, such as grocery shopping or taking a child to or from school? (Affects the choice of frame and wheels and the number of spokes so the bike handles well under a load.)

Frame

For commuting, virtually any style of frame will do, so choose what you like. If you want to own just one bicycle and you want to use it for recreational riding as well as commuting, choose a bike suited for the recreational purpose and then make do with it as a commuter. Why? Because if you have fun on your bike, you'll hardly be able to wait to get on it each day, even for the commute—but if you don't find it fun to ride on the weekends, you'll be less likely to ride it for commuting.

If you want one bike just for commuting, however, go with a frame that can be equipped with racks and whose geometry (angles made by the various principal tubes) is designed to be stable while carrying loads: road-touring, hybrid, or mountain bike frames are all good choices.

Standard upright bicycles have two common frame designs: the diamond and the step-through. The most common is the diamond frame, so named for the diamond shape created by the front and rear triangles. The front triangle consists of the top tube between the headset (where the front fork and handlebars are inserted into the frame) and the saddle, the down tube between the headset and the bottom bracket (where the pedals attach to the frame), and the seat tube between the saddle and the bottom bracket. There are two divergent rear triangles, one on each side of the rear wheel; both share as one side the seat tube and have as their other two sides the seat stays (between the saddle and the left and right sides of the rear hub) and the chain stays (between the bottom bracket and the left and right sides of the rear hub).

Bicycle frames come in a variety of sizes based on the length of the seat tube. The frame of a road bicycle is considered to fit when the rider can stand astride the top tube and still have about one inch clearance to the crotch when the feet are flat on the ground; a mountain bicycle frame is considered to fit if there are three or more inches of clearance. Some mountain bikes have top tubes that slant downward to the rear to offer even greater stand-over clearance.

The diamond frame, which once was called the men's frame, is now generally ridden by most women as well. The old-style V-shaped "women's frame," which had no top tube, is no longer widely manufactured because of the structural weakness resulting from the absence of one arm of the front triangle. Women who don't like the diamond frame, however, may prefer a step-through frame. Step-through frames either have a lower top tube that slants downward to the rear or have the top tube replaced by two parallel thinner tubes slanting downward from the handlebar all the way to the rear hub (a design known as the mixte). Both designs preserve much of the strength and rigidity of the traditional diamond frame while still offering more room for a skirt.

The most desirable bicycle frames are both very

strong and very light in weight. Frame tubes on the most inexpensive bicycles are made of relatively heavy carbon steel. On moderately priced bicycles, the tubes are made of lighter-weight, thin-walled, high-tensile alloys such as chrome-molybdenum (cromoly) steel and molybdenum-manganese steel. On somewhat more expensive bicycles, tubes may be made of even lighter-weight aluminum alloys. Aluminum, however, is not as strong as steel, so aluminum alloy tubing must have a larger diameter and sometimes must be oval in cross section to offer the

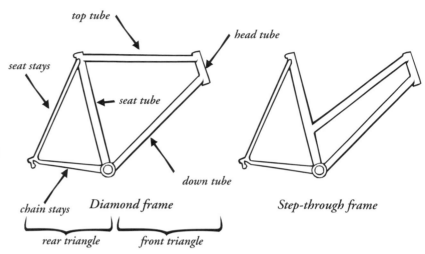

Upright bicycles have two common frame designs, diamond and step-through .

same strength as steel alloy tubing. Some of the most expensive super-lightweight bicycle frames, usually for racing, are die-cast in one piece (known as a monocoque frame) out of carbon fiber and epoxy composites or magnesium alloy. The lightest racing bikes of all are made of titanium-steel or titanium-aluminum alloy tubing, which is up to half the weight of stainless and other alloy steels.

Frames for Small Riders

The smallest stock road bicycle frame is typically 19 inches, which can be too long in both the seat tube (for the legs) and the top tube (for the reach) for adolescents or for men and women shorter than about 5 feet 4 inches. The best known manufacturer of high-quality frames for small riders—especially proportioned for women with shorter torsos and longer legs—is Georgena Terry (of Macedon, New York; 800-289-8379). Some of these bicycles

have a standard 26-inch or 700 C wheel in the rear and a 24-inch wheel in the front. Many other manufacturers also have become aware of the needs of women and small male riders, among them Bianchi, Bridgestone, Cannondale, Fuji, Marinoni, Miyata, Mongoose, Rivendell, Rodriguez, Specialized, Trek, Univega, and Waterford.

With the trend in mountain biking toward smaller frames for nimble, tight, almost BMX-like handling, you may be able to put together a setup for your needs from a bicycle shop's stock. Also, don't ignore well-made mountain bikes intended for adolescents, which may have 24-inch wheels and proportionately smaller frames, smaller brake levers and bar-end shift levers, ultrashort handlebar stems, and other small-proportioned components. Consider also custom or semi-custom framemakers and makers of folding bicycles with 20-inch wheels, such as the Bike Friday by Green Gear Cycling, Inc. in Eugene, Oregon.

Gears

For a commute that is essentially dead flat or only gently rolling, a one-speed, three-speed, or five- to seven-speed bicycle will suffice, as long as you don't have stiff headwinds (headwinds have been accu-

rately likened to hills that don't quit).

Single-speed (fixed-gear) bicycles feature a single chainwheel in front centered on the pedals and only one sprocket in the rear centered on the rear hub. Three-speed bicycles have one chainwheel (a sprocket in front centered on the pedals) and an internal planetary gear mechanism inside the rear hub. Five-, six-, or seven-speed bicycles typically have one large chainwheel and a rear derailleur that moves the chain across five, six, or seven toothed wheels known as cogs on a freewheel centered on the rear hub. The gearing on one- to seven-speed bicycles is high and intended primarily for riding fast on flat terrain—that is why their riders often walk the bikes up hills of any real grade.

For moderately rolling terrain, an old ten- or twelve-speed will give you some lower gears for the uphill stretches by virtue of being equipped with a second, smaller chainwheel that adds a lower range of higher-leverage gear ratios. For a truly hilly commute or if you have bad knees, however, nothing is better than a "triple crank" —bicycle jargon for a setup having three chainwheels, including a tiny sprocket called an alpine or "granny" gear.

Gearing 101

Here's a quick mini-course on gearing for standard upright bicycles.

On most multispeed bicycles, gears are changed by means of derailleurs that, when activated by levers mounted on or near the handlebars, mechanically "derail" the chain by pushing it toward or away from the bicycle's frame so it moves from one cog to another. For many bicycles, the rear derailleur moves the chain across the freewheel cogs for the finer differences in gear ratios needed for most shifting; a spring-loaded arm under the freewheel takes up or lets out slack in the chain to hold the chain under consistent tension regardless of the gear ratio chosen. The front derailleur moves the chain across the chainwheels to alter the whole range of available shifting (to change, say, from a fast downhill cruise to an uphill climb).

The "speeds" of a bicycle refer to the number of gear ratios possible for that particular bicycle. The gear ratios are the ratios between the number of teeth on each of the chainwheels and the number

of teeth on each of the freewheel cogs. A ten-speed bike, for example, has two chainwheels and five freewheel cogs; in theory, the chain could be set on any one of the five rear cogs when it is on either the larger or the smaller chainwheel: $2 \times 5 = 10$ possible gear ratios or speeds. A twenty-four-speed has three chainwheels and eight freewheel cogs: $3 \times 8 = 24$ potential gear ratios.

In practice, not all those speeds are usable, particularly on bicycles with a triple crank. Why not? Because some of those gear ratios are very low to make it easy for the cyclist to climb hills with minimum effort; others are very high to make it easy for the cyclist to cover ground fast on a flat road or a downhill. It would thus be counterproductive to set the chain on a chainwheel intended for climbing hills and on a freewheel cog intended for high speed. It is also bad practice; such "cross-chaining," as it is called, pulls the chain at a diagonal, eventually stretching the chain and—more expensively— grinding down the gear teeth.

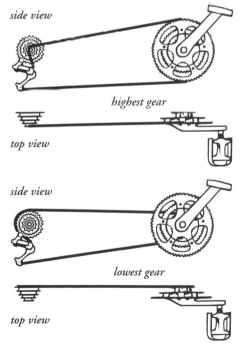

Highest gears are the farthest from the bicycle frame; lowest gears are closest.

How can you tell which gears are low and which are high? For both the front and rear, the sprockets closest to the bicycle frame are the lowest gears (for hill-climbing) and the ones farthest away from the frame are the highest gears (for high speed). In other words, for climbing hills you will want the chain set on the smallest of the front chainwheels—the granny gear if you have a triple crank—and the largest of the freewheel cogs; for flat or rolling terrain, you'll want the chain on the middle chainwheel and on any one of the freewheel cogs; and for high-speed riding, you'll want the chain on the large chainwheel and the smallest freewheel cogs.

> *One of the best-kept secrets is that you can change the options on a new bicycle just as you can on a new car.*

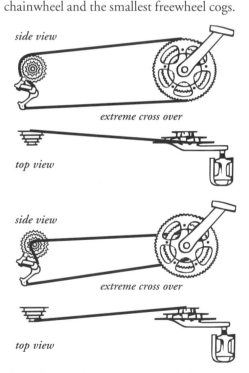

side view

extreme cross over

top view

side view

extreme cross over

top view

Cross-chaining (gear ratios where the chain is stretched at a diagonal) ruins gear teeth.

Customize Your Gearing

Bicycles from before about 1990 had standard chainwheels with 52 and 42 teeth with a granny gear of maybe 28 teeth if the bicycle was a triple crank; freewheels typically ranged from 13 to 28 teeth. On such a stock setup, the ratio for the highest gear (largest chainwheel and smallest freewheel cog, both to the outside of the bicycle frame) was 52:13 or 4:1. One rotation of the pedals drove the rear wheel around four times, propelling the bicycle twenty-eight feet (the 27-inch diameter of a bicycle wheel $\times \pi \times 4$). Such a high gear gives great speed on the flat, but ordinary mortals would have a tough time using it to climb even a modest hill. The lowest gear (smallest chainwheel, largest freewheel cog, both the closest to the bicycle frame) was 28:28 or 1:1, meaning that one rotation of the pedals drove the rear wheel around only once, propelling the bicycle only seven feet. You can't go very fast on the flat, but riding up hills is actually easier than walking the bike.

Gearing can be customized. One of the best-kept secrets is that you can change the options on a new bicycle just as you can on a new car, for just the difference (if any) in cost between what's stock and what you prefer. Don't feel you have to accept the manufacturer's specifications, especially if you have bad knees or live in a hilly area and know you must have low gears. Actually, getting adequately low gears on new bikes is less of a problem now than it once was, as mountain biking has revolutionized manufacturers' views on low gears even for hybrids and road bikes. (You can also replace the gears on a bicycle you already own, but at a much higher price.)

For example, I am a fan of low gears for bicycle touring and bike camping. My eighteen-speed Univega Sportour has a triple crank with 48, 38, and 24 teeth and a freewheel with six having 14 to 34 teeth. That means that my lowest gear has a ratio of 24:34, or 0.7:1, meaning that one rotation of the pedals drives the rear wheel around only 0.7 revolution, propelling the bicycle less than five feet. Yes, I sacrificed top speed, but with this setup I have yet to meet a hill I can't climb, even when hauling 25 pounds of camping gear.

If you commute in a hilly area, don't be afraid of arriving at a unique solution. For one job, California commuter John K. Bell, whose hobby is long-distance endurance rides of 100-plus miles but whose "knees are aging before the rest of my body," rode sixteen miles each way over hills with 1,500 feet of vertical climb. For the commute, he rode an ultra-lightweight Specialized carbon-fiber road-rac-ing frame complete with aerodynamic handlebars; but to make life easier on the steep grades, he replaced the stock high-geared racing cluster and short-arm rear derailleur with a long-arm mountain bike rear derailleur and a triple crank. The low gearing drew stares from traditional racers, remarked John, "but my knees are happy."

Wheels and Tires

Many commuters (although by no means all) prefer moderately wide to wide wheels and tires over thinner wheels and tires. Wider wheels resist being knocked out of true by potholes and wider tires give more traction over gravel and wet pavement and are good shock absorbers over uneven surfaces. Popular commuting sizes are 700 × 28 C (1⅛-inch wide) 700 × 32 C (1¼-inch wide) wheels and tires for road bicycles and 26 × 1½-inch to 2-inch wide wheels and tires for hybrid (cross) or mountain bikes. (The 700 C size allegedly stands for 700 mm but in reality these tires range from 666 to 686 mm in diameter, smaller than the no-longer-used nominal 27-inch tire.) If the roads in your area tend to be really chewed-up by large trucks, lack of maintenance, or frost heaves, you may want true mountain bike wheels and tires.

The tradeoff, of course, is that even with today's high-tech lightweight materials, wider wheels and tires are inevitably heavier than narrower ones, requiring more effort to stop and to get rolling again. Moreover, wider tires have lower air pressure than narrower ones, with a larger "footprint" on the road and correspondingly greater rolling resistance. Aggressive (high-traction), low-pressure mountain bike tires two to three inches wide have so much rolling resistance on pavement that they can be tiring on a long commute, and deep-treaded knobby tires roll with a high-frequency humming and vibration that can be wearying for the hands and body.

The usual way of eliminating that vibration and humming is to purchase mountain bike tires either with an inverted tread (smooth outer surface cut

"City bike" tire (left)—knobby with a smooth central ridge—is twice as wide as the road touring tire (right).

deeply) or tires with knobs only on the curved sides and a smooth central ridge down the middle that is the only part of the tread that contacts smooth pavement.

There are also more exotic alternatives. Lakeland, Florida cyclist Jim Arth likes riding his flat five miles on a mountain bike with 26 × 1½-inch wheels, because it eases his mind to know that in an emergency on residential streets he could sure-footedly jump a curb without ruining the rims. But instead of using knobby tires, he has installed slicks—tires whose tread is perfectly smooth. Slicks give him the same quiet ride as narrower

17

road tires, but with their lower pressure are better shock absorbers over uneven surfaces and—even without deep tread—give more traction over gravel or wet pavement. Most important to Jim, "If I happen to go off a shoulderless road, the wider mountain bike tires can navigate through the sandy dirt—stuff that grabs a narrow tire like a vise."

If you're using just one bike for both commuting and recreational racing or off-road riding, you can get the best of both worlds by buying a second pair of wheels. One set would have sturdy tires for weekday commuting. The other set would have the tires for weekend fun—true knobbies for the mountain bike or high-pressure racing tires or a perhaps a disk wheel for the road racer. Either can be exchanged in minutes with quick-release attachments. Sure, wheels are expensive, but a second pair is likely to be less expensive than a second bike and will take up less space, too. Plus, a quick change of wheels is less work than changing just the tires every weekend.

Spokes and Truing

Most bicycle wheels consist of a circular rim attached to both sides of a central hub by wire spokes under tension. The spokes usually hook into the hub's flange tangentially to convey the tangential force from pedaling most efficiently from the hub to the rim; the spokes are usually laced over and under one another to maintain their tension and to reduce their tendency to loosen.

Keeping the spokes under tension allows the bicycle wheel to be exceptionally strong while also being exceptionally light in weight. But this combination of benefits lasts only as long as the rim is both radially true (perfectly circular) and laterally true (in one plane). If a spoke loosens or breaks, the balance of tensions among the remaining spokes is broken, and further riding will rapidly cause the rim to be distorted or even irreparably bent into a characteristic potato-chip shape.

If you and your stuff weigh more than 200 pounds and if you commute over potholed terrain, you're putting a lot of stress on your bicycle's wheels. This stress can cause them to go out of true, especially in the rear, which bears most of the weight. Women and lightweight male commuters may find that their bicycle wheels stay true for years. Heavy riders, however, may find themselves breaking spokes and truing wheels several times a year.

If this is you, consider commuting on a mountain bike, whose 26-inch wheels are just enough smaller than 700 C wheels to be more durable with the standard 36 spokes. Alternatively, try substituting a more durable 40- or 48-spoked 700 C rear wheel such as are used on tandem bikes to support the 400-plus pounds of two riders.

Breaking spokes and having wheels go out of true is less of a problem, even for heavy riders with heavy loads, on the smaller wheels characteristic of most recumbent bicycles.

Handlebars and Riding Position

If you're commuting along roads or streets congested with rush-hour traffic, you'll want to be as visible as possible. Moreover, you will want a high vantage point to be able to watch for patterns in the traffic—not only the behavior of the car next to you, but also the cars behind it, ahead of it, and to its left. For this, you may prefer a bicycle with upright handlebars, which allows you to ride at an angle of about 60 degrees from the horizontal, raising your eyes at least to the level of the driver in many types of cars.

Some riders even attach special vertical handles to the tops of handlebars so they can sit up almost vertically and really survey the situation.

True, a more upright position is less aerodynamic, and the wind will catch you full in the chest. But on an urban commute, wind resistance is not likely to be uppermost in your mind when you are being stopped by red lights every few blocks and are looking for the flashing left-turn signals of impatient drivers trying to beat oncoming straight-ahead traffic—including bicycles—having the right-of-way.

If you'll be riding on lightly traveled rural roads, or if your commute requires you to ride into a prevailing headwind, or if you ride fifteen or twenty miles a day and like to vary the positions of your hands and back, go for standard drop handlebars. By resting your hands on the brake hoods instead of on the drops, you can get a reasonably high viewpoint while being bent forward at about a 45-degree angle. Note: Aerobar attachments, which allow a rider to rest the forearms on a curved bar that projects forward of a standard handlebar so as to be bent as far forward as possible in an aerodynamic tuck, will lower your visibility as well as your wind resistance; they may be a hazard in urban traffic.

On recumbent bicycles, depending on design, the handlebars may be in front of the cyclist's body or below the cyclist's hips. Preference and comfort should dictate your choice.

Saddles

Until the 1980s, the only readily available saddle on a new standard high-quality bicycle was a narrow racing saddle designed for the male anatomy. Many women found riding such a narrow saddle over potholes as comfortable as sitting astride a bucking three-inch pipe, bruising to the ischial tuberosities ("sit bones") of their wider pelvic structures.

Avocet was one of the first companies to recognize this need of half the adult population by offering a saddle that was somewhat wider in the back. Today, manufacturers are aware that cyclists come in all shapes and sizes—including the size XXL cyclist who is taking up bicycling to lose weight. Good, comfortable saddles and seat covers are now available in all shapes and sizes.

Female commuters, take note: Numbness of the outer labia now is also a discomfort of the past, as some models of saddles for women have a hole cut in the upper part of the nose where it encounters those soft tissues. Some men also find that saddles with central holes relieve pressure on the prostate or the testicles. Among the manufacturers of such saddles are Avocet, Halo, Miyata, San Marco, Selle Italia, Terry, T-Gear, Vetta, and Viscount. Many choices are available in bike shops, from mail-order houses, and directly from the manufacturers.

Saddles are highly individual. Some cyclists swear at designs of saddles that other cyclists swear by. Everyone is shaped differently and may need a central hole—if one is desired at all—in a slightly different configuration from someone else. For maximum comfort, find a saddle that fits your shape: try many types and see which one is most comfortable for you (see also "Health and Personal Safety," page 130, for information on saddle soreness).

Some cyclists like Brooks leather saddles. Although the 500-mile break-in period is famous for its discomfort, eventually the leather deforms into a shape that uniquely fits your anatomy and provides legendary comfort. Alternatively, John Forester, in his classic book *Effective Cycling,* (6th ed., Cambridge, MA: MIT Press, 1992), describes in detail a way in which you can buy an inexpensive plastic saddle and cut it to modify it to your own anatomy. (See "Riding in Traffic" and Appendix II, "Additional Resources," for more information on *Effective Cycling.*)

Choose the narrowest saddle that is comfortable. Both men and women want a saddle that is not too wide: Your "sit bones" must support your weight in order for pressure to be relieved on softer tissues. Moreover, a narrower saddle will weigh the least and will offer the least impediment and risk of chafing to your legs while pedaling. Those foot-wide, super-fat, spring-loaded saddles enjoying a resurgence of popularity in the "cruiser revival" are too wide to be practical for any commuter.

Saddles are less of a pressing issue (pun intended) for recumbent riders because the cyclist leans against a back support rather than leaning forward on genitalia. Adequate lumbar support and ventilation are the main considerations for recumbent riders. Again, try all the available choices—among them, whether you straddle foam or are cradled in mesh—to determine what is most comfortable for your anatomy.

Upshot: If don't like the saddle on your old or new bike, get thee to a bike shop and try different saddles until you find one you do.

Brakes

Four principal braking systems are used on bicycles: coaster, caliper, disk, and drum brakes.

Coaster brakes, which are mounted inside the hub of the rear wheel, are usually seen only on single-speed utility bicycles or on children's bicycles. Coaster brakes are operated by rotating the foot pedals backward half a revolution until they lock, expanding a mechanism inside the hub that creates friction on an internal brake sleeve.

Caliper brakes are almost universal on multi-geared bicycles. They have a pair of arms anchored to a pivot on the frame, whose ends are fitted with brake pads; the pads close onto the metal wheel rims in a scissorlike motion when controlling cables are operated by hand levers mounted on the handlebars. Friction between the pads and rims stop the bicycle's movement. Caliper brakes are available with either side-pull or center-pull cables. Side-pull brakes are frequently used on road racers and touring bikes because their braking force is easily feathered (finely adjusted). Center-pull brakes are sometimes found on recreational and light touring bicycles—especially older ones you might find second-hand—because they could accomodate for the larger clearances required for wider tires and rims.

One category of caliper brakes—always of a center-pull design—are high-leverage cantilever, cam, and U brakes. They are distinguished by having exceptionally large brake pads and leveraging mechanisms to increase the amount of braking force delivered. High-leverage brakes are found most commonly on mountain, touring, commuter, hybrid or cross, and BMX bicycles, where a premium is placed on retaining braking ability even when the bicycle is ridden through dirt, water, or mud.

Disk and drum brakes, which operate much like the disk and drum brakes on automobiles, are less common but are sometimes used on tandems, utility bicycles, mountain bicycles, and recumbents that must carry heavy loads.

Of the commonly available brakes, cantilever brakes or side-pull caliper brakes are the ones you'll most likely find or want on a commuting bike.

Side-pull brakes are common on road bikes.

Cantilever brakes are common on mountain bikes or hybrids.

Coaster brakes, such as those found on one-speed cruisers, have a number of practical annoyances that to me make them undesirable. Their stopping distance is longer than that of all hand brakes (which could be a problem on long, fast downhills); when you step off the bike at a stop, the brake is disengaged and the bicycle can roll, which can cause the pedal to scratch or bruise the back of your ankle; and if you throw the chain, you have no brake at all. Their single advantage is that a coaster brake's operation is unaffected by water, mud, or oil, which—if splashed onto the bicycle's rims—reduces the braking force of any caliper brake.

This May Sound Stupid, But . . .

What you absolutely don't want for commuting is a bike with no brakes. That sounds sensible, but you'd be amazed how many folks navigate through traffic on brakeless, fixed-gear track-racing bicycles. Track bikes, intended to be raced on the banked wooden or concrete track of a velodrome, have one set gear (corresponding to the highest gear of the typical road bicycle), no freewheel (so it is impossible to coast—the pedals are always moving as long as the bike is moving), and no brakes (the bike is slowed only by the cyclist exerting backward force on the always-rotating pedals). A track bike has such a long stopping distance, in fact, that riders using them on city streets—including some bicycle messengers in midtown Manhattan— count on their fast reflexes and agility in steering and dodging to get themselves out of trouble. But such macho weaving between taxis and buses is nothing less than Russian roulette on wheels.

Pedals

The pedals couple human muscle power into the drive train of the bicycle. Some pedals—such as the metal "rat trap" pedals on utility bicycles and old ten-speeds, and the more recent ATB (all-terrain bicycle) or platform pedals found on some mountain and BMX bicycles—are designed so the feet simply rest on them. Motive force is conveyed only when the feet push down on the pedals during the front half of each pedal stroke.

Much mechanical advantage is gained, however, if the cyclist can also use muscle power to pull up on the pedals in the back half of each pedal stroke. Two of the oldest (decades old) ways of attaching the feet to the pedals are toe clips and cleats.

Toe clips are curved, springy cages, commonly of metal or high-impact plastic, that bolt to the front of a counterweighted pedal to enclose the toes of the cyclist's shoes. The toe clips are cinched down with a leather or fabric side strap to grip the shoe with the desired amount of force. The optimum force is that which holds the foot onto the pedal with minimum play but still allows the cyclist to free the foot as needed when coming to a stop. Toe clips work with virtually any type of ordinary walking shoe, allowing the cyclist complete freedom off the bike.

Cleats are permanent attachments projecting from the soles of special hard-soled cycling shoes. The cleats have a slot that slips over the rear edge of the pedal under the toe clip. Cleats allow a cyclist to deliver power to the pedals more efficiently than with toe clips alone, making toe clips with cleats long popular for racing. Toe clips without cleats, however, have long been preferred in touring, commuting, and ordinary recreational cycling because walking in cleated shoes is virtually impossible.

Since the 1970s, manufacturers have devoted much attention to developing "clipless" or "uncleated" systems. The cyclist must still wear special shoes, but the shoes attach to devices that replace conventional pedals and toe clips. The cyclist inserts or removes the foot from the attachment with a twisting motion of the ankle. Unlike cleats, however, the attachment mechanism on the shoe is recessed into the sole instead of projecting from it. Such clipless or uncleated systems yield the efficiency of cleats without impairing the cyclist's ability to walk, which is an innovation that has been widely embraced. Indeed, some manufacturers have developed shoes for clipless pedals that are nearly indistinguishable in appearance from normal sneakers or loafers.

One disadvantage of the clipless system is that the attachments that replace the pedals make it difficult or impossible to ride the bicycle while wearing ordinary walking shoes or winter boots. Shimano's 323 pedal system and Performance's Campus Pedals, however, get around this disadvantage. With either system, one side of the pedal is designed for Shimano SPD clipless shoes and the other side of the pedal is a standard platform for any shoe at all. They may be used with or without toeclips or cleats.

Pedal Cranks for Small Riders

Crank-arm length is the key factor to proper fit for small riders, according to Larry Black of Mount Airy Bicycles in Mount Airy, Virginia, who fits child and adolescent "stokers" (rear riders) on tandem bicycles. Shortening the crank arms reduces the diameter of the circle described by the feet while pedaling. Thus a small rider's hips no longer must rock to reach the bottom of the pedal stroke, and the knees are no longer overly stressed by being bent up to the chest at the top of the stroke. The pedal crank arm in millimeters should be no more than 10 percent of the rider's height; so a commuter who is 4 feet 10 inches tall—or 139.2 cm—should use a crank arm no longer than 140 mm. Standard crank arms are 150 to 165 mm long, however, and shorter ones are expensive custom items.

A cheaper solution is to bolt a crank-arm shortener onto a standard crank arm. A crank-arm shortener is a piece of metal with several threaded holes into which the pedal can be screwed farther up the crank arm.

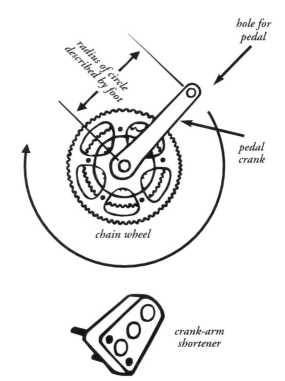

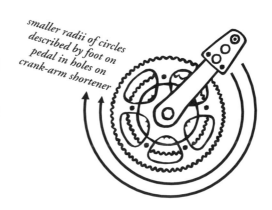

Crank-arm shortener and its effects.

Chapter Three

REHABILITATING A SECOND-HAND BICYCLE

Author's "junk" three-speed was found on the street in Maplewood, New Jersey, on "scavenger" day and was rehabilitated into a reliable commuter for $50 in materials.

Get Rolling for Under $100

Let's face it, new bicycles are expensive. Not everyone can afford to shell out $500 to $800 for today's average decent riding machine. You may not be able to afford even an entry-level bike from a bike shop (ones from Cannondale, Mongoose, Schwinn, Specialized, and Trek run $200 to $350).

If you truly can't afford more than $100 for a commuter bike, what can you do?

Bad Bargain: Department Store Bikes

Assuming that $100 is a fixed budget, don't cheap out and buy one from a department or toy store. You'll only live to pay for this mistake.

You know the adage about getting what you pay for? It was written about bicycles. Dollar for dollar, the quality of the materials is better in a bike shop. According to Scott Harlow, former owner of the East Coast Bicycle Academy and of Cool Breeze Cyclery in Harrisonburg, Virginia, a bicycle sold in a department store includes a profit mark-up of 100 percent, whereas a bike sold for the same price at a bike shop has a mark-up of only 10 percent (bike shops make their money on accessories, not bikes).

Better quality means:

- The brake levers are metal instead of plastic.
- The brakes actually close on the rims to stop the bike.
- The spokes are of hardened steel and are properly laced.
- The wheel rims are of hardened steel or aluminum with reinforced holes so the spokes can be tightened enough to keep the wheels true without pulling through the metal.
- The headset and bottom bracket have ball bearings instead of nylon bushings.
- The gear teeth don't bend or break.
- The chain doesn't stretch out of shape.
- The bike frame is of high-tensile alloy steel or aluminum and is internally butted to give a combination of strength and light weight, so it can take a beating instead of bending at the first pothole while not being a heavy chore to pedal uphill.
- The saddle can be slid forward on rails for better fit instead of only pivoting at an angle.
- The kickstand is long enough to hold the bicycle upright instead of at an angle, so it won't fall over when stuff has been strapped onto the rack.
- The frame carries a lifetime warranty instead of only thirty to ninety days.
- The purchase includes assembly and a free safety check of all the components after thirty days of riding.
- The list goes on.

Better quality also means that the bicycle is put together by a professional mechanic, not by a stockroom clerk—or by you, when you get the box home and find the thing was shipped unassembled. A professional bike mechanic knows that every screw must be greased before being inserted, knows just how tight is tight enough but not too tight for the headset and hubs, and knows not to install the handlebar stem backward.

All these factors add up. According to New Jersey bicycle mechanic Brad Ford (this book's illustrator), new department-store bicycles commonly need repairs or adjustments every few months, which, if done in a shop, could well run you the cost of the bicycle again in a year. That is false economy.

Much Better Bet: A Good Used Bicycle

A better inexpensive alternative is a real bike shop bicycle purchased used or maybe even obtained for free. If you're mechanically inclined, a second-hand bike can get you commuting easily within your $100 budget.

Actually, there's a lot to be said for commuting on an old clunker. You won't care whether it gets splattered with mud, scratched by locks, knocked over by a truck backing into a too-tight parking space, or dissolved by salt in winter's snows. It may look so worn and old that it won't be attractive to bicycle thieves on the lookout for shiny new models that can turn a quick sale. (Just make sure that the dusted-off "trashmobile" is not one now valued as a classic!) A 1960s- or 1970s-vintage one-speed, three-speed, five-speed, or ten-speed may have fenders and a chain guard (no longer standard equipment), which may be quite useful to a commuter riding in dress clothes.

A drawback is that the frames of older bicycles are usually carbon steel and tend to be heavy compared with today's high-tech aluminum and steel alloys. However, they are also nearly indestructible.

Too-high gearing may also be of concern. The lowest gear of a typical 1970s-vintage ten-speed, for example, is likely to be 42:28, or 1.5:1, high enough that a fair number of novices would still end up pushing the bike up a very steep hill (for a discussion of gearing, see "Selecting Bicycle Components," page 12). Three-speeds and five-speeds are geared even higher (the single chainwheel on a five-speed is the equivalent of the 52-tooth larger chainwheel on a ten-speed). The fixed gear of a one-speed is the equivalent of a ten-speed's highest gear, making it laborious to get it rolling each time you stop at a red light. These factors may be important if your commute involves a lot of traffic lights, stop signs, or hills, or if you have poor knees.

Where to Find a *Good* Used Bicycle

Just as with buying a used car, buyer beware: second-hand bikes are usually sold "as is" with no warranty and essentially no recourse of returning it to the original owner. On the other hand, compared with cars, bicycles are mechanically simple and relatively easy and inexpensive to fix and maintain.

Bicycling Outlets

The least risky place to look for a used bicycle is in the classified section of the newsletter of a local bicycle club or in one of those free regional bicycling newspapers distributed to bicycle shops. Less commonly, you might find a used bike on the sales floor of an especially large bicycle shop that accepts trade-ins or offers to sell used bikes on consignment for members of an attached club. In some sports meccas, you may also find a place that specializes in selling used or reconditioned athletic equipment.

Used bikes from such sources are likely to have been owned by experienced riders who are selling them to trade up to a sleeker machine. As such, they are likely to be good-quality machines that were well cared-for during their previous ownership and are thus probably in as good a condition as a second-hand bicycle can be. The flip side is that the owners or outlets know their worth, and so

such bikes are likely to be as expensive as the market will bear—possibly more than $100—although certainly inexpensive compared with a similar machine new.

Yard Sales and Police Auctions

You can also look for second-hand bikes in the classified ads in your local newspaper or at yard, garage, or tag sales. A little-known fact is that many police departments have periodic fund-raising auctions of unclaimed found or confiscated stolen property—including bicycles—where the owners could not be traced.

Bikes found at yard sales or police auctions run the gamut in quality and condition, from top pro models in mint condition to discount outlet specials that have been left out in the rain. Occasionally you make out: At a yard sale in Ohio, I picked up a five-speed tandem plus child seat for $80, and at a police auction Florida bicycle commuter Jim Arth found a nearly new Montague folding bicycle for under $100!

"Junk" Bicycles for Free

If you're vigilant, you may even find an old bike *for free* on the street during your community's periodic "junk" or scavenger pickup day—a day scheduled for disposal of appliances, furniture, and other items. Some areas pick up such items weekly; in other areas, scavenger days are scheduled only several times a year, but are pubicized in advance. Call your community's municipal offices or local trash-disposal authority for details.

Typically, items for disposal may be set out on the curb early on the evening before the pickup. On those evenings, slowly cruise up and down the streets, keeping alert for bicycles. Taking these discarded items is not stealing; in fact, owners sometimes will even attach signs like "this still works," hoping the item will be rescued before the disposal trucks roll by the next morning.

One "junk day" in Maplewood, New Jersey, I located a red three-speed Drake English racer that, after $50 of new tires and inner tubes and a thorough lube job, served me well on a five-mile commute in New York City. Who cared that it kept popping out of first gear into second and third? Instead of spending money for a repair, I just wound a strap around the handlebar and shift lever to hold it in first gear all the time, which was the gear I preferred anyway.

Obviously, bicycles found on a junk day may be in tough shape, otherwise their owners wouldn't have considered them to be trash. And sometimes the owners are right, especially if the bicycle is a department-store or toy-store special. There's little point in rehabilitating a bicycle that was of poor quality to start.

But if you're lucky or if you make a point of cruising around affluent neighborhoods where people often throw out something perfectly good just because they no longer want it, you may find a bike whose only real problems are deteriorated tires and a dry, sagging chain.

One helpful way to tell whether a bicycle was sold by a bike shop or a department store is by its labels. Look for brand names seen now or in ear-

lier days in bike shops or mail-order houses, such as Bianchi, Cannondale, Giant, Miyata, Mongoose, Nashbar, Panasonic, Performance, Raleigh, Ross, Schwinn, Specialized, Trek, and Univega. (Of course, the brand name alone tells you nothing about whether the particular model was bottom or top of the line, and some models may have been intended for the masses rather than for serious cyclists.) But avoid toy-store or department-store brands (walk through several major chain stores in your area to compile a list of names of avoid).

How to Check for Fit

Looking for a used bike is not at all the same thing as shopping for a new one. Don't even think about being choosy about style or color. All you care about are two things: acceptable fit and decent mechanical condition.

The most important thing is to make sure that the bicycle's frame is not too big. A bicycle that is slightly too small is safer and preferable to one that is too large.

First, make sure that when you stand astride the top tube with your feet flat on the ground, there is at least an inch of clearance between the top tube and your crotch. Second, see if the saddle can be lowered (or raised) enough so that when you are seated with your feet on the pedals, your leg is nearly straight at the bottom of the pedal stroke. Third, make sure that when you sit on the saddle with your hands relaxed around the brake levers, your elbows are comfortably bent and you are not stretching all the way forward with straight arms.

Many police departments have periodic fund-raising auctions of unclaimed found or confiscated stolen property— including bicycles.

Note: If you find a bicycle in good mechanical condition (see below) but too large or too small to fit you, you might consider taking it anyway to sell or trade to a fellow tight-budget commuter or a shop.

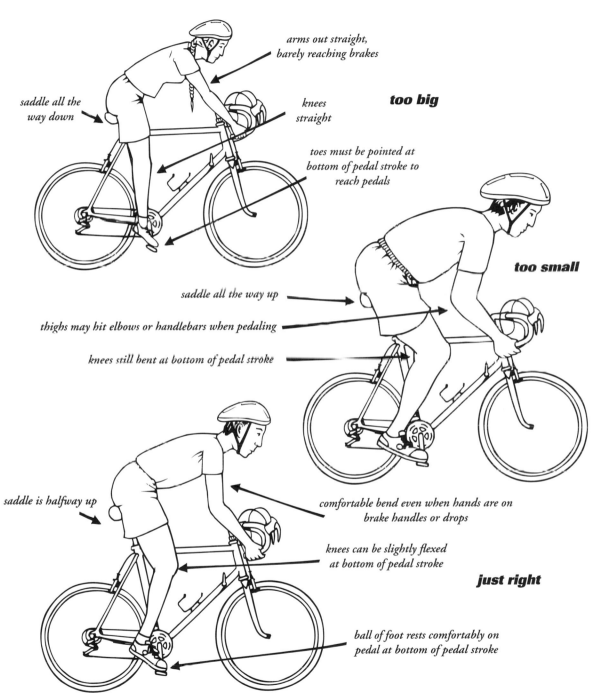

*arms out straight,
barely reaching brakes*

too big

*saddle all the
way down*

*knees
straight*

*toes must be pointed at
bottom of pedal stroke to
reach pedals*

saddle all the way up

too small

thighs may hit elbows or handlebars when pedaling

knees still bent at bottom of pedal stroke

*comfortable bend even when hands are on
brake handles or drops*

saddle is halfway up

*knees can be slightly flexed
at bottom of pedal stroke*

just right

*ball of foot rests comfortably on
pedal at bottom of pedal stroke*

*Acceptable fit is determined by standover height, leg extension, and reach.
Here three different riders try the same bicycle.*

How to Check Mechanical Condition

When checking the condition of a second-hand bike, the most important thing is to make sure the expensive parts of the bike (frame, fork, headset, hubs, wheels, derailleurs, saddle, handlebars, pedal cranks) are in decent mechanical shape. However, plan to replace all the parts of the bike that normally wear or age: tires, inner tubes, brake pads, gear and brake cables, and chain. And plan a major cleaning of everything.

One way to evaluate the condition of a used bike is to have a bike shop check it out for you and give you an estimate of what it will take to put it into good shape. An estimate alone may cost $20 or $25, but is likely to be free if you let the shop do the reconditioning (of course, this will put a real dent in your $100 budget).

If you have fair knowledge of bicycle mechanics yourself, a less expensive way to evaluate a used bike is to follow the variation on the American Youth Hostels' weekly "two-minute bike check" presented in the following table.

The steps in the table are listed roughly in order of decreasing seriousness. The tests in steps 1 through 4 are the most critical for safety and function, and repairing the involved parts of the bike are the most expensive. If the bike flunks one or more of these four tests, repairs may not be within your budget unless you know enough and have the necessary tools to do the work yourself.

Steps 5 through 16 cover routine repairs that are commonly necessary to recondition a used bike; they range from being moderately expensive to free. They probably should not deter you from buying a second-hand bike that has passed steps 1 through 4. There are many excellent bicycle-repair books; see Appendix II, "Additional Resources," from some suggestions.

In the descriptions in the table, a slash (/) means check first one and then the other, not both at once. In each step, the potential problem is followed by advice or a remedy along with an estimate of its cost. If you want to test whether loose parts just need a little tightening or are truly stripped, take along a headset wrench, a bottom-bracket wrench, and a pedal crank. Just remember, if the bicycle you're examining is at a yard sale, be sure to ask the owner's permission before you begin tinkering.

Evaluating the Condition of a Second-Hand Bicycle

Potential Problem	Solution
1. *Overall Condition.* Is the bicycle significantly rusted? Is the frame's paint nearly absent, with the handlebars, chainwheels, and wheel rims pitted with brown dots? If so, it has been stored in a damp place or even left outdoors in the rain. Worse than the visible rust may be the rust unseen inside the hubs, headset, and bottom bracket. With a bicycle that has seen such poor care, it is likely that the original grease packing the bearings in those locations may never have been replaced. The resulting rust may even have eaten away and weakened the frame.	*Avoid paying money for a seriously rusted bike* unless you really know what you're about or unless you deliberately want the degraded appearance to discourage theft. You cannot evaluate its true condition until you take it apart. If you can get the bike for free and it seems to have been a once-expensive model, carry it along until you find something that is clearly better. The cost of rehabilitating a bike rusted inside as well as out may be so high that it is prohibitive.

Potential Problem	Solution
2. *Frame.* Place your head alongside the frame to sight along the tubes and stays. In addition, carefully examine the paint. Does the metal frame show any signs of having been dented or bent, and subsequently straightened? If so, then the metal has been irremediably weakened.	*Avoid paying money for a bike with a bent or once-bent frame; it is unsafe.* But before discarding it altogether, examine the general condition of the front fork, components, and accessories (pedals, chainwheels, freewheels, derailleurs, handlebars, saddle, racks, reflectors, and so on). Are they made by a decent manufacturer (such as Shimono, Suntour, or—lucky you—Campagnolo), and are they free from rust, bends, broken teeth, and the like? If nothing seems to be wrong with the components and accessories that a good cleaning wouldn't fix and if the price for the bike is exceptionally low or zero, you may want to consider cannibalizing the bike for its parts.
3. *Headset.* Stand in front of the bicycle with the front wheel gripped between your knees. Place both hands, palm up, under the handlebars. Try to lift the handlebars straight up out of the frame. There should be no slight movement or click. Rotate the handlebars through a 180-degree arc to determine if there are flat spots on the headset bearings.	If there is a slight but perceptible click, gently tighten the headset with a headset wrench, taking care not to overtighten it; you want the front wheel and handlebars to be able to turn freely under their own weight when the front end of the bicycle is lifted. If the headset cannot be tightened and continues to feel loose no matter how many times you've used the wrench, the threads on the front fork may be stripped; that means that the front fork must be replaced. *The front fork is second only to the frame in cost; replacing it may run $100 or more* if done by a shop. If you're mechanically knowledgeable, you may know how to find and install the right replacement fork for cheap; otherwise, the cost of repair is prohibitive. You may want to pass over this bike or consider cannibalizing it for parts.

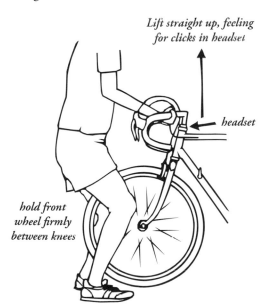

Lift straight up, feeling for clicks in headset

headset

hold front wheel firmly between knees

(continued)

Evaluating the Condition of a Second-Hand Bicycle (continued)

Potential Problem	Solution

4. ***Bottom Bracket.*** Grasp the pedal crank arms with your hands and try to move the cranks in and out perpendicular to the plane of the frame of the bike, that is, perpendicular to the plane in which the chainwheel(s) spin(s). The pedal cranks should not move.

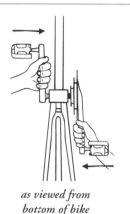

as viewed from bottom of bike

Solution: If you sense any slight movement or a perceptible click, tighten the bottom bracket. Really crank it down; it should be the tightest thing on the bike. If the bracket cannot be tightened, then look for stripped threads; if the threads are stripped, then the frame will have to be rethreaded or discarded altogether unless it is an exceptionally good frame. If the pedal cranks cannot be tightened, disassemble the bottom bracket to check for a broken axle, which is a moderately expensive repair; make your own judgment depending on the condition of the rest of the bike.

5. ***Chainwheels and Freewheel Cluster.*** Carefully examine each chainwheel for broken or worn teeth. Perform the same examination of the freewheel cluster.

Solution: If any individual sprocket has worn or broken teeth, it must be replaced—a moderately expensive repair. Make your own judgment depending on the condition of the rest of the bike.

6. ***Wheels.*** Lift the front/back end of the bike and spin the wheel. When you sight directly down from the tire to the hub, the wheel should appear to rotate in exactly one plane. If the wheel appears to wobble or has an obvious potato-chip shape, or if the rim rubs one brake pad left or right during only part of each revolution, it is out of true.

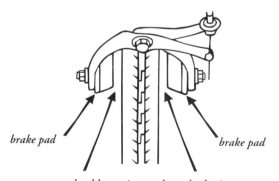

brake pad   *brake pad*

gaps should remain equal as wheel spins

Solution: Tighten the appropriate spokes to true the wheel or take it to a shop to have it trued. The cost to you if you know what you're doing is nothing. The cost at a shop for truing ranges from free to about $10 per wheel depending on severity. *Do not ignore this problem; riding on untrued wheels can break spokes and bend the rims beyond repair* and replacement wheels start at $50 to $100 each, which is a perfect example of an inexpensive fix staving off a costly replacement.

Potential Problem	Solution
7. *Derailleurs.* Check that all the nuts and bolts attaching the derailleurs are secure. Lift the rear wheel or take the bike for a short spin, shifting the rear derailleur into lowest gear, that is, onto the largest cog on the freewheel cluster. Make sure the derailleur arm does not hit the spokes or ride on the cogs. While turning the pedals, shift through all the gears with the rear derailleur to make sure all are accessible without the chain jumping off the largest cog into the spokes or off the smallest cog onto the axle.	If the chain jumps off, tighten the rear derailleur stop screws a quarter turn and try it again. If the rear derailleur rests on the sprockets, the spring holding the arm may be worn and weak and may impede proper shifting; the cost of a new derailleur is moderate.
• Repeat the test with the front derailleur to make sure the chain can make all transitions between chainwheels without jamming, rubbing, or falling off.	Adjust the front derailleur stop screws and adjust the angle of the derailleur. Cost of adjustments: nothing if you do them; a few dollars if a shop does them.
• If the derailleurs and gears seems to be in good shape but the shifting is really sloppy, see how far you must push the gearshift lever to make the chain shift. If the distance seems excessive before you get a response, the cable may be stretched or the cable housing may be too long. If the lever pulls the cable with no response at all or there seems to be some obstruction, the cable may be broken or frayed.	Shorten the cable housing and replace the cables, greasing them well before inserting them into the housing. Cost of new cables: a dollar or two, plus labor if done at a shop.
8. *Hubs.* With the bike resting on the ground, push against the top of the front/back rim perpendicular to the plane of the wheel. You should not feel any movement nor hear any clicks in the hub bearings. *press on rim on top of stationary wheel, perpendicular to plane of wheel, feeling for any click from the wheel's hub*	If there is a slight movement, tighten the hub cones with a cone wrench, taking care not to overtighten. Cost to you if you know what you're doing: nothing. Cost of adjustment at a bike shop is a few dollars per hub. If you really want to do the job right, disassemble the hub and examine the cones for pitting, replace the cones as necessary, and repack the hub with new white lithium grease and properly sized bearings. Cost of cones, bearings, and grease: a few dollars, plus labor if done at a shop.

(continued)

Evaluating the Condition of a Second-Hand Bicycle (continued)

Potential Problem	Solution
9. *Brakes.* With the bike stationary, squeeze the right/left brake levers as if you were braking hard. At its lowest point, there should be about an inch of clearance separating the lever from the handlebar grip.	If there is less than half an inch, tighten the rear/front brake cable. If you really want to do the job right, remove both cables and inspect them; if frayed, replace them with new cables, greasing them well before inserting them into the housing. Cost for new cables: a dollar or two per cable, plus labor if done at a shop.
• Make sure that the brake hoods are firmly anchored to the handlebars.	If the brake lever assembly can be slipped or rotated around the handlebar, tighten it in the proper position. Squeeze the brake lever to expose the anchoring screw inside the assembly. Cost of repair: nothing.
• With the brake lever squeezed, note the position of the rubber pads pressing against the rim. Their entire braking surface should be against the metal of the rim, not partly on the rubber tire or partly in the air below the rim.	Loosen the brake pad holder nut to adjust the position of the brake pads in the brakes. Cost of repair: nothing.
• While moving the bike forward, grip the right/left brake lever hard. The bike should stop securely, with no slipping of the brake pad on the rim and with no squealing of the brakes. (Note: If the bicycle is a one-speed with a coaster brake, it may have been junked solely because the brake no longer works. Ride it slowly and test the brake by backpedaling half a revolution. If the bike stops well at low speed, try it at progressively higher speeds. If the bike stops only after an excessive distance or does not stop at all, the coaster brake will have to be replaced. This is a moderately expensive repair that may be worth the money if the bicycle is otherwise in good shape.)	Replace worn pads for a couple of dollars each. To eliminate squealing, adjust the angle of the brake pads so that the leading edge touches the rim a little before the trailing edge. Also, make sure the rims and pads are completely clean by rubbing them with a lint-free cloth soaked in alcohol—one of the best, cheapest, and safest grease-cutters around. If one pad persists in rubbing one side of the rim, adjust the tension springs on the proper side of the brakes. This adjustment can be an exercise in frustration but is easily and cheaply done in a shop.
10. *Tires.* If the rubber tires and inner tubes are supple and have no splits or signs of rotting, consider it a bonus—and a very unusual one.	Most used bicycles have deteriorated tires, so expect to replace both tires and both tubes. In fact, tires and tubes are items that wear out and should be replaced routinely every couple of years or after several thousand miles, depending on the length of your commute. Cost is $10 to $20 per tire and about $3 per tube for average-quality items, plus labor if done at a shop.

Potential Problem	Solution
11. *Handlebars.* Stand in front of the bicycle with the front wheel gripped between your knees. Try to twist the handlebars from side to side while holding the wheel still. They should not move. Also, the handlebars should be at right angles to the front wheel.	If the handlebars are loose, tighten the bolt on top of the handlebar stem. Cost: nominal or zero.
12. *Pedals.* Spin the pedals on the ends of their crank arms. They should spin freely unless they are designed to stop in certain positions.	If the pedals resist movement, they may need to be repacked with grease. This repair is not very common.
13. *Saddle and Seat Post.* Try to move the saddle up and down in the seat tube, try to rotate it, to push its nose up and down, and to slide it backward and forward on its rails. The saddle should remain firm.	If it moves, tighten the appropriate bolts. If the bolts won't tighten, replace the appropriate attachment parts, which may be worn. Cost: a dollar or two.
• Check to make sure that with full leg extension the seat post is not projecting beyond the safety marking. Generally, at least three inches of seat post should remain in the seat tube.	If you still need more height, consider buying a new long mountain-bike seat post for a few tens of dollars.
14. *Chain.* Plan to replace the chain unless you know for a fact that it is essentially new.	A bicycle chain wears and stretches and should be replaced routinely every few thousand miles, that is, every spring, if you commute year-round more than three to five miles each way. Why? Because a worn and stretched chain will grind down gear teeth, and gears are expensive while chains are cheap. Cost of a chain: $8 to $15 plus labor if done at a shop. (Note: A new chain will not always work if the gear teeth are extremely worn.)

Evaluating the Conditions of a Second-Hand Bicycle (continued)

Potential Problem	Solution
15. *Drive Train.* Check to see if the drive train squeaks while you pedal.	Oil each joint in the chain and the axles of the pulleys on the derailleur. If the drive chain is dirty or sandy, remove the freewheel, derailleur, and chain and clean them in solvents before lubricating them—a messy job best done at a shop if you don't have the right tools. Such a thorough cleaning, however, is moderately expensive in labor. If the used bicycle is an older type without sealed freewheel bearings, oil the freewheel. (See "Bonehead Maintenance," page 146.)
16. *Accessories.* Check to see whether there are white (clear) reflectors on the front of the bicycle and on the spokes, and a red reflector on the rear; they are required by law.	If not, replace them; the cost is a dollar or two each. If there are racks, a light, fenders, or other accessories, consider them a bonus.

The Bottom Line

How does rehabilitating a "beater bike" translate into real costs? If you can obtain a rust-free, mechanically sound second-hand bicycle that fits you for $0 to $50 and give it new tires and tubes, new gear and brake cables, a new chain, new brake pads, new reflectors, touch-up truing to the wheels, and a complete cleaning and lube job, you have yourself a good deal. The total cost for the bike plus parts should indeed come in at under $100, if you can do the reconditioning yourself.

Chapter Four

ACCESSORIES FOR SAFETY AND COMFORT

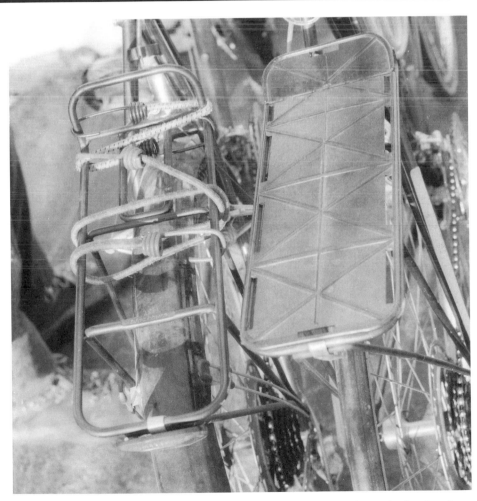

Rear rack with bungees (left) is a necessity for carrying loads; the rack may be fitted with a snap-on RackMate splash protector (right) to keep your clothes dry on wet pavement.

What Do You Really Need?

Accessories are those items that are not strictly necessary for the act of riding the bicycle but do allow you to use a bike as practical transportation.

The accessories and other equipment most fair-weather commuters may want to consider fall into six categories:

- Items for safety (for protection in a fall and for being visible to motorists).
- Items for comfort and convenience.
- Racks, packs, and fasteners (for carrying work-related items to and from your job).
- Child and grocery carriers (for errands on the way to and from work and at lunchtime).
- Locks (for securing the bike while it's parked).
- Tools (for fixing routine mechanical problems en route).

That sounds like a lot of stuff. Well, it may or may not be, depending on what you actually need each day and how cleverly you organize your life.

Here are two considerations that may make commuting easier. First, spend a little time and thought each evening on organizing and packing your stuff to allow you to leave quickly and easily the next morning. As you gain experience, refine your kit and get into a routine. This nightly organization eventually will take less time and will become second nature. Without initial forethought, however, you risk being so hurried and frustrated every morning that you just grab the car keys or fare card instead.

Second, examine the routine of your work and errands to see if there are ways to avoid carrying heavy stuff when not necessary. For example, if you're an urban commuter who needs a heavy-duty lock to secure the bike outdoors at the same pole every day, why not leave the four-pound vinyl-coated chain and lock around the pole instead of lugging it on the bike? Then carry just a lighter-weight cable lock to hold the bike at stops for brief errands.

Accessories for Safety

Even if your commute takes you along only isolated country lanes, you can still be thrown off your bike by an unexpected pothole, a blowout, or a freak collision or near-collision with a deer, goose, squirrel, cat, or chipmunk (yes, it has happened).

The chance of injury can be minimized by proper equipment for protection in the event of a fall, for increasing your own view of the road, and for being noticed by motorists and pedestrians.

Helmet

The single most important safety accessory is a helmet. If you bicycle regularly, it is not a matter of "if" you will fall, but of "when" (I have averaged a fall every year or two as a result of common hazards, such as gravel, wet pavement, potholes, taxi doors being flung open into my path, and the like). A helmet can make the difference between a concussion (or worse) and just some pulled neck muscles. Many states now also mandate bicycle helmets for all children below a certain age. Check with a local bicycle shop or your department of motor vehicles for details of the law in your state.

Most helmets have an interior lining of crushable foam designed to absorb the force of an impact. This is surrounded by a thin outer shell of high-impact plastic. The helmet is usually perforated for ventilation. Most good bicycle helmets meet impact standards set by the American National Standards Institute (ANSI). For maximum protection, buy a helmet that has a sticker inside indicating that it has also passed the particularly rigorous safety standards of the Snell Memorial Foundation. Do not buy such a vital safety accessory for either yourself or your child from a department or toy store unless it has the ANSI or Snell stickers; go to a local bicycle shop or order it from a reputable sports mail-order house. Do *not* use a toy football helmet or otherwise unsuitable substitute.

Helmets come with several sizes of sponges that attach with hook-and-loop closures (Velcro) inside the foam shell to alter the fit. The helmet is properly snug when, with the chin strap unfastened, you can bend over upside down and the helmet stays on your head. Adjust the chin strap so it is loose enough to be comfortable when your neck is extended forward in riding position, but taut enough so that the helmet cannot be pushed backward off your forehead.

The old complaints about helmets being hot and heavy no longer pertain with today's lightweight, high-impact plastics and styles with generous ventilation. A white or yellow helmet will reflect the sun's heat the best and offer maximum visibility at night. In spite of the sharp appearance, avoid a black helmet, which will absorb heat and be unbearably hot in the summer and will be invisible at night. Some helmets can be fitted with optional visors to keep the sun out of your eyes, which is particularly useful if you live west of where you work, because you'll be commuting into sun both morning and evening.

Most important, of course, is that you wear the helmet every time you mount the saddle, so it becomes a habit with no exceptions. A helmet is not talismanic—it does your head no good if it is packed in a bag or dangling from your handlebars.

Gloves

Fingerless, padded cycling gloves serve two purposes: They minimize abrasion when you fall, and they buffer road shock to the palms and heels of your hands every time you ride—thus preventing repetitive stress injury (including carpal tunnel syndrome) to nerves and tendons.

Gloves are the right size when they are just large enough to slide on and off easily without being too loose. Padding may be of gel, leather, foam, or some other material; the backing may be of Lycra, terry cloth, or crocheted thread. If you ride a bicycle with drop handlebars, make sure the protective padding extends to the inner sides of index fingers (which are under pressure when you ride on the brake hoods) and to the inner sides of your thumbs (which are under pressure when you're riding on the drops with your fingers outstretched to the brake levers). There are nerves running along those spots, too. Mountain bike gloves are longer in the fingers and thumbs than road bike gloves.

As with a helmet, don't skimp on quality with gloves. Buy them at a bike shop. The better ones will be more expensive, but they will also have thicker, wider, and more durable padding

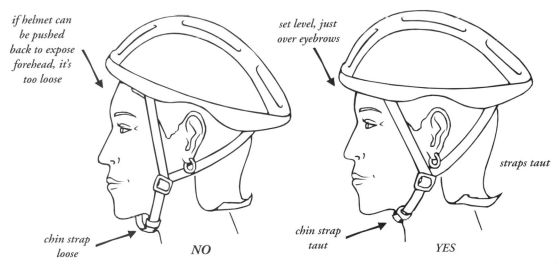

Make sure the helmet sits level on the head and the chin strap is snug.

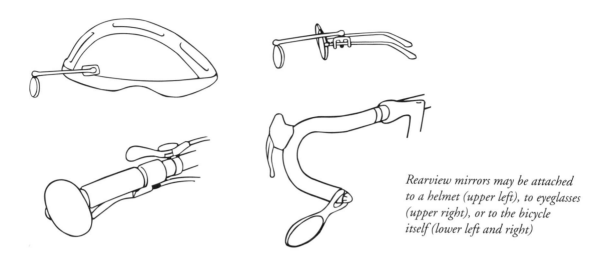

Rearview mirrors may be attached to a helmet (upper left), to eyeglasses (upper right), or to the bicycle itself (lower left and right)

than the cheaper ones. With hard daily usage, a pair should last you more than a year.

To prolong the life of the leather, make a practice of turning the gloves inside out when you remove them so the inside can dry between wearings. In my experience, gloves with the crocheted backing are very comfortable but they also seem to have a shorter lifespan than other designs, because the thread disintegrates long before the padding wears out. If you know how to crochet, you can effect repairs.

For extra cushioning, wrap your handlebars with padded handlebar tape or slip cushioned grips (such as those made by Spenco) around the handlebars and brake hoods.

Rearview Mirror

A rearview mirror allows you to watch for automobile traffic approaching from behind without taking your eyes from the road ahead. This is particularly valuable if your commute involves a fast downhill run or heavy traffic or if you are riding a recumbent bicycle (it is almost impossible to turn far enough in the upright seat to see adequately behind). With a rearview mirror, you will not be startled if a car quietly materializes to your left and honks.

In my experience, the most effective rearview mirrors mount to your helmet or to your eyeglasses.

Make sure such a mirror has a large field of view and does not tend to slip out of position. On bumpy roads, mirrors that mount to the bicycle handlebar itself may vibrate too much to stay aligned or to produce a clear image, although some commuting cyclists really like them. Try all types and choose the design you like best.

Some of the plastic helmet-mounted rearview mirrors break easily. You may want to buy two or three of the design you like best and hold onto the broken pieces. They don't always break in the same places and eventually you'll be able to assemble a new one from the parts.

By the way, don't rely exclusively on a rearview mirror to keep you informed (in fact, the "Effective Cycling" courses offered by the League of American Bicyclists actually discourage the use of rearview mirrors). Just as is good practice in an automobile, physically turn your head to look behind you before you change lanes, not only to judge the distance of approaching cars accurately, but also to help inform overtaking drivers that you are aware of their presence and you intend to make a move.

Reflectors

New bicycles sold in the United States must be equipped with front, side, and rear reflectors per regulations of the Consumer Product Safety Commission. Front and side reflectors are usually white and the rear reflector is red; the side reflectors are usually attached to the spokes of the wheels. Some types of pedals also have small amber reflectors that can be seen from the front and rear. But these minimal reflectors are by no means adequate, especially if you intend to commute after night falls or in the rain (see "Riding After Dark," page 81 and "Riding in Foul Weather," page 93).

In winter, I sometimes sport an international orange hunting jacket, which makes me a brilliant orange spot in sunlight on a grey day. If you do the same, criss-cross it with reflective tape to make it also light up at night.

Flags

At a bike shop, you can buy an attachment that bolts to the left side of your rear hub and holds a five-foot-high rod with an international orange flag that waves over the tops of cars. Such flags are good especially if you are carrying a child.

Flags that mount horizontally are also helpful because they make cyclists seem wider, so that motorists allow a bit of extra clearance when they pass. The best kind of horizontal flag—now hard to find—has a spring mechanism that allows the flag to be clipped down onto the left seat stay when not in use.

A horizontally mounted flag makes cyclists seem wider.

Bells and Whistles

A bicycle bell may be required by the motor vehicle law in your state. It's a good idea to have one even if it isn't.

Buy the loudest bike bell you can find. Some are even battery powered to amplify their ringing. Bells are more recognizable in signaling a bicycle's approach than a horn. Also, bicycle horns often sound comical—like those used by circus clowns—and thus may not be taken seriously by motorists. Bells may also be somewhat safer in traffic than a horn: A bell's lever can be triggered by a thumb instead of requiring you to take your hand off the handlebar to squeeze the horn's rubber bulb (although an electric horn also can be activated by a thumb button).

Do not, under any circumstances, buy a police whistle. In some areas, it is actually illegal for an unauthorized person to blow a police whistle in traffic. Moreover, many of the motorists or the pedestrians in crosswalks whom you are trying to warn of your presence may think the whistle is not directed at them; when they find it is, they may become indignant that you had ordered them around so peremptorily.

Most pedestrians do, on the other hand, respond favorably to a bicycle bell, recognizing what it is and glancing around to see where you are before moving out of your way.

Keep in mind that bicycles are nearly silent and seem to materialize out of nowhere to pedestrians or motorists wrapped in their own thoughts. Most cyclists don't think to use a bicycle bell until faced with an incipient emergency. In midtown Manhattan, however, I felt far safer adopting the approach of an anonymous bicycle commuter I once saw; she sounded a preventive ding every time she passed a parked car with people inside, approached a crosswalk with people on the curb, and the like. This bicycle commuter sent out a continual gentle "radar pinging" reminder of her presence as she rode down Park Avenue, just as a car's engine warns one of its approach.

Accessories for Comfort and Convenience

Bicycle commuting can have its annoyances: getting saddle sore, breathing bus exhaust, getting chain grease on your right leg, and the like. Not to worry, technology to the rescue. Just note: As with all bicycle accessories, products come and go. Keep your eyes open for new ones that may do the job better than any described in this book, and be prepared to stock up when you suspect an old classic is disappearing from the market.

Padded Seat Cover

Saddle soreness is caused by road shocks being transmitted through the bicycle seat and constantly bruising your "sit bones" (ischial tuberosities) at the ends of your pelvis. Saddle soreness is a problem particularly pronounced for women, who have wider pelvic structures than male riders.

To minimize or even eliminate saddle soreness, buy one of the slightly wider saddles designed for the female anatomy (Avocet was a pioneering designer). For extra padding, cover the saddle with a seat cover, either of the gel type (such as those by Spenco or Vetta) or of Merino wool fleece. Either works fine, although the gel is less bulky and has a longer life (over time, the wool fleece tends to rub off when you pedal). Unless you are greatly overweight, do not buy one of the extra-wide, spring-mounted saddles commonly seen on adult tricycles; your inner thighs will rub on it and it will interfere with your pedaling. (See also the section on saddles in "Selecting Bicycle Components," page 19, and the saddle-soreness section in "Health and Personal Safety," page 130.)

Chain Guard

A chain guard is a piece of metal or plastic that covers the bicycle chain to prevent clothing from being torn or soiled. Chain guards once were standard equipment on old one-speed, three-speed, and ten-speed bicycles.

A more modern version of the chain guard is a metal disk slightly larger than the largest chainring

that mounts on the outside of the chainring, so that its smooth circumference extends beyond the teeth.

Kickstand and Flick Stand

Racing cyclists abhor kickstands as dead weight; they would rather lean their bikes up against a tree or a wall or lay them on the ground. But just try lifting a bicycle off the ground with loaded panniers or just try to place a toddler into a bike seat when the bicycle is leaning against a wall; once is all you need to be convinced that kickstands definitely have a purpose in life.

Buy a kickstand from a bike shop—Greenfield is one well-known brand; the ones sold at department stores tend to be flimsy and about an inch too short to hold the bicycle upright under load.

Some kickstands bolt onto the bottom of the rear triangle of the bicycle between the seat tube and the rear wheel. For this design, use two wrenches to make sure the bolt is fastened securely; a loose kickstand will rotate and the bicycle will

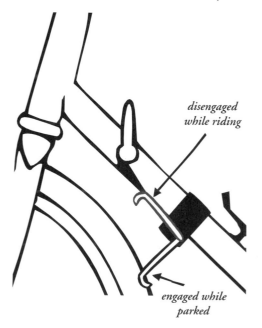

disengaged while riding

engaged while parked

Flick Stand holds the front wheel securely in line with the frame when the bicycle is parked.

topple. Others may attach near the rear hub where the chainstay and seat stay meet. Some are adjustable in length. Whatever design you buy, make sure it is strong and sturdy.

The partner to the kickstand is an ingenious device tradenamed the Flick Stand. It is fastened to the down tube by a plastic band and consists of a hinged rectangular wire loop that holds the front wheel securely in line with the frame. It is engaged by lifting the wire loop while simultaneously rolling the bicycle backwards an inch, wedging the wire against the front tire. It automatically disengages when the bicycle is rolled forward.

When engaged, the Flick Stand keeps the headset from rotating, thereby allowing you to load the kickstand-supported bicycle without having the front wheel turn and the bicycle fall over. Even without a kickstand, the Flick Stand holds the bicycle rigid when it is leaned against a wall. This inexpensive little device lasts for years and is one of cycling's best inventions.

Water Bottle and Cage

On a hot and long commute with climbing, you may regularly down an entire bottle of water before reaching home. At the very least, the water would help you wash up if you had to make any dirty repairs.

Water bottles come in two standard sizes: a pint and a fifth (really!). Before buying a new water bottle, open it and sniff it to make sure it is completely odor-free. A new bottle that smells like plastic will always smell like plastic and it will make the water taste like plastic, too. Color makes no difference, except avoid black: it will absorb the sun's rays and heat the water more than a bottle of a light color.

Water bottles are carried in cages affixed to the bicycle's down tube or seat tube, either by brazed-on attachments that are part of the frame or by extra attachments that come with the water bottle cage. Most bicycles can be fitted with at least three water bottle cages (one on the seat tube, one on the upper side of the down tube, and one on the lower side).

Items for Cleanliness

You never know when you're going to have to mess with your grease-covered chain or fix a flat. If you're in business clothes, you can't just wipe the dirt onto your pants or skirt—and in a city, there may be no nearby grass to help out.

Be prepared. Carry one of those portable boxes of a dozen baby wipes, such as "Wet Ones." They are excellent bike-grease cutters—far better than many of the products advertised for that purpose at bike shops. You might also want to fold a couple of paper towels and sandwich bags into a small plastic bag and wedge it into the rails under your seat; the towels can help with some clean-up jobs and the plastic bags can isolate the filthy refuse from the rest of your stuff until you find a garbage can. You might also want to carry a small first aid kit. Many camping and sporting goods stores sell a light nylon pouch with samples of all the basics. Although no one plans to be injured, it's nice to know you could clean and soothe the road rash right when it happens. Or, you might be able to help a fellow bicycle commuter.

The baby wipes "Wet Ones" are excellent for removing bike grease from your hands.

Chapter Five

CARRYING LOADS WITH THE BICYCLE

Rear panniers on author's '85 Univega Alpina Sport are loaded for commuting from Lakewood to Cleveland, Ohio. Note fenders.

Turning a Bicycle into a Workhorse

Many commuters who drive or take public transportation must take stuff to and from work—papers, work tools, samples, a lunch, gym clothes, maybe a laptop computer. As a bicycle commuter, you will likely tote some of the same items plus a change of clothes and some bicycle tools.

Although carrying weight may reduce the enjoyment of riding a bike for some riders, other cyclists philosophically reason (as I do) that riding a heavy bike is just that much more exercise. A willingness to carry weight allows you to make bicycling an integral part of your daily life.

Just remember, fasten everything securely! Washington, D.C. commuter Michael Leccese (who now lives in Boulder, Colorado) learned that lesson the hard way. "I had put my lunch into Tupperware containers and tucked them under the rack strap on my rear rack. My commute took me down Connecticut Avenue, which has a long, high, narrow bridge with no shoulder and no sidewalk," he recounted. "This one day, I was riding fast over the bridge to keep ahead of the advancing wall of cars when suddenly I hit a very big pothole. I heard a WHUMP! and looked into my rearview mirror—just in time to see a Tupperware container hit the ground and split open, my tuna sandwich going open-faced in mid-air and landing on someone's windshield, and the windshield wipers turning on."

Michael lost only his lunch, but other cyclists have lost original artwork and expensive tools for not following this simple advice. Don't let it happen to you.

Racks

Essential to carrying loads of any kind are the proper racks. For an upright bicycle, do not buy cheapie silver colored school-kid jobs from a toy or department store; buy durable, sturdy ones made by a reputable maker such as Blackburn or Rhode Gear from a bicycle shop. For a recumbent, have racks fitted at the time of purchase. Serious racks are designed to support forty pounds or more without bending or sagging. They have threaded eyelets for attaching them to your bicycle frame, and they can take as much abuse as your bicycle frame. They also (if you're into vanity) look better.

Rear Racks

At minimum, on any upright bicycle you'll need a rear rack. Most rear racks are bolted to the tops of the bicycle's seat stays just below the saddle and to eyelets on both sides of the rear hub. Stuff can be strapped onto the top of the rack, and panniers (see page 45) can be hung on the sides. Alternatively, a child seat can be installed on the top (because of the design of a child seat, which must accomodate the child's legs, panniers cannot be used at the same time).

A brilliant invention is the portable or removable rear rack. Seatpost racks by Blackburn and Performance can carry up to fifteen or twenty pounds, while the Headland Utility X Rack is sturdy enough to carry up to 40 pounds.

A removable rack is convenient if you commute on a racing bicycle whose frame is not equipped with eyelets for supporting a permanent rack and you want the bike to be free of racks for your weekend training rides. A removable rack may also be useful for carrying your stuff—or your child's stuff—on the back of a child's trailer bicycle, whose horizontal attachment member prevents you from using the top of your own rear rack, although you can still attach panniers.

Another brilliant invention is the Load Llama, a hinged device that attaches to a rear rack. When unfolded, four arms stick up vertically, allowing you to strap large, heavy, or awkwardly shaped items securely (the advertising pictures show it holding a basketball).

Front Racks

Front racks come in two varieties: standard and low-rider.

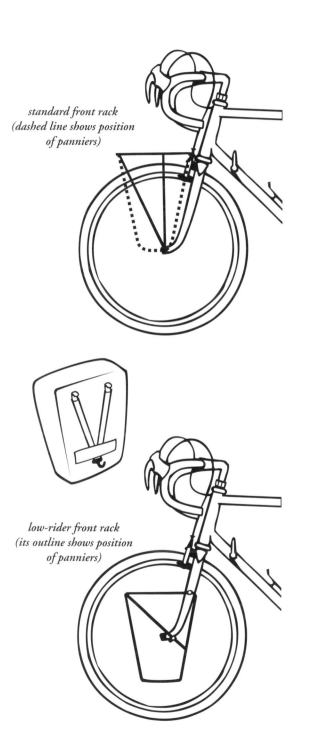

*standard front rack
(dashed line shows position
of panniers)*

*low-rider front rack
(its outline shows position
of panniers)*

A standard front rack looks like a shorter version of a rear rack and fastens to the front fork and both sides of the front hub. Again, stuff can be strapped onto the top of the rack and panniers can be hung on the sides.

Low-rider front racks carry panniers only; there is no provision for a load to be carried atop the front wheel. Well-known manufacturers include Blackburn, Bruce Gordon, Vetta, and Voyager.

Both types of front racks have advantages and disadvantages. A standard front rack can carry more, but because the load is placed high, it significantly degrades the steering and handling of the bicycle. Low riders carry a bit less, but the symmetrical placement of the load closely around the front hub makes the bicycle more stable.

Please remember to never use just one pannier on a front rack. You will constantly be fighting the bicycle's tendency to turn in the direction of the loaded pannier. Even if you don't have much to carry, distribute the load as equally as possible between two front panniers. Use of one pannier on the rear, however, is fine.

Cargo Trailers

If you have so much stuff that you cannot carry it all on the bicycle, you might consider a bicycle trailer. Bicycle trailers can carry a remarkable amount of weight. I've even seen a photograph of a cyclist using a homemade trailer to pull a kayak!

Probably the most compact commercial cargo trailer is the eight-pound Wheele. Basically, it is a diagonal pole that fastens at the top to your seat post and has a small wheel at the other end. Up to 35 pounds of gear can be slung in the bag under the pole.

For hauling loads of up to 100 pounds, look into the B.O.B. trailer or the various trailers designed for one or two children (see "Using Your Bicycle for Errands," page 50). Many attach to the left side of the bicycle's rear triangle close to the hub.

If you own a Bike Friday along with its suitcase, you can purchase additional hardware and two small wheels from the manufacturer, Green Gear Cycling, Inc., for converting the suitcase into an enclosed trailer.

Be forewarned, though, that a trailer itself can weigh in at more than 20 pounds, even when empty, thus adding to your load. If you anticipate using a trailer often, make sure you have super-low gears and allow more time for your ride to work.

Packs for the Bicycle

Small objects, clothes, and papers you will want to carry in zippered packs or bags rather than just strapping them onto the racks where they're exposed to the weather. Bags can also make your packing highly efficient. Develop the habit of always keeping the same items in the same compartment of the bag on one particular side of the bike, and soon you'll be able to pack and locate everything with ease.

Some of these zippered bags are available from local bicycle shops; a wider selection can be ordered from mail-order houses.

Please do not assume you need one of each of the following types of bags! Many of them duplicate functions, and some cannot be used in conjunction with others. These descriptions just give you a list of options from which to choose for your own specific carrying needs.

Note: In most bike bags that see heavy use, the first part to give out is commonly the zipper—which either sticks or starts to separate even after being zipped closed. Don't assume that you must throw out an otherwise serviceable $50 bag when that happens! Take it to a good tailor at a reputable dry cleaner. In five minutes, the tailor can realign the zipper and attach a clip to make the fix permanent (cost: about $1); at worst, the tailor can replace the entire zipper at well under the cost of a new bag.

Panniers

Panniers (pronounced "PAN-yers," not as the French might expect) are soft-sided saddlebags, usually with an internal frame, designed to clip onto racks for quick installation and removal. The most common ones are made of heavy-duty Cor-

dura fabric, which is somewhat like a tight-weave lightweight canvas with a semi-waterproof lining.

Smaller panniers may be used interchangeably on front or rear racks (although the fastening mechanisms may have to be repositioned for use on low riders); larger ones are exclusively for the rear (otherwise your toes might hit them while pedaling). Panniers are usually sold in pairs. Some panniers snap together for easier carrying off the bike.

Panniers have an internal tension mechanism that is stretched and attached to the flat, horizontal rod forming each side of a rack and to an inverted J-hook or other attachment on the rack on each side of the hub (such J-hooks may come with the panniers; if not, they can be bought for pennies from a bike shop). The tension mechanism may be either a shock cord or a metal spring. I have heard that over time the shock cords may tend to lose their tension, allowing the pannier to come loose; they may, however, be replaceable. I've never had any problem with the metal springs weakening or rusting, although others have sometimes complained. Before buying, check with the pannier's manufacturer for warranty and details.

Some panniers are single compartments; others have all sorts of wonderful zippered side pockets and even a detachable kit (intended for toiletries and valuables while touring). The downside is, those side pockets limit the versatility of the use of the space; go for one big and one small pocket on each pannier and use stuff sacks to organize the rest of your gear.

For commuting, try the smallest panniers first so you aren't tempted to stuff them with non-essentials just because you have that wonderful volume, unless you also want them to double for

Front panniers on low-riders are centered around axle.

loaded touring. Common brands, especially for serious touring, are Cannondale, Jandd, Kirtland, Madden, Ortlieb, and Performance.

The angled cut of the lower forward corner of rear panniers, which provides heel clearance, may make it difficult to carry large books, binders, or a notebook computer. Smaller square-angled front panniers used on the rear may actually give you more usable room for such objects.

Although panniers may be advertised as waterproof, do not necessarily believe the claims. Yes, they will keep your clothes and papers dry in a light drizzle, but a heavy downpour may seep through the seams and zippers. The only ones reported to be fully waterproof are Cobb and Ortlieb. With all others, play it safe: Line the panniers with small or medium-size kitchen garbage bags (the ten- or fifteen-gallon white kind) and twist the bags closed at the top.

Handlebar Bags

A handlebar bag is useful for lightweight items that you want easily accessible—a windbreaker, a first aid kit, a snack. Handlebar bags come in two basic designs: ones intended to fit drop handlebars and ones for upright handlebars.

The ones for the drop handlebars of road bikes can be quite voluminous indeed, but don't be tempted to pack them with heavy items. I learned this the hard way. Their high center of gravity may destabilize the bicycle's steering, particularly on wet or gravely pavement at high speed. Also, make sure there is some way of adequately anchoring the bottom of the bag to the bicycle frame so that it won't bounce up toward your face every time you hit a pothole. Note that it may not be possible to strap items onto the top of a standard front rack if you use a very large handlebar bag.

If you must park your bicycle outdoors, look for a handlebar bag that can be readily removed, and fit it with a detachable shoulder strap. Then when you lock your bike, you can remove your odometer and headlight, zip them into the handlebar bag, and sling it over your shoulder as you walk in to work.

Rack Trunks

A rack trunk is a firm-sided rectangular pack with a zipper around the top that is commonly fitted with straps that pass under the rear rack and fasten with hook-and-loop closures for easy removal. Some rack trunks have an expandable central cavity as well as numerous side pockets for carrying everything from extra tools to a pump and U-locks. The rack trunk can be carried along with panniers.

Usually insulated, the rack trunk is useful for carrying a lunch and keeping it reasonably cold for a few hours. Hint: If your workplace has no refrigerator, freeze a box of juice the night before and stick the frozen juice in between your tuna sandwich and yogurt; by lunch time the juice will have thawed but will still be refreshingly chilled, and the mayonnaise and yogurt will have been kept cold enough to be safe. (Don't try this with bottled or canned beverages; the containers will explode in the freezer.)

Duffels

A duffel can carry a tremendous volume for its diameter and is particularly well-suited for gym clothes and shoes—items that don't have to be protected from wrinkles.

A bicycle duffel attaches to the rear rack in much the same way as a rack trunk, although you might find you need an additional fastener because of its larger size. If you go to the gym on only certain days, air the duffel out between uses.

Attaché Cases

For the spiffily dressed business crowd there actually is a cyclist's briefcase, which is almost indistinguishable from the soft-sided, zippered Cordura cases carried by many business people. This is a good choice for white-collar professionals who feel self-conscious carrying a backpack or other evidence of bicycle commuting into a board meeting.

The cyclist's attaché case differs from an ordinary one primarily in having hooks and a concealed tension mechanism for attaching it to a rear rack like a pannier. It also has pockets for pens, calculators, computer disks, and papers so that everything is not shaken and disordered after you bounce over potholes.

Garment Bags

Garment bags for the bicycle are a great solution for those who must be nattily dressed on the job but have a long and sweaty commute getting there. Fold your business clothes neatly as for a garment bag taken on an airplane; then lay the bag across the rear rack with each end attached to the hub hooks for rear panniers. A bicycle garment bag will keep a suit and dress shirt or a blouse protected from the elements and free of wrinkles while in transit; there are also special compartments for dress shoes.

The only disadvantage of a bicycle garment bag is that you cannot carry anything else on the rear rack.

Of course, this is not necessarily a problem if you have front panniers, a handlebar bag, or a backpack.

Wedges

Wedges—so named because of their triangular shape—are zippered bags that fasten to the rails under the saddle. They are intended primarily for carrying bicycle tools. Some are so tiny they barely accommodate a patch kit; others are large enough for all the tools you'd need on even the longest, most isolated commute. Some are soft-sided; others are reinforced with stiff plastic.

Choose the size of wedge you need by the number of tools you intend to carry for your commute (see "Emergency Roadside Repairs," page 151). Modest sized wedges usually will not interfere with most stuff you might carry on a permanently mounted rear rack.

Some wedges attach only with hook-and-loop closures, others with some kind of augmenting buckle. I strongly recommend the latter. Tools are heavy for their size, and even when anchored as well as possible, they swing and bounce enough to reduce the "stickiness" of the hook-and-loop closures well before the zipper or the rest of the bag wears out, rendering the wedge prematurely useless.

Racks and Packs for Recumbents

Some creativity may be required for mounting racks and packs on a recumbent bicycle, because most gear is standardized for upright bicycles and different brands of recumbents are designed quite differently. "It's possible, but you have to improvise," notes Juneau, Alaska, commuter John Andersen. "My computer is between my knees, my headlights are five feet in front of me." Some recumbent riders may prefer towing a trailer, although—depending on which type of recumbent—you may want to check where this puts your center of gravity and whether it adds to or detracts from your stability.

Packs for the Rider

Fanny packs, backpacks, and messenger bags differ from all the bags discussed so far in that they are carried by the cyclist instead of the bicycle. Thus, in addition to carrying capacity, you also want to consider the pros and cons of comfort, ventilation, stability, and visibility—and even wearability on a recumbent.

Fanny Packs

Fanny packs are zippered bags attached to a strap that buckles around the waist or hips, with the bag itself carried over the small of your back where it won't interfere with pedaling. This placement can help keep your lower back warm in winter, although it also can expose the bag to the elements (unless you cover it with the tail of your cycling jacket).

Unlike a backpack or handlebar bag, a fanny pack does not significantly raise your center of gravity. It can carry a remarkable amount and is very comfortable. It is useful for everything you'd normally carry in a purse or suit jacket—wallet, keys, pens—plus maybe even a water bottle. Some commuters also like to carry their tolls and lunch in an extra-large fanny pack, thus doing away with a wedge and handlebar bag.

A convertible fanny pack has a separate zippered compartment on top that contains a lightweight shoulder pack, which is perfect for stowing unexpected extra work or a loaf of bread picked up on the way home. (The straps may be too narrow and the foldable pack too lightweight, however, for daily use.)

For maximum comfort, make sure that the fanny pack has a true hip belt, not just a narrow waist strap, so its weight is distributed and stabilized over your whole pelvis.

Backpacks

A backpack or "book bag" is worn on the back and supported by two padded shoulder straps.

Larger models also have an internal frame, a hip belt, and a sternum strap to better support the load.

A backpack provides a great amount of room, especially if you need to carry manuscripts or documents. A backpack also has a number of disadvantages. If heavy, it raises your center of gravity and can affect your steering. If stuffed, a large backpack can interfere with your ability to see traffic over your shoulders. If your commute is long, the straps can chafe the front of your shoulders and under your arms; the pack's rubbing across your back can even irritate the skin over any projecting vertebrae. In the winter, a full backpack over heavy clothes can feel tight and confining. All this being said, a backpack has so many arms-free advantages off the bike that I used one for years.

If you don't mind carrying a backpack while on the bike, but you'd prefer the appearance of an attaché case when off the bike, some sporting goods stores carry Cordura attaché cases with concealed straps and hooks that convert into backpacks—one alternative to the cyclist's attaché.

Messenger Bags

A messenger bag resembles a soft-sided attaché that has a long shoulder strap, allowing it to be carried over one shoulder. While riding, the case itself is stabilized over your back with a waist strap. The messenger bag opens at the top, allowing you to carry oversized packages or mailing tubes—something that may be important in some professions. Off the bike, the shoulder strap can be dropped inside the bag, giving it the more traditional appearance of an attaché. One type of messenger-style bag, the Performance Metro Clip, also converts to a pannier. The permutations and combinations are endless.

Fasteners

Objects are most commonly strapped onto bicycle racks with shock cords commonly known as bungee cords: stretchy cords of differing lengths and widths having a vinyl-coated steel hook on each end. One hook is fastened somewhere onto the rack, the cord is stretched over the load, and the second hook is fastened elsewhere onto the rack, so the load is bound onto the rack by the tension of what amounts to a giant cloth-covered rubber band.

The bungee cords found in bicycle shops are commonly ¼-inch thick and either two or three feet long. You can find a wider variety in an auto or RV supply store or in the auto supply section of a major department store, such as Sears. These include bungee cords up to four feet long, a "spider" of a dozen bungee cords tied to a central steel ring, and packages of very small bungee cords perhaps only ⅛-inch thick and six to fifteen inches long—all of which are extremely useful.

The "spider" of cords (which you can also make yourself by knotting two or more three-foot cords together in their centers) is useful for lashing boxes or other rather large, heavy, or irregularly shaped loads onto your rear rack. In the simplest configuration—two bungees knotted together—hold the knot or the ring on the top of the package while you bring the four hooks down under the rack, one down each of the box's four sides. Attach the hooks around various parts of the rack. For extra security, wrap another bungee cord horizontally around the box to prevent the box from slipping out between two cords should you ride over potholes.

The small bungee cords are useful for little, miscellaneous repairs that you can't always predict. I keep a couple with some safety pins in my handlebar bag. The first time you use them, you'll know why you carry them.

Always use two hands to fasten any kind of shock cord.

Similar to a bungee cord is a stretchy shock cord known as a Rack Strap made by Blackburn. It consists of two flat stretchy shock cords about three feet long whose ends are joined at an angle to double hooks. The flat cord resists rolling and may stay in place better over irregular packages; the double hook is specially designed to fit under the base of a rack near the hub. But don't try to just tuck something under the Rack Strap; its tension may not be sufficient to hold it in place.

For safety, always use two hands to fasten any kind of shock cord—one to stretch the cord from the first hook and hold it under tension, and the other to attach the second hook—until you are absolutely sure the second hook is secure. When fully stretched, bungee cords pack a lot of energy. If the second hook unexpectedly releases, its fast-flying end can cause serious damage, gouging out a deep chunk of your flesh or worse (scars of experience here). Holding onto the stretched cord with a second hand limits its flying travel. Don't think you may be saved because the hook's end is covered by a vinyl protector; the vinyl protector is the first thing to come off and get lost, and the side of the flying hook can still hurt if it smacks you upside the head.

(By the way, bungee cords can have a million uses, including simple temporary repairs. While en route home from my daughter's nursery school, a screw supporting her child seat backed out of the rear rack and the rear eyelet of my bicycle frame; I noticed its loss only when the rear rack sagged under her weight and dragged on the rear tire. When I could not find the screw along the road, I hit on the idea of slipping a bungee-cord hook into the two screw holes to hold the rack in place—and it worked flawlessly for the two miles home.)

Chapter Six

USING YOUR BICYCLE FOR ERRANDS

The capability of carrying children and groceries allows a bicycle to be truly practical transportation. Note commuter's fanny pack and bicycle's low-rider front rack and handlebar bag.

Groceries and Children

Like car commuters, you may want to combine bicycle commuting to and from work with errands —shopping for groceries, shuttling your child to and from daycare or school, and the like. Or you may become such a cycling enthusiast that you want to do many of your weekend errands on the bike as well.

Properly equipped, it's amazing how much a bike can carry; I myself have carried up to six bags of groceries. You'll learn how in this section.

Once again, be ingenious about handling the necessities. If you take a child to a sitter or to school on your way to work, why not ask if it's okay to store the child carrier there during the day? Not only will that lighten your load, but bicycle-commuting couples can trade off who picks up the child on the ride home, and both can use the same carrier.

The more you take into account your life's practicalities, the more likely you'll be to reach for the bicycle rather than the car keys.

Carrying Groceries

As an impulse buyer, I always walk out of a grocery store with far more than I intended to buy. But amazingly, I have always managed to get it onto the bicycle and home in one piece—including such delicate and oddly shaped items as eggs, cantaloupes, and pizza shells. You can, too.

Grocery Baskets

The oldest form of carrier is the metal wire basket. Commonly you will see one-speed and three-speed bikes dating from the 1950s and 1960s equipped with a front basket fastened to the handlebars over the front wheel, or a pair of rear baskets that bolt over the rear rack, with one permanently open basket on each side of the rear wheel. Fixed, open wire baskets once were standard equipment for bicycles, and they still can be found at yard sales. Bicycle shops also sell folding metal grocery baskets by Wald, which close flat against the bicycle when not in use.

Wire baskets have distinct advantages and disadvantages. The rear ones each nicely hold a standard grocery bag, and they are as durable as racks—even protecting your produce should the bicycle fall over. But wire baskets are heavy (compared with panniers with their hard plastic frames and Cordura fabric); they are not easily removable (compared with the quick-release system of panniers); they are not remotely waterproof (compared with the coated Cordura fabric of panniers, especially if lined with plastic bags); their open tops allow small or unsecured items to bounce out (instead of being held in by zippers); and in some circumstances they can make it difficult to lock the bicycle securely.

The upshot is, if you have an older bicycle equipped with front or rear wire baskets, by all means use the rig. Plenty of commuters do, with great success. And if you're on a tight budget and can pick up a pair of rear wire baskets for cheap at a yard sale, do it and save yourself some big bucks. But if you're shopping for new equipment, think twice about making them your first choice.

Grocery Panniers

Similar in concept to rear wire baskets are open-topped grocery panniers. Made of Cordura fabric stitched around a frame, they fold closed against the side of the rear rack when not in use.

The open top and extra width of grocery panniers means that you can just slide in your full paper or plastic grocery bags and ride off. (In contrast, because of their narrower width and zippered openings, regular panniers usually will not accept a full paper grocery bag, requiring you to repack the individual items into each pannier.)

Improvisation

I found that a surprisingly good grocery carrier was my daughter's empty rear child seat (see next section on child carriers). The secret was to request that the groceries be packed in double plastic bags, not paper.

Fat, heavy items, such as a gallon of milk and a half-gallon of orange juice, could sit snugly on the seat itself, secured by the horizontal arm rest. Long, thin, durable items such as boxes of spaghetti or bags of carrots could stand upright in the foot wells, secured by the hook-and-loop foot straps. Boxes of muffin mix could be wedged here and there in between, with other items in bags secured under the seat's shoulder straps. Canned goods fit well into the fanny pack section of my convertible fanny/backpack; lighter-weight bulky items, such as boxes of cereal, or breakables such as eggs, were protected well in the backpack section. Small dense items, such as cans of tuna and juice boxes, could be zipped into my handlebar bag. Everything else could be tied to the child seat's straps by knotting together the handles of the plastic bags. Bags can be tied onto other bags and even hung over the rear of the seat, if you don't mind some degradation of the bicycle's handling.

A child seat can also carry several bags of groceries.

In a pinch, a small rider can slip his or her arms through the plastic grocery bag handles to improvise a backpack, with fruits and veggies hanging down between the shoulder blades—uncomfortable, yes, but tolerable for a mile or two home. (Remember this trick if you pass a farm stand on a summer weekend ride and don't want to bounce the vine-ripened tomatoes into juice on your rear rack.)

Carrying a Child

A child old enough to hold his or her head up to sit upright (nine to twelve months on average) may be a passenger on a bicycle. In bicycling circles, there is a heated debate about which is safest for a very young child (and the adult cyclist), a rear child seat or a trailer.

The debate usually centers on the fact that a child in a child seat raises your center of gravity, which can require a fair amount of upper body strength, good reflexes, and experience for confident handling. There is no denying this fact.

A child trailer has a low center of gravity, making for stable handling. Some cyclists claim it even makes the bicycle handle better than without the trailer. And if the adult cyclist falls, the trailer may not even tip over—or may do so in only a slow roll.

A trailer is about three feet wide, however, possibly compelling the adult cyclist to ride a bit farther away from the right-side edge of the road than he or she might normally do to keep the right-hand trailer tire on smooth pavement. Even though a trailer is usually brightly colored and heralded with a waving flag, its width may cause some parents to fear that it is in danger of being clipped by cars passing too close. Riders with trailers counter by noting that motorists usually give a

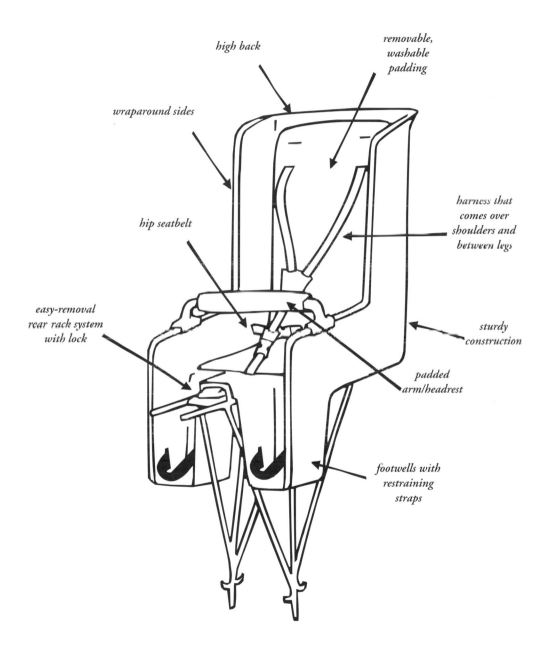

high back

removable, washable padding

wraparound sides

harness that comes over shoulders and between legs

hip seatbelt

easy-removal rear rack system with lock

sturdy construction

padded arm/headrest

footwells with restraining straps

Key features to look for in a child seat.

trailer a wide berth, knowing that its occupant is a child.

Child seats are more compact and do not lengthen or widen the profile of the bicycle. A child seat is also much lighter than a trailer, which can top 20 pounds empty—a factor that may be important in hilly areas. A child seat also costs one half to one third what trailers do (some trailers approach the price of a lower-cost bicycle). But a trailer allows you to carry more than one child plus luggage and can also shield the child from the weather.

Try both and—with the intimate knowledge of driver habits in your area plus your own needs (especially if you have more than one child)—make your own decision.

Child Seats

A child seat allows a toddler or young child—usually no more than 40 pounds—to be carried on top of the rear wheel of an adult's bicycle. My own daughter was able to use a child seat from eighteen months to age four-and-a-half; a child who is very tall or very heavy will grow out of a child seat at a much earlier age, while some petite children can still use it at age six.

The safest child seats have a back that comes up above the child's head (to prevent whiplash), sides that wrap around (to protect the child in a fall), straps that come up between the child's legs and over the shoulders as well as across the lap (so the child won't dangle when snoozing), and straps for securing the feet in the foot wells (so little toes don't get hurt in the spokes). Some child seats also have a padded bar that fits across the front at the child's elbow height; such a bar is very nice if the child dozes off, because it pillows the head during the ride.

Once again, for maximum safety, buy a child seat from a bicycle shop instead of from a toy store or department store. Rhode Gear, Troxel, and other manufacturers are well known for their excellent products.

Some child seats bolt permanently onto the back of the bike. Better ones fasten onto a rear rack with two or more locking devices and can be slipped off and on without much trouble (do watch your fingers to prevent them from being pinched, though). Some child seats require a rack with a particular feature, such as a front section that rises from the flat surface vertically instead of at the usual 45-degree angle. So if there are two bicycle commuters who might be trading off shuttling the child to and from day care or preschool, make sure to fit both bikes with the proper type of rack, which often can be bought separately.

With a child seat, your luggage-carrying capacity is limited to front panniers and whatever type of pack you care to wear. The rear rack is completely removed from service.

Hint from experience: Even if the child seat can recline, never use that feature. Always keep the seat in its full and upright position (to use airline lingo). When the seat is reclined, the child's weight extends beyond the rear axle, causing the bicycle to fishtail and degrading its handling.

Child Trailers

A child trailer, which is usually fastened to the left side of the rear triangle near the axle, is towed behind the bicycle. The child is secured on a seat inside with shoulder, lap, and crotch straps. The major advantages of a trailer are that it can be fitted to carry an infant, it can carry a child's toys and other gear on longer trips, and some designs can carry two children totaling up to 100 pounds. A trailer also can be fitted with netting or plastic to protect its young occupant from wind, dust, rain, or cold.

The safest trailers have a protective metal frame and roll bar. Some have a frame that can be folded so it will fit into the trunk of a car. Designs with inflatable 16-inch or 20-inch wheels give the smoothest ride for the child, and the larger wheels won't hang up in potholes. Several well-known manufacturers include Burley, Rhode Gear, and Koolstop Original (formerly Winchester).

With a trailer, you can also carry stuff on top of your rear rack and in at least one rear pannier (on the right side, opposite the trailer's connection).

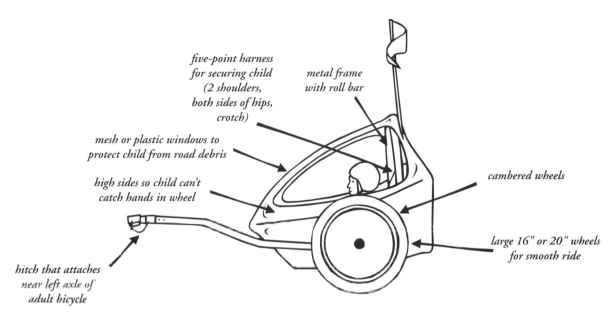

*five-point harness
for securing child
(2 shoulders,
both sides of hips,
crotch)*

*metal frame
with roll bar*

*mesh or plastic windows to
protect child from road debris*

*high sides so child can't
catch hands in wheel*

cambered wheels

*large 16" or 20" wheels
for smooth ride*

*hitch that attaches
near left axle of
adult bicycle*

A child trailer can carry one or two children up to 100 pounds.

Trailer Cycles

A trailer cycle is essentially a child-sized rear half of a bicycle that can be clipped to an adult's bicycle, instantly turning your steed into a three-wheeled tandem. The trailer cycle allows you to use the bicycle to shuttle your child to and from school through those awkward years when the kid is too big for a child seat or trailer but is still too young to be pedaling alone in traffic or for any real distance.

The trailer cycle comes complete with handlebar, pedals, and a saddle whose positions can be adjusted to accommodate the child's growth from ages four through ten years. Unlike a standard two-wheeled tandem, the trailer cycle has its own freewheel, allowing the child to pedal or coast as he or she chooses. Like a trailer, the trailer cycle itself weighs some 20 pounds; but with verbal coaching and some judicious bribery (Fig Newtons, etc.), you can induce your child to pedal up hills—which is a big help.

Trailer cycles attach either to the seatpost or to the top of a rear rack of the adult's bicycle. Therefore, a trailer cycle precludes your carrying stuff on the top of the rack; however, you may still be able to use rear panniers. You might also try using a detachable rear rack on the trailer cycle (a permanent rack designed for BMX bikes cannot be made level on a trailer cycle without some custom metalworking).

The pioneer of trailer bicycles is the Canadian-made Adams Trail-a-Bike. Fitted with a standard 20-inch BMX bicycle wheel and sliding handlebar, the models range up to ones suitable for up to three children and capable of five-speed shifting. The cost is comparable with that of a child trailer or a lower-end adult bicycle from a pro shop but is far cheaper than a standard tandem with a child-kit adapter.

A similar item is the Ally Cat Shadow II. It also has a 20-inch wheel, but its handlebar can only be rotated to different positions. It costs about half that of the Adams models.

Burley, the well-known maker of child trailers, offers the Piccolo, which fastens with a proprietary attachment to the top of a custom heavy-duty rear rack. Because the attachment point is directly over the rear axle, it has a lower and more stable center of gravity than the seat post–attachment models offer, thus avoiding some of the torquing movement the adult cyclist otherwise feels when the tail-gunner decides to lay on a burst of power.

Avoid the look-alikes marketed by department stores or toy stores. Not only are they comparatively flimsy, but the child is a completely passive passenger; there is no drive train allowing you to benefit from some back-seat pedaling.

If you and another commuting cyclist share child-care duties, buy two of the mechanisms that attach the trailer cycle to your bike—one for each commuter. If you can arrange to leave the trailer cycle at the school with the child, the two adults can easily share the drop-off and pick-up duties.

Children's Bicycling Accessories

A child in a child seat, trailer, or trailer cycle is exposed to the same hazards as an adult cyclist and so must have the same protections.

Number one is a good child's helmet—in fact, helmets are now mandated for minors on bicycles in at least 15 states: Alabama, California, Connecticut, Delaware, Florida, Georgia, Maryland, Massachusetts, New Jersey, New York, Oregon,

Give your kid a choice. Make the helmet a fashion accessory.

Pennsylvania, Rhode Island, Tennessee, and West Virginia. Legislation is pending in other states, although local jurisdictions have already passed laws. For details in your area, check with a local bike shop. Several makers produce helmets for children that meet all the same stringent Snell standards as helmets for adult cyclists; their concession to young riders are decorations in all the favorite garish designs, neon colors, and imaginative characters. Give your kid a choice. Make the helmet a fashion accessory. Again, however, do not buy such a vital safety accessory at a toy store unless you can find one with a Snell sticker inside; go to a bicycle shop.

Once a child graduates to a trailer cycle, his or her hands are also exposed to the same road shock and risk of falling as yours. Go back to the bike shop and invest in a pair of padded, fingerless bicycling gloves just like mama's or daddy's. And since your pride and joy is now bringing up the rear, make sure he or she is dressed in light colors adorned with the same highly reflective trim as you are.

Hint: If your child has long hair, bind it at the neck and ends to prevent wind-blown tangles—and tears at combing-out time.

Part Two

TECHNIQUES

Dennis Coello

Chapter Seven

CHOOSING A
GOOD COMMUTING
ROUTE

San Diego, California, commuter Jerry Schad enjoys a fast section on the shoulder of an interstate.

What Makes a Route Good for Bicycle Commuting?

"Selecting a commuting route is not like selecting one for a Saturday ride. You pay attention to efficiency, not scenery, fancy hillclimbs, or lack of traffic," observed John Forester, in his classic book *Effective Cycling.*

. . . You may start with the idea that you want to avoid traffic, but it won't work that way. More than most motorists, you need a route with minimum stops and slow-downs, because these tire you as well as delay you. So you will ride the main streets because they are protected by stop signs, have signals set in your favor, and have better sight distances at hazardous places, which are also the reasons motorists choose these routes.
. . . [Y]ou soon enough realize that with regular riding cycling in traffic is not particularly difficult or dangerous as long as you follow the traffic-safe cycling techniques . . . Just like everybody else commuting, you'll attempt to find a

better route or short-cut. Your criterion will be speed or effort, not scenery or lack of traffic.

Forester is generally correct in saying that your main criterion will be speed or effort. I would respectfully point out, however, that there are many circumstances in which commuting along the main roads with major amounts of motor-vehicle traffic is not more efficient—or even wiser—than taking a side road with a lesser amount of traffic. Moreover, road conditions and the quality of the neighborhoods through which you pass may also be considerations.

In my view, the best commuting route is one that is the most direct, with the least traffic, the fewest road hazards, and the greatest personal safety. You must examine the roads in your own area and make your personal choice based on the specific circumstances between your home and your place of work.

Evaluating Possible Routes

Look first at the route you already take to work by car or public transportation. If the main road between home and work is essentially a straight line, and if bicycles are allowed on it, then it may well be the best choice for two wheels as well as four. Commuters in Maryland and Oregon, for example, are especially blessed in this regard: Many of the main highways in those states have smooth, lane-wide, paved shoulders specifically marked for bicycles.

Even if you don't like the main road because of its traffic, you may be stuck with it because it's the only route that exists. For example, there is only one road that links Greenport, Long Island, with points east on the north fork. Likewise, there is only one road that links Clearwater, Florida, with Madeira Beach and points south to St. Petersburg Beach. Similarly, in relatively new (post-1960) suburbs such as the tract housing common in California and Florida, the residential streets meander endlessly through the homes without taking you any place in particular, limiting you to one main road for traveling any distance.

In any region crisscrossed by many secondary and tertiary roads, however, you might have more—and better—alternatives available than you know, especially if you now drive only one route by rote. It's worth some time to do a bit of research.

Maps—and Their Limitations

You cannot decide which route is best for bicycle commuting from only looking at a map. Maps show you only where roads go—and some maps don't even show all the roads or don't show them accurately or indicate which roads are one-way. Moreover, only in the roughest way do maps give clues about road conditions, traffic, or local topography. They give no information about routes available to bicycles but not to cars (such as a paved bike path through a park) nor about the quality of the neighborhoods through which roads pass. Furthermore, they do not show how some factors, such as traffic, vary with the time of day or night. Last, maps can be rife with errors ranging from the spelling of names to the placement, presence, or absence of entire streets.

In selecting a route, however, you must start somewhere, and a map is a start. Get a street map or a county map that shows all the local roads. Make a point of finding the most recent map published; in some areas, construction is so rapid that recently built roads may not be shown on maps that are only a year or two old.

In some cases, you may need more than one type of map to fully explore all potential routes. For example, the wonderfully accurate, large-scale, black-and-white county maps from the Planning

Division of the Department of Highways in West Virginia show only numbered county roads, omitting all named streets within towns and cities! So if you are commuting from rural to urban West Virginia, you'll need a separate map to plot your route through town.

Try to find a bicycle-suitability map. Such maps, if one exists for your area, are often published by a local bicycle group or a state's bicycle coordinator; they may be sold at local bike shops. Not only will such a map show all local streets and roads, but it will also code them for traffic loads and other factors relevant to cyclists.

Weekend Test Ride of Potential Routes

Once you've chosen several candidate commuting routes, take a Saturday or Sunday to cycle the different options to determine the mileage and the minimum time needed to pedal the distance. Keep an eye out for general road conditions and situations that might pose a problem during rush-hour traffic or in poor visibility.

Choosing Among Main Roads

Some main roads may be distinctly superior to others for bicycle commuting. For example, the roadway or shoulders may be smoother, the visibility is better on curves, there's a genuinely safe bike lane, the neighborhood is safer, or the lighting is better after dark.

A case in point was the part of my bicycle commute southeast of Central Park from 59th Street to 48th Street toward the United Nations building in New York City, I had no choice but to ride along one of midtown Manhattan's main north-south avenues. After trying them all—one-way Fifth Avenue, Lexington Avenue, and Second Avenue for riding south, and one-way Madison Avenue, Third Avenue, and First Avenue for riding north on the return—I settled on two-way Park Avenue for traveling in both directions. Two crucial factors dictated that choice: the lanes are significantly wider

than on the other avenues, and—most important —no buses are allowed north of 46th Street. That meant I never had to breathe diesel exhaust, I was never in danger of being overtaken and cut off by a bus passing me and then ducking right to reach the curb, and I never risked being squeezed between a bus and a car or between two buses, which were ever-present hazards on all the other north-south avenues.

Similar practical considerations should help you determine your route for your commute.

Choosing Among Side Roads

There are circumstances in which parallel side roads are distinctly superior to a main road.

In midtown Manhattan—and probably in other cities that are laid out in a grid—the numerous, narrow, one-way side streets are superior to the few main two-way crosstown streets for heading east or west. Why? Because there are no buses and only relatively light local car traffic and the same number of traffic lights. Not only are the side streets easier on the nerves, but for a bicycle the travel time also is faster.

In older suburbs built before it became fashionable to slow or discourage car traffic by creating cul-de-sacs and circular entrances and exits, side roads may be just as direct as main roads—with far less traffic. In the relatively old (old by California standards) suburbs of Los Angeles, for example, there seems to be a category of "main side road" ideal for bicycle commuting. Such side roads parallel the main four-lane roads; their two-lane width and 25-mile-per-hour speed limits discourage automobiles, and they are protected from cross traffic by stop signs at intersecting side roads.

Much of the flat farm land across the nation is laid out in regular grids with north-south and east-west roads bounding every square mile. The lesser-traveled side roads are often just as direct as the main highways. Moreover, because they have few if any commercial enterprises (rural towns tend to be laid out along one main road), they have fewer turn-offs and far less traffic—especially suction-producing trucks. Although rural side roads usually don't have shoulders, riding in the lanes is less treacherous than riding on the shoulders of the main roads, which can be badly chewed up, essentially rendering them unusable.

Bicycle Paths—Pros and Cons

In some cases, a paved bicycle path may give you not only a more pleasant commute, but also a shorter travel distance. In the case of a commute from Kensington, Maryland (or even from Rock-ville, Maryland) into the heart of Washington, D.C., for example, pedaling along the paved bike path running the length of Rock Creek Park is far more direct than traveling along any combination of main roads. Riding a bicycle path even only part of the way can make a surprising difference if the bike path runs at an angle across streets laid out in a grid or joins two streets that are not connected by another road.

Bike paths may also have disadvantages. If bike paths are not well-maintained, they may become covered with slippery leaves in the autumn or blocked by snow in winter (unless you're lucky

You cannot decide which route is best for bicycle commuting from only looking at a map.

enough to live in an enlightened city where bike paths are routinely plowed). On beautiful sunny days, your progress may be impeded by crowds of joggers and families with dogs and strollers. Alternatively, the route may be too isolated or unlighted to make you feel comfortable riding alone after dark.

Again, you must be the judge for your case. Even if the path is not suitable at all times of the day or the year, it may be ideal for other times.

Bicycle Lanes—Pros and Cons

There are vocal cyclists—including John Forester—who are adamantly opposed to striped, on-road bike lanes, claiming that such lanes are actually anti-bicycle. According to their arguments, bike lanes imply to motorists that bicycles do not belong on the roadway itself and that bike lanes may ultimately lead to mandatory sidepath restrictions. They also argue that bike lanes are dangerous: They might lull a cyclist into feeling as safe as if riding on the sidewalk, they can create uncertainty in the minds of motorists at intersections (such as motorists wishing to make right turns), and they encourage incompetent cyclists by removing the motivation to ride according to good vehicular principles.

I do not subscribe to such an extreme viewpoint. That being said, there are certainly places where bike lanes do not perform as they should because they are poorly designed (such as being placed on the left side of a one-way roadway or are striped for two-way traffic on just one side of the road), because they are poorly maintained and thus accumulate sand and other debris, or because delivery trucks and other motor vehicles double-park in them.

If you are fortunate to commute in an area with well-planned bike lanes, enjoy them in good health. Until you are familiar with the ones in your area, however, do not assume that just because a bike lane is striped it is safe. If lanes begin and end unexpectedly, are placed on arbitrary sides of the road, invite unexpected meetings of bicycles and motor vehicles, or simply collect glass and other hazards, just ride as if they don't exist. You're smart; you'll figure it out.

When Longer Is Better

In some areas you might choose to bicycle by a route that is longer than the route you commute by car—and not just because you want to get more exercise. For example, you may be compelled to lengthen your route if bicyclists are prohibited from using a bridge or tunnel on the most direct route.

Another reason is safety or the perception of safety: Perhaps the most direct route has S-curves around which motorists cannot see a cyclist, or it goes through an undesirable neighborhood in which you feel vulnerable, or it passes a junkyard with a watchdog that barks so viciously you worry about the strength of its restraining chain.

If something on the most direct route annoys you or makes your heart pound, keeping the distance short may be secondary to maintaining peace of mind. After all, you're commuting by bicycle not only to get exercise and save money, but also because you enjoy it. If basic enjoyment is sapped by tension each day, you might begin finding excuses for not commuting by bicycle at all, when the real solution is simply to find a more acceptable route.

Odd Routes for Odd-Hour Commuters

Do you work in an office with flexible hours where you can choose your own starting and ending times? Or do you work evenings and weekends at a retail establishment? Or do you work a swing or graveyard shift? If so, as a bicycle commuter you are freed from traveling at the peak of traditional rush hours.

That freedom may, in fact, allow you to use routes unavailable to your nine-to-five counterparts. In some cities—New York City among them—roads through parks may be closed to automobiles between the traditional morning and afternoon rush hours, allowing cyclists to rule the pavements. Some main four-lane highways may also be closed to cars early on Sunday mornings, especially in the summer, allowing weekend commuters the best main roads of all.

At the very least, you may be able to use main roads when they have the least traffic—before or after most people are already at work.

Telecommuters or the self-employed may also take advantage of these odd hours. "I work from home, so I don't commute, so to speak," recounted Salt Lake City and St. Louis freelance photographer Dennis Coello. "But this allows me the wonderful hours from 9:00 to 11:30 AM and 1:30 to 4:00 PM to go to the post office, UPS, Fedex, or Office Depot while getting in a real workout."

Checklist of Miscellaneous Factors

As you ride along each potential route, examine it for a host of other factors. These differ a bit depending on whether your commute is primarily urban, suburban, or rural.

Questions for an Urban Commute

- Does any part of the route go through an "undesirable" or unsafe neighborhood? Can that be avoided by shifting your route a few blocks?

- Is any part of the route on one-way streets? If so, how must the return trip differ from the outbound trip? On one-way streets, always plan to ride with traffic. Riding against the traffic is illegal and just asking for a head-on collision; moreover, you cannot see the traffic lights change because they face vehicles only in one direction.

- Where must you turn left across traffic? Are the signals timed so that traffic turning left is protected? Or is the signal a come-on booby trap where an unwary cyclist is at risk of being hit by a car proceeding legally? Left-turn hazards exist especially at three-way intersections with badly planned signals and at busy four-way intersections with no separate left-turn lanes.

- How much broken glass is there on the road? Use Kevlar-belted tires reinforced with a heavy plastic strip—Mr. Tuffy is one brand—and puncture-resistant inner tubes. The sharp splinters from broken bottles are more damaging than the obviously rounder pieces left by the shattered tempered glass of automobile windshields. If you do accidentally ride through broken glass, stop immediately, then walk your bike a few feet while rubbing the leather palm of your gloved hand on the riding surface of each tire. With luck, your glove should dislodge slivers of glass that might otherwise burrow into the tire and inner tube and cause a flat. If there seems to be a lot of broken glass along your commute, consider installing a loop of stiff wire on your downtube and seat tube that has a horizontal inch of wire that lightly touches each tire to knock off anything picked up by the tire before it can make one revolution and be wedged into the rubber by your weight. And always carry tire levers, an extra tube, a patch kit, and an air pump and know how to use them.

Questions for a Suburban Commute

- Do you pass by a local elementary, junior high, or senior high school? If so, what are its hours? Avoid commuting past a suburban school during the half hour surrounding its opening and closing. You may be slowed by up to five to ten minutes because automobile traffic increases unbelievably as parents drop

Avoid commuting past a suburban school during the half hour surrounding its opening and closing.

off and pick up their offspring; local police may even be directing cars.

- Where can you shorten your route by cutting through a college campus or a park? Is that a good choice all year around? Cutting through a college campus might be good only in the summer when the pedestrian student population is low. Make sure that bicycles are allowed through the park; don't risk a summons by violating a local ordinance or by riding where signs command you to dismount.
- Is the commute near the ocean? Your bicycle's frame is exposed to corrosive salt air that can rapidly eat away the metal where paint has been nicked. As attractive as a commute along the beach might be at sunrise or sunset, be aware that the sand kicked up by your wheels will cling to your chain and brake pads and rapidly wear down your gears and rims, requiring some cleaning once you reach home. Also, is there a route several blocks inland where on windy days you can avoid sand being blown onto the road or into your eyes?
- Are there any aggressive dogs on the route? Is there a leash law in the neighborhood? If not, can the dog be avoided by taking another route?
- Examine the drainage grates: Do the grills parallel the curb and are they spaced about two inches apart? Do any of the grates extend several feet out into the roadway where you might be riding? Especially, is a grate hidden around a corner? If so, memorize that turn, approach it with caution, and always plan to take that corner wide. Drainage grates with grills parallel to the flow of traffic and about two inches apart are one of cycling's most common road hazards, especially in suburban and semirural areas. The grills are just far enough apart for your bicycle tire to drop into the slot right to the axle, ruining an expensive wheel and throwing you for a nasty spill. Never ride over these grates—you can't win. Extra warning: In some areas where

the roads have been widened, there may even be a double-width drainage grate three feet into the road from the curb. This is truly hazardous. Contact your local town planning commission and lobby for replacing the grates with a safer grillwork to prevent cycling accidents.

safe grate

watch out!

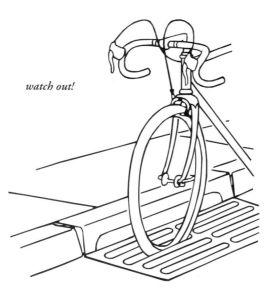

Watch carefully for unsafe drainage grates—some of which can grab a front wheel and cause a serious accident.

Questions for a Rural Commute

- Are the roads cracked and pocked from heavy farm machinery? Frequently the local idea of rural road maintenance is simply to throw on another series of asphalt patches, making for very bumpy riding. The surfaces of some roads may be dramatically better than others, so for speedy commuting seek out the smoothest roads—or attack the ones you have with a true mountain bike.

- Must you ride on the shoulder of an interstate highway for some of the commute? In some parts of Arizona, California, and other western states such riding is legal and even specially marked because there is no alternative route. If an interstate highway is part of your route, how strong is the suction from trucks barreling by at 70 mph? Do vehicles kick up gravel? How visible are you after nightfall?

- Must any part of the route be made on dirt or gravel roads that are periodically oiled? If so, are there any alternate routes? Riding on a freshly oiled dirt road is guaranteed to gunk up your tires, brakes, and frame; it can take an hour or more to clean the mess.

- Are you commuting in Texas or other western states where roads are littered with tack-sharp thorns? Use Kevlar-belted tires reinforced with a heavy plastic strip and puncture-resistant inner tubes. And always carry tire levers, an extra tube, a patch kit, and an air pump and know how to use them.

- Is there a deep drainage ditch only a few feet from the pavement's edge, as is common in Ohio farm country? If so, is there a white "fog line" painted along the pavement's edge to mark the boundaries of the road for easy visibility after dark?

- Are there any cattle guards? In farm country, a road may have a cattle guard: a three-foot-wide grating made of steel rails spaced about six or eight inches apart laid across a shallow pit that crosses the entire road. Most cattle guards are laid perpendicular to the road, so you can ride across them with impunity—although you should slow down to minimize the washboard bumpiness. Be especially cautious crossing a cattle guard in the rain; the wet steel rails can become very slippery.

- Are there railroad tracks? Railroad tracks are a hazard primarily when they cross the road on a diagonal. Slow down as you approach them. You want to ride across the rails perpendicularly. If you try crossing them at a more acute angle, your tires may slip off into the slot beside the rails, possibly ruining your wheels and throwing you off the bike. If traffic does not permit you to head into the lane diagonally when you cross the tracks, then dismount and walk your bicycle across. Be especially cautious crossing railroad tracks in the rain; the wet steel rails can become very slippery.

    Note also that some rural railroad crossings are *not* protected by flashing lights, a clanging bell, and gates! Do not just blithely barrel across such crossings. Listen carefully for an approaching train and look both ways. If a train is heading toward the intersection just as you are, never try to beat it. Trains are always moving faster than they appear to be, and their stopping distance can be half a mile or more depending on their load and speed. Better to be late to work than to be dead.

- Where do you regularly find sand or fine gravel? A mixture of gravel and sand congregates in neat triangles at intersections and at the mouths of driveways in semirural and rural areas. Also, automobile tires tend to throw it to the right onto the road shoulders, particularly in early spring in areas where sand or gravel is spread on the roads in winter to improve traction on snow and ice. In some states—West Virginia for example—the shoulders of the main roads are themselves of large gravel, and so a lot of one-inch rocks also end up on the pavement. When rounding

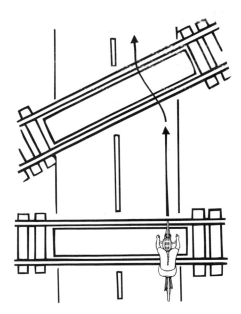

Cross railroad tracks at right angles.

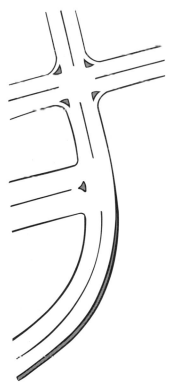

Watch when riding through areas where sand and gravel accumulate.

corners, don't ride over the triangle of gravel and don't cut too close to the curb or shoulder. Reduce your speed and commute on a mountain bike or beach cruiser with wide squishy tires to maximize traction.

- Are there aggressive dogs on the route? Can they be avoided by taking another route? Rural areas seldom have leash laws, and dogs may be left to roam free to protect a large expanse of property.
- Are there other animals of which you must be wary—such as unfenced cattle or horses or sheep? What about deer that suddenly might bound across the road? Colliding with any of these large beasts could result in serious injury. Even a squirrel dashing into your spokes could ruin your day.
- When is hunting season? Make a point of *not* wearing a white helmet; hunters sometimes shoot at moving white targets, thinking they are seeing the tail of a bounding deer. In Vermont, for example, cyclists can buy international orange covers for their helmets.

Begin to Commute by Bicycle

Riding your candidate route or routes over the weekend will give you an idea of the distance and road conditions. But a weekend ride tells you nothing about the commuter traffic or even about the timing of the traffic signals, both of which may differ on weekends and weekdays.

A day or two before you start commuting by bicycle, drive the entire route (if the entire route is on public roads) during the time of day you would be bicycle commuting. Note the traffic, the buses, and other road conditions from a cyclist's viewpoint. See if there are any other commuting cyclists taking parts of the same route and observe their techniques for handling the traffic.

Choose a lovely morning for your first try on two wheels. Unless the commute is very long or unless the nature of your work prevents you from eating after you arrive, you will likely find it most comfortable to ride on an empty stomach and then relax with coffee and breakfast after getting to work.

If you have more than one candidate route, try the alternate route either on the return home or on the next day. You may well find, in fact, that one route works better in one direction and another for the return home, depending on traffic patterns, street lighting, sun angle, steepness of hills, distance, and other factors. You may also find that the day of the week makes a difference: for example, travel along one street may be dicey on Wednes-days because all the businesses there have deliveries that morning and the street is blocked with trucks.

At first, you may wish to start bicycle commuting only two or three days per week and then work up to all five. Gradually, as you become familiar with the rhythm of the traffic, the timing of the traffic lights, and your own riding speed, you'll learn how to pace yourself so you hit all the lights green without racing and braking, and your commuting time will shorten accordingly.

Key to Happiness: Start Early

The first day you pedal the route as an actual bicycle commuter, give yourself plenty of time so you won't feel rushed—a whole extra hour beyond the time you clocked on the weekend. Because you're unfamiliar with the whole process of bicycle commuting, everything will take longer. Moreover, this first day, you'll also want to allow extra time once you arrive at work to figure out the best way to lock your bike, freshen up, and eat.

If you and most of the city where you live work from 9 AM to 5 PM, I can't emphasize enough what a difference it makes to beat the rush hour by getting an early start. If unrestricted by other factors (such as the opening of your kids' schools), you will likely choose to leave early all the time. In a city, even half an hour can make a dramatic difference. If I left my

New York City apartment by 7:00 AM, I was at work by 7:30 AM; the streets were pleasantly deserted of cars, and the time of my ride was set only by potholes and traffic signals. When I arrived at work, the elevators were empty and so I could take my bicycle up to my office.

But, heaven forbid, if I left merely half an hour later, at 7:30 AM, I never arrived before 8:15 AM—lengthening a thirty-minute commute to forty-five minutes. By the time I was riding through Manhattan's east side, the traffic was at its horn-screeching heaviest. Worst of all, in my office building all the elevators were jammed with other employees,

meaning I had to leave my bicycle in the basement. And all the good food in the cafeteria was gone.

If your city has a very early rush hour, however, and you have some flexibility in your hours, exactly the opposite tactic might work better. In Cleveland, for example, the heaviest rush hour is between 7 and 8 AM for people needing to be at work at 8. I have found my seven-and-a-half mile commute from Lakewood into Cleveland to be dramatically freer from traffic if I leave home at 8 AM instead of 7. (Leaving at 6 AM would also work well, if day care were available that early.) Upshot: Sense the rhythms in your own city and work around them.

Seasonal Road Hazards: Familiarity Breeds Alertness

Once you select the route that works best for you, stick with the same route day after day. Yes, it may get boring, but we're not touring the sights here; we're trying to get to and from work as quickly and as safely as possible. Navigating the familiar demands less psychic energy than finding your way through the unfamiliar, allowing you to arrive at work mentally refreshed instead of drained.

In addition to coming to know the timing of the signals and the rhythm of the traffic, on a route you ride daily you'll also become alert to other hazards that may develop—such as the exact location of a sinkhole slowly growing deeper and wider, or a steel plate whose lip is starting to raise, or a construction site where sand coats the entrance, or the junkyard where a big guard dog always throws itself onto its confining fence with heart-stopping growls.

If you're intimate with a route, you'll be physically and psychologically prepared to deal with such conditions. On an unfamiliar route, though, you may be so focused on seeking out the correct turn, you'll be less attuned to potential hazards and thus run a slightly greater risk of a surprise unpleasant encounter.

You may not be able to evaluate some bicycle commuting conditions on your test weekend ride or even your first few weeks of actual commuting

because they depend on the weather or the season. But as they come to your attention, make a mental note of them.

Sun Direction

Do you live west of where you work? If so, and if you commute at traditional hours, at least some part of the year you will be riding directly into the sun both morning and evening. Not only will the sun in your eyes interfere with your own view of the road, but motorists will also be blinded and may not see you. Equip your helmet with a sun visor and plan to wear flashers or other devices to increase your own visibility.

Flood Areas and Puddles

Are there poorly drained road areas that always flood during a rain? Can you design your route to circumvent those places?

Are there huge potholes that regularly become huge puddles? Never ride a bicycle through a puddle. A small puddle may just fill a pothole; a larger one may hide a drainage grate. Even if the water doesn't obscure a greater hazard, it may be topped with a thin film of motor oil from the road surface—oil that can coat your rims and dangerously reduce your braking power, doubling or even quadrupling your braking distance.

Moreover, if the water splashes up inside the bicycle's bottom bracket—the mechanism where the pedal cranks mount to the frame—the bottom bracket really should be disassembled, drained, and repacked with grease. If the water is left in the bottom bracket, accompanying grit may grind down the internal parts or the water itself may eventually rust the bicycle frame from the inside out.

Wet Surfaces

During the summer in the suburbs, are there residential sprinklers that wet the road surface as well as the lawns? Such wet pavement can present an unexpected slippery hazard when you round a corner. In cities, metal plates, grates, and manhole covers can become treacherously slippery in the rain.

Most astonishingly, painted traffic lines—features intended to enhance safety—can also pose a hazard. Some reflective traffic paint is not really paint. It may be tape or it may be a kind of plastic put down while molten, then sprinkled with sand-sized reflective plastic spheres. If wet, some types of traffic lines can become extraordinarily slick.

Watch especially if part of your commute involves a downhill coast on a road whose border is defined with a white line. One of the worst cycling falls I've suffered was on a rainy evening on just such a downhill when both my tires crossed the wet white line nearly simultaneously; they slid right out from under my bike as if they'd hit ice and down I went, barely rolling out of the way of a following car.

Ice

If temperatures in your area drop to the low thirties in the winter, even if you (as I) draw the line at riding through snow, you may well find yourself commuting when standing water has frozen into ice. Surprisingly, the overnight low does not even

Never ride through a puddle. The water may obscure a pothole or dangerous grate.

need to reach 32 degrees Fahrenheit for water to freeze; if the sky has been clear, radiative cooling may cause ice to form at a higher air temperature.

Most treacherous of all is the "black ice" (so named because it is invisible on asphalt) that forms on cold, clear nights on rural roads. Motorists, thinking the black road is safe, drive at their usual speed only to find that their brakes fail to stop the car at an intersection.

If the nighttime temperature has been anywhere close to freezing, allow a little more time the next morning and ride more slowly on your commute. Ride a mountain bike or beach cruiser with wide tires inflated to the lower specified pressure to maximize traction. Avoid riding on obvious patches of ice and steer clear of areas you know to have poor drainage or regular runoff. If a car is simultaneously approaching an intersection where you have the right of way, anticipate what you must do to protect yourself should the car slide right through the stop sign. Above all, ride watchfully and defensively.

Steep Hills

Are there steep hills that may be treacherous in winter's freezing conditions? Might you have to forgo the hill-climb when the weather turns cold enough to freeze puddles into ice?

And if you are coasting down a long steep hill or mountain on an extremely hot summer day, apply your brakes intermittently—the heat of braking friction has been known to cause the inner tube to explode.

Fallen Leaves

Do mounds of fallen leaves collect on your route? Never ride through them. They may obscure a pothole, puddle, drainage grate, broken glass, or ice. Moreover, wet leaves—even just a few of them—can be very slippery and can cause a fall.

High Winds

Does your community have high winds? Is there a risk that such high winds might blow you into the path of traffic—especially on an exposed bridge?

Manure

Do horses or cows travel along the road? No joke. Fresh manure can make the road surface slippery and is as likely to be encountered in cities that have mounted police and recreational livery carriages as it is in farm country. Moreover, if you ride through manure in the rain—as I did once (only once!) when taking a shortcut down the carriage lane in New York City's Central Park—your tires will spray the stinking slurry up onto your bicycle's frame and your back. The only way I found to remove the stench—which does not go away when the frame dries—was to put the bicycle into my apartment's tub shower. Learn from experience.

Dogs

Although strictly speaking a dog is not a seasonal hazard, canines are more likely to be outdoors in good weather than in bad. There is nothing more heart-stopping than to hear aggressive barking and to see a dog streaking right at you across a lawn.

Your instinct will be to pedal like hell, but few cyclists can outrun a big dog. Take advantage instead of the psyche of dogs: Dogs are territorial and set up a ruckus because you entered their turf.

At the first warning bark of a dog bounding toward you, shout, "Go home!" in an authoritative tone. Dismount, put the bicycle between you and the dog, and walk along the road, continuing to command, "Go home!" A walking figure is one with which the dog is familiar and used to obeying, and normally the dog will prance alongside you barking until it comes to the edge of its territory. When you've walked past that boundary, it will just stand and bark, allowing you to safely remount and ride off.

As scary as this sounds, it is the practice followed by organized tour groups, and in nearly two decades of riding, I've never had it fail.

Still, as a commuter, do you want to do this twice a day, five days a week? If it is not possible to alter your route to avoid passing the dog, see if you can approach the owner, and with courtesy and respect, ask if the dog might not be restrained at the hours you are most likely to be riding by. Failing that, try to make friends with the pooch itself.

Don't even think of using one of those eye-irritating pepper sprays sold for self-defense; if the wind direction is wrong, it could disable you instead, and anger the dog. If an unrestrained dog impresses you as being truly vicious, call the local police and see if blue uniforms can convince the owner to keep it chained.

With frequent stops and spewing exhaust, buses are not the best commuting companions.

Intermodal Bicycle Commuting

"Intermodal" bicycle commuting is a fancy Department of Transportation term for combining bicycle commuting with some other means of transportation. This may be an attractive option especially if your commute is longer than ten miles each way.

Bicycle Commuting Plus Public Transportation

Some enlightened cities have made provisions for combining bicycle commuting with public transportation.

Washington, D.C., offers bike racks at its outlying Metro stations; people can pedal from their homes to the Metro station, lock their bikes, and then take the Metro train into the city.

San Diego and other cities have equipped buses with racks for carrying bicycles as well as human passengers. People pedal to the bus stop and then ride with their bikes into the city.

In New York City, the Long Island and Metro-North commuter trains, New Jersey Transit trains, the PATH (Port Authority Trans-Hudson) tube lines between Manhattan and New Jersey, the Staten Island ferry, and some private bus lines will take bicycles. This option works best for people working nontraditional hours, however, because public transportation is off-limits to bicycles during peak standard commuter hours.

Contact your local public transportation carriers or your state's bicycle coordinator for guidelines about the hours that bicycles are allowed and restrictions on the equipment. Some carriers, for example, allow only folding bicycles that will not obstruct the aisles. A folding bicycle with 16-inch or 20-inch wheels actually can be quite discreet, especially if you can slip it into a Cordura carrying bag and sling it over your shoulder before boarding.

Bicycle Commuting Plus Driving

Even if you work in an area that does not have obliging public transportation, you might be able to devise your own personal intermodal system for a commute too long for bicycling the whole way. Here are just a few suggestions.

Put your bicycle into your car, drive part of the way to work, park in a public lot, and ride your bike the rest of the way.

Arrange to carpool with a colleague who lives closer to work than you do. On the days that it is your colleague's turn to drive, ride your bicycle to his or her house.

■ *If both you and a colleague are cyclists, one of you can drive one car to work while the other pedals. Then switch off for the return home.* ■

■ Arrange to drive a nearby colleague to work in your car along with your bike, and have your colleague drive your car home solo that evening, allowing you to pedal. Your colleague saves wear and tear on his or her own car and drives only one way, and you get to ride your bike home without losing the use of your car.

■ If both you and a colleague are cyclists, one of you can drive one car to work while the other pedals. Then switch off for the return home. Trade cars every other day. You won't get to ride together, but you'll both save gas and you'll both enjoy some long miles. And if one of you absolutely must arrive at work fresh and pressed on certain days, that person can arrange to bicycle only the leg home.

Chapter Eight

RIDING IN TRAFFIC

Bicycle and car commuters share the roads in San Francisco.

Sharing the Road: Some Ruminations

Bicycle commuters in England have as much right to the road as do motor vehicles. And automobile drivers respect that, even in the center of busy metropolitan London.

Yet in the United States every cyclist probably has at least one harrowing tale of a motorist's deliberate pranksterism (a car sneaking up alongside a cyclist and then honking to watch the cyclist jerk or jump), rudeness (throwing trash, yelling, or shaking a fist), or even injury (such as the time Brooklyn bicycle commuter Richard Shuldiner was actually chased and his bicycle deliberately hit by a car whose driver then stopped and got out with doubled fists intending to finish the job).

What accounts for such international differences in the attitudes of motorists toward cyclists?

One likely reason is historical necessity: With the England's shorter distances (compared with the vast ones in the United States), the bicycle remained a practical mode of transportation long after the invention of the automobile. Moreover, England's population has had a lower average disposable income than working-class Americans, so fewer families have chosen to buy a car—much less one for each adult and teenage driver.

Another likely reason is marketing history. In England, the bicycle was never reduced to the status of a kid's toy—as it was by Schwinn in the United States to rejuvenate flagging sales in the 1930s and to claim the juvenile market in the 1950s.

On the contrary, in England and Europe, bicycle racing has remained a popular spectator sport—and an image of male virility. Thus, there the automobile did not take on the American mystique of raw male potency that Detroit bestowed upon it in the 1950s and 1960s.

In the United States on the cusp of the 21st century, that testosterone-powered image still fuels a rape-of-the-highway mentality: Only the big and powerful and important own the road, so getouttamyway,yafugggintwerp! (How many overtly rude female drivers have cyclists encountered? Think about it. This may be changing for the worst, however, now that it's becoming socially acceptable for a woman to wield traditionally masculine power.)

A third reason for more civilized relations between motorists and cyclists in England is that English cyclists are obligated to obey the same traffic laws as motor vehicles—otherwise they get a traffic ticket. American cyclists visiting England must do the same, in full recognition of the precious rights to the road such behavior confers. Such traffic-law enforcement on cyclists in the United States is almost unheard-of.

Fortunately, deliberate acts of threatening behavior or violence by motorists toward cyclists are rare—maybe a once-a-year occurrence even for an urban bicycle commuter. That's the good news.

The bad news is the spreading prevalence of a general heedlessness by motorists toward the consequences of bending or breaking traffic laws. In many regions, traffic laws are no longer strictly enforced, and motorists routinely get away with speeding 15 miles per hour above the limit, not yielding before turning left with oncoming traffic, and running red lights. Some impatient motorists even take wild chances, such as veering into a left-turn lane to pass traffic and then turning right before the other cars. Such perilous audacity is, at least in some parts of the United States, becoming a daily occurrence.

Many bicyclists don't help. They feel that traffic laws are for cars, not bicycles. They drift through stop signs and red lights after glancing both ways to make sure the way is clear, while the cars wait for the green light. Or they circle in front of cars doing track stands instead of coming to a halt until the light changes. Some law-abiding drivers (some do still exist) could interpret such behavior as insolence; why should they, in turn, respect a bicycle as a vehicle if the cyclist doesn't act as if he or she is driving one?

Like it or not, every bicyclist—like every motorcyclist—is seen by many drivers as a representative for the whole minority category of bicyclists. And an automobile driver steamed by a past encounter with an unrelated cyclist may decide to exact revenge on innocent you.

One lesson I learned in spades as a bicycle commuter is that traffic laws exist for good reasons.

Speed limits, stop signs, traffic lights, all those seeming annoyances against total freedom of the road are really and truly your only defense against chaos. Obey them. Nay, cherish them. As a motorist and cyclist both, do your part to keep order—for your own protection.

Moreover, as a bicycle commuter, go beyond simply obeying the law. Be pleasant. Make eye contact with motorists. Smile. Wave a "thank-you" to a considerate driver who waits to pass or gives you wide berth or performs some other little courtesy. On your commute, you will likely be taking the same route day after day at roughly the same times—and so will the motorists. Thus, you'll be encountering the same people day after day. Make friends with them by your lawful and respectful behavior.

Give cyclists a good name. Drivers will grow accustomed to seeing you on the road. Some may come to genuinely look out for your safety as they approach and pass. And they may also pass this consideration on to the next cyclist they meet as well. Come spring, one or two motorists may even be inspired by your example and take up bicycle commuting themselves.

And then you've won the biggest prize of all: one fewer car on your road.

The Bible for Safe Riding in Traffic

The most widely recognized authority on cyclists' sharing the road with motor vehicles is John Forester's *Effective Cycling*. This 600-page book is widely available at bike shops, book stores with a good sports/travel section, and mail-order houses.

The book is also the fundamental text for the series of "Effective Cycling" courses offered under the sponsorship of the century-old safety and advocacy group, the League of American Bicyclists (based in Washington, D.C., and, until 1994, known as the League of American Wheelmen). The original basic course required a commitment of thirty hours of class time over ten weeks; the League revised the curriculum in 1995 and 1996 to break it into three nine-hour classes (Road I, II, and III) to make it more widely accessible to busy cyclists who couldn't commit to a semester but who could manage to spring loose for an occasional whole-day seminar.

Each course has both a lecture part and an on-road part, plus final tests on both parts. Students who complete the series of courses learn many techniques useful for their own safety as commuters. There are now more than 500 Effective Cycling Instructors (ECIs) around the country.

The information in this section is only a brief summary of the fundamental principles that should govern a bicycle commuter's behavior on the road. For details behind the theory of vehicular bicycle driving as well as detailed discussions of common traffic situations likely to be encountered by bicycle commuters, I urge you read chapters 26 through 32 of Forester's *Effective Cycling*.

Act Like the Driver of a Vehicle

The fundamental premise of *Effective Cycling* is: "Cyclists fare best when they act and are treated as operators of vehicles."

On the one hand, being the operator of a vehicle means that bicyclists have the *duty* to obey all traffic laws: riding with traffic, stopping at every stop sign, signaling turns, and the like, all of which you have presumably learned when you took driver's education and passed the written and driving exams for your driver's license. (If you do not drive and have never taken driver's ed, then obtain the standard booklet from your local department of motor vehicles office and memorize the traffic laws for your state.)

On the other hand, being the operator of a vehicle also means that bicyclists have the lawful *right* to the lanes on the road. And as with a car, their position in the lanes should be determined by their speed and their intent. For the most part, cyclists travel more slowly than cars, and so generally should stay near the right in the right-hand lane.

But where the cyclist's speed matches that of the automobile traffic—such as on a fast downhill—the cyclist has the lawful right to move left into the flow of traffic to claim the entire lane. Similarly, where the cars slow down to match the cyclist's speed—such as approaching a stop sign or red light—the cyclist again should move left to take his or her proper turn in the order of traffic. The cyclist should not coast past the line of waiting cars to go to the front of the line.

Cyclists wanting to turn left from a four-lane road with left-turn lanes also have the temporary right to the left-hand lane. In fact, they should behave exactly as they would if they were driving a car: signaling left, scanning (looking back over the left shoulder) to see that the next lane left is clear, moving into the next lane, signaling and scanning again, and moving into the left-turn lane to make the turn.

To novice cyclists, all this lane-claiming may seem radical and putting one's self into the path of cars. On the contrary, it is part of predictable vehicular behavior, which is recognized by most motorists and is also recognized by law. And it really works.

Traffic Statutes for Bicycles

Since the 1970s, when the first edition of Forester's book was published, its vehicular principle for cyclists has come to be adopted in the motor vehicle statutes of most states. In general, state statutes specify that "bicycle drivers" or "operators" have all the *rights* to the road and all the *duties* to obey traffic laws as motor-vehicle drivers. In fact, in many states, the bicycle is explicitly classed as a vehicle.

While the details and thoughtfulness of the parts of the vehicle codes specific to bicycles vary from state to state, all state statutes expressly rule that bicyclists must:

- Ride with the flow of traffic.
- Ride "as far to the right as practicable"—with specific exceptions (more on the meaning of "practicable" later).
- Keep at least one hand on the handlebars at all times.
- Signal a right or left turn at least 100 feet before that turn, and while stopped waiting to turn.
- Equip the bicycle with a warning bell or horn, but not a siren or whistle.
- Equip the bicycle with reflectors visible from the front, side, and rear for use in twilight and dark—and preferably lights as well (see "Riding After Dark," page 81).
- Not ride more than two abreast on a roadway.

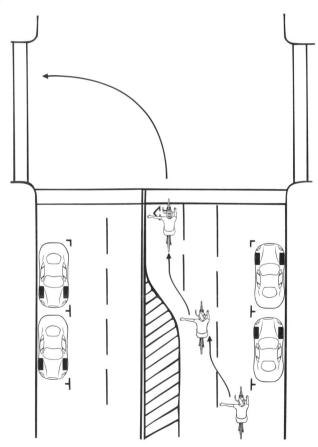

Cyclists may use left lanes to turn left, exactly like motorists.

- Not attach themselves to motor vehicles for hitching an informal ride.
- Not plug both ears with earphones or headphones (hearing aids and one-eared communication systems excepted).
- Not carry more passengers than the number for which the bicycle is intended and equipped (so worded as to make tandems and child attachments legal, but not a person sitting on the handlebars or on the rear rack).

For a copy of your state's statutes, contact the department of motor vehicles or bicycle/pedestrian coordinator (generally in the department of transportation in your state's capital). While you're at it, also ask for a list or map of all bridges, tunnels, and roads that are off-limits to bicycles; such regulations could affect your choice of a commuting route.

Many state statutes are based on the federal government's Uniform Vehicle Code (UVC), a national set of statutes that can be used as a model for state governments in devising their own statutes. The UVC is strongly based in the vehicular principles of *Effective Cycling*. In the absence of access to your own state code, you'll do okay just by following the terms of the Uniform Vehicle Code, whose simplified text is reprinted in Appendix I (page 161).

How Far to the Right?

The Uniform Vehicle Code (as well as individual state statutes) specifies that anyone operating a bicycle on a roadway at less than the normal speed of traffic must ride "as close as practicable to the right hand curb or edge of the roadway."

The UVC does, however, recognize specific exceptions:

- When overtaking and passing another bicycle or vehicle proceeding in the same direction.
- When preparing for a left turn at an intersection or into a private road or driveway.
- When reasonably necessary to avoid conditions, such as a substandard width lane, that

make it unsafe to continue along the right-hand curb or edge.

In the experience of many cyclists, even in ordinary conditions the words "as far right as practicable" do not mean clinging to the far right-hand edge. Not only is a gutter or road's edge often broken or littered with sand and gravel, but motorists cannot see you, nor do they expect to see a vehicle moving at the curb or shoulder unless it is slowing down to stop. Cars tend to blow right by you and cut you off when they turn right.

Many main roads and residential areas have lanes that are wide enough for both a car and a

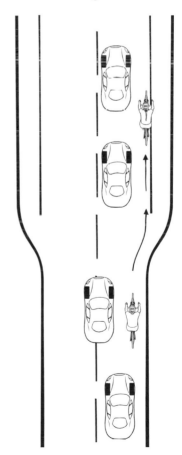

When a lane is narrow, ride about a third of the way to the left (bottom), moving farther right when the road widens (top).

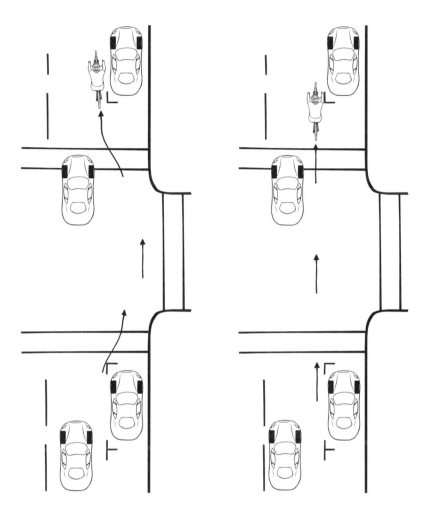

Don't weave in traffic (left); ride a straight line at all times (right.)

bicycle to proceed safely side by side. On narrow, shoulderless roads or bridges, however, many experienced cyclists advise riding about a third of the way to the left—about where the passenger in an automobile would be. Thus, cars approaching from behind must slow down and move left a bit to pass you, so you will not be squeezed off the right-hand edge of the road.

When passing parked cars, ride two or three feet to their left, out of range of an opening door. As you approach each parked car, glance inside for the silhouette of a driver who might suddenly open a door in your path. Also, never pass on

the right-hand side of a taxi that has stopped mid-lane to discharge a passenger—that is just asking to be "doored."

It also is essential that you ride a straight line. Don't duck to the right to be closer to the crosswalk in an intersection or to be closer to the curb on long stretches between parked cars. Keep riding straight as if all the parking spaces—whether marked or not—were occupied and doors were opening. Driving (yes, driving) your bicycle in a straight line keeps you visible and predictable, and is expected vehicular behavior—exactly what motorists do.

Silence Isn't Golden

As discussed earlier in "Accessories for Safety and Comfort" (page 39), a bicycle bell is an important accessory. And while using your voice has mixed results, there are times when a word or two can prove to be a useful safety technique. In a city, amid all the chatter on a sidewalk or inside a car, a voice does not penetrate like a bike bell. Yelling can raise hackles against perceived rudeness. In the quieter suburbs and the country, however, a gentle and polite verbal warning such as "Excuse me" can be very effective. Avoid using the athlete's common shorthand "On your left," meaning that you are passing on the left; half the time, unathletic pedestrians will interpret your words as a command to move to the left, directly into your path. You usually get a better response by slowing down enough to be more explicit: "Hello, I'm coming up on your left."

Riding on Interstate Highways

Whereas the eastern United States as well as much of the Midwest is crisscrossed by numerous secondary and tertiary roads, some of the more western states have vast distances linked by only one artery, which may well be an interstate highway. If your commute offers you no choice but to ride on an interstate, don't assume that this eliminates the possibility of your commuting by bicycle. In a third of the states, cyclists can indeed legally ride the interstates.

Five states explicitly permit bicycles on the shoulders of all parts of interstate highways: Idaho, Montana, North Dakota, South Dakota, and Wyoming.

Another nine states permit bicycles on the shoulders of selected portions of interstates. To be safe, request details about the permitted portions from the state bicycle/pedestrian coordinator. These states are Alaska, Arizona, California, Colorado, Nevada, New Jersey, Oregon, Utah, and Washington.

Oklahoma and Texas as well as the District of Columbia have no official policy, but unofficially discourage the riding of bicycles on interstates; in Texas, bicycles are tolerated on interstates outside of cities, although cyclists are prohibited from interstates inside cities.

Thirty-four states prohibit bicycles from all interstate highways: Alabama, Arkansas, Connecticut, Delaware, Florida, Georgia, Hawaii, Illinois, Indiana, Iowa, Kansas, Kentucky, Louisiana, Maine, Maryland, Massachusetts, Michigan,

Minnesota, Mississippi, Missouri, Nebraska, New Hampshire, New Mexico, New York, North Carolina, Ohio, Pennsylvania, Rhode Island, South Carolina, Tennessee, Vermont, Virginia, West Virginia, and Wisconsin.

For updates or changes, consult your state bicycle/pedestrian coordinator. Also, the annual *Cyclist's Yellow Pages,* published by the Adventure Cycling Association (known as Bikecentennial until 1994), Missoula, Montana, keeps a tally of interstate highways on which bicycles are permitted for the benefit of touring cyclists.

Helmet Laws

Fewer than half of the states have enacted mandatory helmet laws for cyclists. Mostly these apply to children—the effective age varies from under 12 (in Connecticut and Tennessee) to under 18 (in California). Some local communities within these states have even stricter laws; helmets are required for cyclists of all ages, including adult commuters.

Even in those states that do not have statewide helmet laws (such as Arizona, Ohio, and Virginia), specific cities have enacted their own local helmet ordinances—and again, some apply to cyclists of all ages. Because this legislative situation keeps changing, contact your state bicycle/pedestrian coordinator for information about ordinances in your own area.

Bicycling Among Lawless Drivers

By practicing vehicular behavior, you will be conforming with the law, easing your interactions with motorists, and maximizing your safety. And of course, the primary purpose of traffic laws is to make every vehicle's behavior predictable so as to minimize accidents and injuries.

But what if you live in an area where creeping lawlessness is eroding the safety of the roads? In this case, there is a disconnect between what motorists are *supposed* to do and how they *actually* behave.

Your task, for your own survival, is to discern whether there is any pattern to the creeping lawlessness. Then, to the extent that the lawlessness itself follows a predictable pattern, be alert for behaviors that may indicate which set of "rules" a motorist is following. Last, be prepared to act defensively as appropriate.

"Predictable" Lawlessness

The specifics of creeping lawlessness may vary by region. In northern New Jersey, the most consistent unpunished offenses by motorists are:

- Speeding (one Maplewood policeman said he will not issue a speeding ticket until a car reaches 15 mph above the speed limit—or 40 mph in a 25-mph residential zone—because speeding is "too widespread for the police to keep up with, and if we spent our time ticketing all the speeders, we wouldn't be able to keep up with real crimes").
- Treating stop signs as yield signs, especially on lightly traveled residential streets.
- Treating red lights as stop signs, especially when traffic is light at night.
- Turning left without first yielding to oncoming traffic (this has become so prevalent in New Jersey since 1990 that at one point I actually telephoned the department of motor vehicles office to see if the law had been changed).

Speeding

The prime danger to a cyclist of a motorist's speeding is that the consequences of being hit are more serious.

On a straight road, the chances of your being hit are not necessarily higher, unless the motorist also commits some other infraction. Harrowing ones I've witnessed in north New Jersey include a speeder passing a speed-limit-abiding driver over a double yellow line in the face of oncoming traffic. Such an action may force an oncoming car to swerve right, perhaps into your path.

On a curvy road speeders may be inclined to "straighten out the curves" by changing lane position, thereby moving closer to the right on right-hand curves and perhaps even onto the shoulder. Keep your ears alert for cars that sound as if they are coming up behind you faster than normal.

Also, speeders are inclined to race traffic lights, even gunning through an intersection instants after the light in their direction has turned red. If you are waiting at a cross street and the light in your direction turns green, look to your left before proceeding to make sure all cars are indeed stopping.

Ignoring Stop Signs and Red Lights

A motorist's not heeding a stop sign or observing the full duration of a red light poses a similar danger to you as that of a speeder racing a light, although it may be done at lower speed.

Even if you have the right of way, watch each car on a cross street as it approaches the stop sign or red light to your left or right. Try to catch the motorist's eye to ensure that he or she actually sees you. Indicate your intention of continuing to ride straight ahead, either with your eyes or by pointing with your hand.

At the same time, be prepared to swerve or brake if the motorist is following the set of "lawless rules." Watch especially when you're grinding slowly up a steep hill, perhaps towing a child or heavy load; a motorist cutting out in front of you not only endangers you but also destroys whatever forward momentum you may have, perhaps forcing a quick dismount in the intersection.

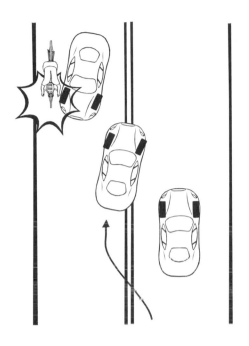

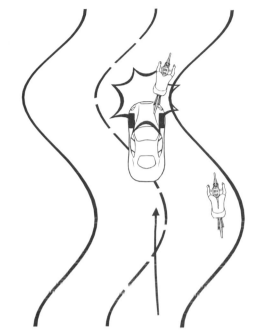

A speeder illegally passing over a double yellow line can pose a danger to a cyclist in the opposite lane.

A speeder "straightening out the curves" may pose a danger to a cyclist in the same lane.

Illegal Left Turns

"Left-turn jumping" as I call it—left-turners not yielding first to oncoming traffic—poses an alarming danger to a bicycle commuter, because it is done at abnormally high speed in order to beat oncoming traffic.

It seems most prevalent at intersections with traffic lights where there is no separate left-turn arrow. A cyclist is most likely to be hit if he or she coasts up to the intersection just as the light in his or her direction turns green. The impatient left-turning motorist, who is intently watching the light for the instant to slam the accelerator to the floor, then broadsides the cyclist entering the intersection.

To avoid such a tragedy, watch for the telltale signs of a left-turn jumper: front wheels already turned left, car creeping forward even while the light is red, motorist's eyes fixed on the light. Avoiding a left-turn jumper is yet another reason for a cyclist *not* to coast up to an intersection

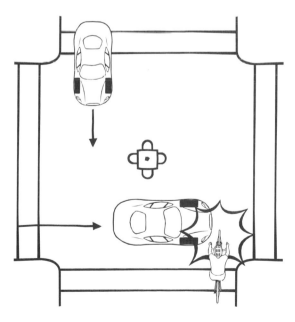

A speeder may race a traffic light, gunning through an intersection after the light has turned red.

along the right-hand side of the cars waiting for the green light.

Erratic Behavior

What about the wholly unpredictable behavior of an occasional motorist who is drunk, on drugs, falling asleep, in the midst of a heart attack, or criminally insane?

Outright erratic behavior is always an acute danger sign: a car weaving back and forth across the lane and into the neighboring lanes, a motorist gunning the engine or honking loudly or squealing the tires at every light, the head drooping over the steering wheel until someone honks.

The danger extends beyond that of the individual erratic motorist. Such behavior is likely to make other motorists nervous as well, and the attention they are devoting to avoiding the erratic driver is attention taken away from watching the road for normal activity—including keeping an eye out for cyclists. Thus, the erratic behavior of one motorist may create temporary erratic behavior on the part of other motorists. In such a circumstance, you may feel safest just pulling over to the side for a moment to let the chaos get well ahead of you.

Last Word: Bicycle Defensively

Above all, keep alert every moment. Use your ears as well as your rearview mirrors.

And remember the definition of defensive driving: Follow the laws, while not expecting others to do the same.

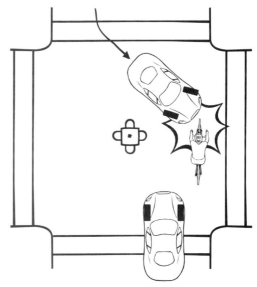

"Left-turn jumping" motorist tries to beat oncoming traffic instead of yielding to it.

Chapter Nine

RIDING
AFTER DARK

A cyclist is not wholly visible at night, even directly in front of a car's headlights.

Seeing and Being Seen

Even if you don't intend to commute after dark, you can easily find yourself accidentally doing so—such as on a night when you work late, or on that record-setting balmy day in early December or January when you just had to get the bike out to enjoy the commute.

Equipping yourself and your bike for riding after dark will allow you to continue bicycle commuting well after the onset of standard time, when—depending on both your latitude and your east-west position in your time zone—twilight or darkness may prevail later than 7:30 AM or earlier than 4:30 PM. Because the law requires that headlights and taillights be used one-half hour after sunrise and one-half hour before sunset, you could need illumination (again depending on your geographical coordinates) as late as 8:00 AM or as early as 4:00 PM.

According to *Lighting the Road Ahead*, a 1990 report on bicycle lighting and night riding by the League of American Wheelmen (now the League of American Bicyclists), "The accident rate for all traffic fatalities climbs from 1.66 deaths per 100 million vehicle miles during daylight to 4.15 deaths per 100 million vehicle miles during the hours of darkness."

A disproportionate fraction—more than 40 percent—of automobile-bicycle accidents also happen after dark, even though fewer cyclists are on the roads. Three-quarters of them happen from the front, although the relatively few that happen from the rear are often fatal. Many of these after-dark accidents occur because the motorist's vision was compromised, the motorist did not expect to see a bicycle after dark (no matter how early it is), and because bicyclists do not always properly equip themselves for night riding.

Warning: A Bicyclist Will See Better than a Driver

Because your vision as a cyclist is not partially blocked by the windshield and metal frame of a car and you can see perfectly well by street light, it is easy—and deadly—to be lulled into thinking drivers can see you equally well.

If you are under 30 years of age, be especially cautious: Do not assume that everyone else sees as well as you do. They don't.

Young people's pupils open very wide: As an amateur astronomer in my teens and twenties, I had enough night vision and dark adaptation even to walk wooded trails by ambient starlight without stumbling. People approaching or past middle age, however, have dramatically less ability to see in the dark—as I am now aware at 45-plus.

Even worse, a motorist's night vision is reduced by being partially blinded by the car's own headlights as well as by those of oncoming traffic. Some drivers may have their pupils further contracted, and thus their night vision further compromised, by prescription medication, such as that for glaucoma, or by the nicotine in ordinary cigarettes. Some illegal drugs contract the pupils to mere pinpoints. Moreover, many people licensed to drive suffer from some form of visual impairment. Most commonly this is red-green color blindness, which is estimated to afflict some 10 percent of men to at least some degree. Color blindness dims a driver's perception of a red rear reflector or light, making it seem to be an inconspicuous brown or gray.

Even if motorists see you, which they may do only at the last moment because they are likely looking for two bright lights instead of a single less-intense one, they may misjudge your speed, not realizing you are clipping along at 20 mph. Thus, they may pull out from a side street in front of you or turn left in front of you.

Therefore, ride even more defensively than you might in the daytime, don't assume that you are seen, and be mentally prepared to stop or react quickly in the event of the unexpected.

What You'll Need

The equipment you'll need for riding after dark depends on the nature of your commute.

Urban areas are commonly so well illuminated by street lights that you actually may be able to see the road and its hazards fairly well. In this case, you need reflectors and lights on your bike primarily so motorists and pedestrians will clearly see you.

Suburban and rural roads, on the other hand, may be sparsely lighted, if they are lighted at all. Thus, without a good headlight, you are literally riding blind. You need not only to be seen, but to illuminate the road itself some distance ahead. This is a much more demanding requirement.

Seeing and being seen are even more imperative if you're riding after dark when it is also foggy or rainy (see also "Riding In Foul Weather," page 93).

Making Yourself Visible

As a cyclist myself, I reflexively look for cyclists even when I am behind the wheel of a car. Yet I've still been spooked by the sudden materialization in my headlights of BMX bikes carrying one or more riders dressed in dark pants, jackets, and stocking caps. I shudder to think of the fate of those teenagers if overtaken by a driver not alert to the momentary warning of the up-and-down motion of the little golden reflectors on the back of the pedals.

Being seen not only helps to prevent an accident, it also speeds your travel past pedestrians if you commute in a place (such as midtown Manhattan) where people on foot routinely step off the curb into the street while waiting for a light to change. They will see you a block away and know to step back onto the sidewalk instead of being surprised—and somewhat put out—when (to them) you suddenly appear to claim your right of way.

What Does the Law Say?

The federal government's Uniform Vehicle Code specifies that every vehicle on a highway from a half hour after sunset to a half hour before sunrise must emit a white light visible from a distance of at least 500 feet to the front. A red rear reflector must be visible for 600 feet to the rear. It also specifies that every bicycle must be equipped with reflective material to be visible from both sides for 600 feet.

State laws, however, are quite inconsistent, and only some are in conformity with the Uniform Vehicle Code. Some states keep their laws up to date, while others haven't changed for decades. Some laws include wholly arbitrary requirements. According to the League report *Lighting The Road Ahead,* "There is not even a common definition of what constitutes darkness!"

All fifty states require a white light be visible from the front, but only forty are in compliance with the Uniform Vehicle Code in specifying that the light be visible from at least 500 feet. The League supports compliance with the Uniform Vehicle Code. (Six states make the additional requirement that the front light also be visible from the side.)

Only thirty-seven states comply with the Uniform Vehicle Code in

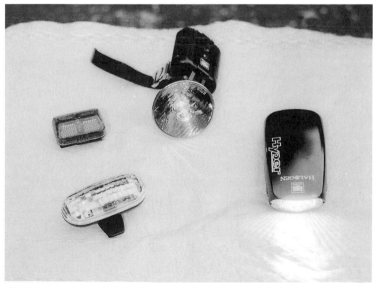

Various headlights and flashers can help a commuter be more visible to motorists and pedestrians.

requiring a red rear reflector; only seven of those conform with the code in actually stating that the approved reflector type "be visible for 600 feet to the rear when directly in front of the lawful low beams of headlamps on a motor vehicle." The League supports the Uniform Vehicle Code provision.

At least five states—Alaska, Florida, New Jersey, New York, and Ohio—require a red rear light to be used. At least three of those states—Alaska, Florida, and Ohio—require both a red rear reflector and a red taillight. A dozen states allow cyclists the option of having a red rear light or a red rear reflector. The League recommends both a red rear light and a red or amber rear reflector, as the two are complementary. The reflector still works even if the taillight burns out (which can happen suddenly and unexpectedly). But a reflector can reflect light only that it receives from another source—and by itself, it may perform poorly when an overtaking motorist's left front headlamp is broken.

Some fifteen states follow the Uniform Vehicle Code and require side-facing reflectors or lights.

Only five states require front and rear pedal reflectors: California, Maine, Minnesota, Missouri, and Montana. Several states allow the alternative use of reflective ankle bands, which can be seen from the side as well as the front and rear.

In conclusion, the League report recommends that "bicyclists riding at night should conform with relevant state laws, and should have at least:

- a white front light
- a rear red light and red or amber rear reflector
- bright and/or reflective clothing
- wheel, pedal or side reflectors, or reflective ankle bands
- any other conspicuity aids that assist early detection and recognition by motorists."

Because this is a reasonable minimum specified by an officially recognized cycling advocacy

For superior visibility, it is worth adding the much larger and brighter reflectors sold at auto-supply stores.

organization with much experience, I'll focus on each of these five recommendations.

Reflectors

The Consumer Product Safety Commission specifies that bicycles must be equipped with a front white reflector, a rear red reflector, amber reflectors on the rear of the pedals, and a white side reflector in the spokes of each wheel.

Upright bikes sold in bicycle shops conform to the Consumer Product Safety Commission's standards (pedal reflectors on recumbents make no sense, because the position of the rider's leg, foot, and pedal blocks the reflector from a motorist's view). The standard front and rear reflectors, however, are not very bright. Moreover, their standard position—in front of the headset and under the saddle—are positions where any handlebar bag or load on the rear rack would obscure them.

For superior visibility, it is worth adding the much larger and brighter reflectors sold at auto-supply stores (they are very inexpensive, a dollar or two at most). Anchor the new red rear reflector at the back of the rear rack where it will not be covered by panniers or gear on the rack. Add amber reflectors to the backs of both panniers or—if you don't carry rear panniers—add a reflector to the left rear seatstay to give some indication of your breadth on the road. Fasten a new white front reflector onto the front of your front panniers, or—if you don't carry front panniers— to the left blade of your front fork. A couple of extra reflectors will ensure that you always have at least one operational, even if one breaks or falls off or happens to be obscured by your stuff.

Some cycling advocates are pushing to allow interchangeable use of either red or amber rear reflectors. Amber is superior to red in that it is brighter: Amber reflects 62 percent of the amount of light returned by a clear reflector whereas red reflects only 25 percent. Amber, neon yellow, and white are the most visible to drivers suffering from red-green color blindness.

If you use a cargo trailer, a child trailer, or a trailer cycle at dusk or later, make sure that it is also fitted with reflectors—ones on the left-hand and right-hand edges if the trailer happens to be wider than your own profile on the bike.

Flashers

Flashing lights for cyclists are readily available in clear, amber, and red. Usually these are bright light-emitting diodes (LEDs) powered by standard AA batteries. The more powerful ones can be seen several hundred yards away. They are lightweight and reasonably cheap and they have a surprisingly long life.

Red flashers as small as an inch across can be attached to a helmet (one brand is Hot Dot). Larger red or amber ones (one well-known brand is VistaLite) can be bolted to your bicycle frame or rack, strapped to your left arm or leg, or attached to your belt or panniers. One theory is that flashing amber lights make motorists instantly think they're seeing a flasher on a traffic sawhorse placed over a large pothole. Amber ones are to be preferred because of their greater visibility in general as well as to red-green color-blind drivers.

Don't try to use a flasher as a substitute for a headlight. Their intermittent light is not enough for illuminating the road. Flashers are meant only to increase your own visibility.

Also, don't try to use a flasher as a substitute for a reflector. They do not return light nearly as efficiently as a true reflector. Moreover, the intermittent bright and dark periods coupled with the change in closing angle may make it difficult for a motorist to interpret your true distance away. A flasher simply draws attention to your presence, whereas a reflector allows a driver to know your exact location.

Some cyclists also use white or amber strobes to call attention to their position. For example, Burton, Washington, commuter Joshua Putnam uses a single D-cell xenon marine safety strobe for riding in fog or rain. Others, however, feel that strobes are not as helpful as the more rapidly blinking flashers.

Visible Clothing

After dark, wear at the very least white or light-colored outerwear: white or light tan slacks or skirt, white shirt or blouse or windbreaker, white helmet.

Better yet, wear clothing designed for cyclists riding at night. Most cyclists' jackets have reflective trim (such as trademarked ScotchLite) across the yoke and the bottom hem. There are also high-tech fabrics, notably the trademarked illumi-NITE and InSight, that make an entire garment or bag reflective. Jackets and vests made of white, brilliant yellow, or high-visibility orange illumi-NITE or InSight fabrics allow a cyclist to be both highly visible in the daytime and reflective at night. When illuminated by headlights, a driver can see immediately that you are a cyclist.

A cheaper option is a cyclist's traffic vest, which is commonly of international orange mesh (for maximum visibility in daylight) trimmed with white or neon yellow reflective trim (for maximum visibility after dusk). Side straps that tie, buckle, or use Velcro hold the vest in place; on some vests, the side straps can be made long enough to allow the vest to fit around a modest-sized backpack as well.

Extra Conspicuity Aids

The minimal reflectors required by the Uniform Vehicle Code and Consumer Product Safety Commission are by no means enough to ensure that drivers can see you in all conditions of lowered visibility. You can do a great deal to increase your visibility further by adopting the League's "extra conspicuity aids."

- Put reflective tape everywhere to be really visible—just like the 16-wheeler semi trucks do. I do mean everywhere. You want headlights to make you light up like a Christmas tree; in my opinion (others differ), it's better to have a driver wake up and think "what a weirdo biker" than to miss seeing you. The average driver is only semiconscious of driving and isn't consciously searching out anything out of the ordinary. Extra reflectivity provides extra visual cues.

Apply neon yellow reflective ScotchLite tape to your helmet and bicycle frame, particularly down the length of the seat-stays facing to the rear. You can also buy reflective tape in precut lengths for an upright bicycle's tubes, stays, and fork blades in black, blue, green, red, and white, plus a set for your helmet and a set for the rims; look for the Reflecto-Nite brand name. Diagonal-striped reflective material used on trucks is commonly available in auto parts stores. It comes in yellow and black, orange and black, and red and silver. Solid-colored material is also available in standard safety colors of orange, red, yellow, blue, green, and silver. A 1-inch-wide strip placed down the length of the center of a fender is wide enough to be seen but narrow enough not to wrinkle when applied. It is also very durable in bad weather—more so, according to some cyclists, than the reflective materials sold in bike shops.

- Attach a reflective "slow-moving vehicle" triangle under your seat or to the rear of your panniers.
- Add reflective trim to your upper arms and wrist bands so your arms are visible when signalling.

> *Some high-tech fabrics make an entire garment or bag reflective.*

- Use reflective straps when binding your pant legs to keep them away from the chain.
- Use one or more reflective bicycle flags that either project to the left side or stand straight up from the left rear hub.
- Consider the type of reflectors that can be taped to the inside of your rims between the spokes that, when illuminated by head lights from the side, will light up the entire circle of your moving wheels.
- If you don't already have a set of panniers or bags for carrying your stuff to and from work, consider buying ones made of illumiNITE. The reflective coating is available in Cordura, the tight-weave canvas-like fabric used to make panniers, rack packs, handlebar bags, and other bags. Such bags are available from mail-order houses. If you already own panniers made of conventional fabric, crisscross them with extra reflective tape. When illuminated by headlights, a driver can see the full dimensions of your bike and packs.

It is also possible to coat your bicycle frame with industrial-grade luminescent paint, which is sold by McMaster-Carr and other outlets. But doing that properly requires three coats: a reflective white base coat, a fluorescent color coat, and a sealer. Be forewarned: it comes only in gallons, and three gallons together cost the same as a low to moderately priced bike.

Illuminating the Road

In older suburbs and in the country, after the sun sets the roads are pitch-dark. After 4:30 PM in winter, you will need powerful head and tail lamps not only so motorists and pedestrians can see you, but also so you can see the road and all its potential hazards.

The variety of lighting systems used on bikes is

daunting. Some are old but still-working generator-powered headlights and taillights of the type common on ten-speed bikes in the 1960s. Others are small, portable, strap-on, battery-operated flashlights that can be removed quickly to discourage theft. Still others are helmet-mounted systems that allow you to direct the beam where you want it (these are especially handy if you find yourself having to change a flat some night). There are high-end dual-beam systems—including those for electric bicycles—that are adaptations of motorcycle headlights and taillights.

Effective commercial battery-operated bike lighting systems, however, routinely retail for more than a hundred dollars. Their steep price tag has inspired some effective home-brew jobs from handy tinkerers who haunt Radio Shack, electrical supply houses, or hardware stores. Bright, long-lasting systems have been home-built out of automobile headlights, lawn path lights, high-brightness LEDs (light-emitting diodes), or even track lighting systems for ceilings, and have been powered by lantern or motorcycle batteries and connected with alligator clips, hose clamps, and clever packaging with foam and Velcro—all ginned together by owners long on electrical cleverness but short on cash. Once again, the watchword is "whatever works."

Power Systems

No power source for a bike's electrical system is perfect. In fact, both the two principal types—generators and batteries—have real disadvantages. Fortunately, the advantages and disadvantages are complementary. Thus, used together, the advantages of one can compensate for the disadvantages of the other—especially on a long commute year-round.

Generators

Generators are devices that convert some of the mechanical energy of your own pedal-power into electrical power. The spring-loaded device presses against the sidewall or tread of the front or rear tire; the rotation of the tire drives a rotor within a magnetic stator, generating electricity that causes the bulb in the headlight (and possibly also a taillight) to glow. (Popular brands are Union and Sanyo.)

Generators work very well as long as you are traveling at a reasonable speed. As you slow down, however, the lights dim, and when you stop, the lights go out altogether, stranding you in darkness. The

10 percent or so extra drag they create is noticeable. Some mount under the bottom bracket; others mount on the front fork or seat stays. Think carefully about their placement if you intend to use front or rear panniers.

That being said, generators are virtually maintenance-free, continuing to work night after night, year after year. Some can produce quite a lot of light. They don't weigh much, so you don't mind leaving a generator on the bike when its not in use. They don't cost much and are bolted to the bike, so they are unlikely targets for theft. And they are inexpensive to run, because no replacement parts are needed beyond perhaps a rare new bulb. If you're mechanically inclined, consider some of the generator modifications described by John Forester in his chapter "Riding at Night" in *Effective Cycling*.

Batteries

Batteries turn chemical energy into electrical energy. The lights stay illuminated even when you slow or stop—meaning that you can rely on batteries for light if you need to make a nighttime roadside repair. When batteries are used to power a halogen or xenon lamp—or an automobile headlight—they can create a beam brilliant enough that oncoming cars dim their brights. They don't create frictional drag like a generator.

The initial and replacement costs for batteries, however, can be high. Some of the more powerful battery systems can occupy a lot of volume (equivalent to a water bottle or larger) and can be quite heavy (some home-brew jobs even use a lead-acid motorcycle or automobile battery on a rear rack). Their principal disadvantage is that their lifetime—especially for a lighting system that is powerful enough to actually illuminate the road—is aggravatingly short, especially at temperatures below 40 or 50 degrees or above 90 degrees Fahrenheit.

It can be surprisingly expensive to run even small battery-operated headlights and taillights that are used only for being seen. In New York City, where I used a compact Cateye headlight and taillight, each powered by two alkaline C-cell batteries, I was nonplused to get only three or four hours of riding out of each pair of batteries. At that rate, I found myself replacing the two pairs of batteries in as few as fifty miles of commuting, or almost once a week—and alkaline batteries are not cheap. (For primary—that is, nonrechargeable—batteries, alkaline cells deliver both greater brightness and longer life than low-budget mercury cells.)

Rechargeable (secondary) batteries also work— as long as you remember to recharge them. For a long commute, that may mean plugging them into an electrical outlet at both home and work. For lead-acid batteries (and for truly high-power lights, many night-riders swear by lead-acid gel-cell batteries), this works well, as you do not want to exhaust them totally because that shortens their life. You also do not want to overcharge them.

A few cautions are in order about nickel-cadmium ("NiCad") rechargeable batteries. Users are commonly frustrated that such batteries lose capacity during recharging, allegedly because of a deleterious "memory effect" that requires them to be fully discharged each time. That supposed reason is widely accepted misinformation.

NiCads, in fact, lose capacity because many products supplied with rechargeable batteries have cheap and inadequate rechargers that rely on timers instead of an automatic cutout that senses when the battery is nearing full charge. Unless the battery is fully discharged, a cheap timer-based recharger will overcharge the NiCads, literally cooking the battery. But exhausting a large multi-celled NiCad fully each cycle also runs the risk of ruining the battery—because one cell might discharge before the others and will get driven backward (known as cell reversal).

The only way to ensure that NiCads reach full capacity and long life is to use a "smart" charger that detects when the batteries are near full charge. Be forewarned: A good recharger will run $35 to $45, depending on the amp-hour rating of your battery. Alternatively, you could use a less expensive, very slow charger that may take a day or two to reach full charge but is unlikely to kill the batteries if you're not precise about turning it off at the right time.

Because the length of a commute does not al-ways neatly coincide with the full lifetime of a battery, you may find yourself having to stop to switch battery packs mid-trip (make sure you have a flashlight along so you can see what you're doing). You'll probably want at least two complete sets of batteries so that one set is always fully charged and ready for use. You'll probably also want separate rechargers for home and for work.

In general, each charge of a secondary battery does not last as long as the lifetime of an equivalent-sized primary battery, although, of course, the total lifetime over many rechargings will be much longer. Also, for NiCad rechargeables, the actual output voltage may be less than the rated output voltage of an equivalent alkaline cell, so the light may not be as bright. As a rule of thumb, count on getting only half the rated energy. Note also that rechargeable batteries do not last forever— just for maybe 30, 50, or 100 cycles. That's a lot, to be sure. But depending on your pattern of use and recharging, you may need to replace all your sets every year or two.

The initial cost for both the rechargeable batteries and a good recharger is much higher than for single-use primary alkaline cells, but the ultimate cost is less than the replacement cost of single-use alkaline cells over that same period of time—not to mention a lot less polluting to the environment. Moreover, advances in battery technology mean that rechargeables are getting better every year.

Generators vs. Batteries

Among generators, primary batteries, and rechargeable batteries, how should you make your choice? Once again, your commute should determine your needs. There are two key factors: the number of stops you must make for intersections on your commute, and the overall length of your commute.

If your commute is short with no stops (say, under five or six miles or taking less than forty-five minutes), you can pick any power supply you like. The generator will burn brightly the whole way, and all types of batteries will have lifetimes longer than your ride.

If you're constantly starting and stopping at intersections, no matter how short the commute, you may prefer a battery system over a generator so your lights stay illuminated at all times.

If you have a long commute—ten or twelve miles each way—with no stops, you can get away with the generator, and may profit well from its low cost and low maintenance, especially if you ride in all temperatures. Carry some kind of a battery-operated light, though, in the event of an after-dark emergency repair.

For a long commute with a number of stops, you'll need a battery-powered system so your lights stay illuminated at the stops. But if the one-way ride is longer than one and one-half hours, you run a substantial risk of running out of juice and having your lights fail before you reach work or home.

Thus, for a long commute you might want to consider using both a generator and a battery-operated system—a combination that works especially well if you're cycling from one town to another through a rural stretch. Turn the generator on and forget about it for the whole ride. Operate the battery-powered system as well when you are riding through each town, so you also have lights at the stops. But once you hit the open road, turn off the battery-powered system and rely exclusively on the generator to conserve the batteries. (If the temperature is colder than 40 degrees, you should remove the batteries and store them in an inside coat pocket next to the warmth of your body to further conserve them.) Using both types of power systems may require having separate headlights and taillights for each system—although you may be able to find or rig up a system that quickly converts from generator to batteries with the flick of a switch.

Regardless of the power source you use, if you ride fast at night—14 or 15 mph—you'll need a system that throws enough light far enough ahead so you're not over-running your headlight beam without seeing the potholes or nocturnal animals.

Advances in battery technology mean that rechargeables are getting better every year.

Which Battery-Powered System?

Lighting systems range from portable strap-on headlights weighing less than 4 ounces and costing about $15 to ones emitting a beam more powerful than that of a car headlamp, topping $2\frac{1}{2}$ pounds, and costing as much as some bicycles (the Cateye Stadium Light retails for upward of $400).

All are suitable for commuting in towns and cities with lighted streets. Only the more powerful systems are capable of lighting back roads or bike paths.

Some systems come with both high and low beams, which can be used singly or together to achieve bright, brighter, and brightest illumination. In this case, the same system will give you different battery lifetimes depending on how often you use the high beams. As revealed by tables of lighting system performance in bicycling mail-order catalogs, typically battery life (which will vary with temperature) for 1- to 6-watt lights is four to eight hours while for 12- to 45-watt lights a battery will drain in one to three hours and sometimes in as little as forty-five minutes.

The "Andersen Acid Test"

Because overtaking traffic frequently must see you against a sea of oncoming headlights, bicycle commuter John Andersen of Juneau, Alaska, offers what he calls "the Andersen Acid Test of taillights." In the dark, lean your bike against the side of your car with the back of the bike next to the headlights. Turn on the car headlights. Turn on the bike taillight. Walk a block away and see if you can see the taillight in the glare of the headlights. If not, get a bigger taillight. Andersen himself uses a 6-inch-wide NightSun taillight, which he says is "by far the brightest I have ever found."

Repeat this test while also shining a small flashlight at the bike to see how well your rear reflectors perform.

In his experience, flashers perform well for visibility in the Andersen Acid Test.

"Andersen Acid Test" sees if taillights and flashers are visible from a block away when placed next to car headlights. The taillight on the left flunks, the one on the right passes.

Other Considerations

The power system is not the only item you should consider for either a commercial or home-brew lighting system.

Bulbs

Halogen or xenon bulbs are much brighter than ordinary incandescent bulbs. They are also more expensive—up to $20 apiece. But you need to carry a couple of spare bulbs, because these delicate spheres of glass can and do go bad on the road, especially if shaken by a big bump or a fall.

For the longest lifetime for halogen bulbs, do not handle the bulb with your fingers, which will leave natural oils on the glass that will cook onto the bulb, causing it to crack and burn out faster.

Pick it up by its base or with a piece of tissue. If you do happen to touch the glass part of the bulb, clean it off with alcohol before using it. Such rigorous procedures may, however, be difficult in the dark mid-ride when your hands are sweaty and dirty.

Note for home-brewers: Halogen flashlight bulbs are usually not powerful enough for use as bicycle headlamps. You can, however, get plenty of up-to-date suggestions for a home-brew electrical system from the good folks who participate in the bike-current@cycling.org listserve.

Spare bulbs can be cushioned in sponge, foam, or tissue paper and easily carried in 35-mm film cannisters.

Also, carry electrical tape on your commute—you may find it as essential as tire levers.

Switches

Make sure that a battery-operated system is easy to switch off and on at will while riding, especially if you intend to shut it off on portions of your route and rely exclusively on a generator.

Some cyclists using only a battery-operated system for a long commute along little-traveled roads like to be able to switch off the taillight separately from the headlight to conserve battery power. They turn the taillight on whenever their rearview mirror reveals the headlights of a distant overtaking car. As soon as the car has passed, they turn the taillight off again.

Mounting Position

In many systems designed for bicycles, the front headlight mounts to the headset-mounted reflector bracket or on top of or just under the handlebars. A helmet-mounted light, while useful for hand-free nighttime repairs, may not properly illuminate the road if you're riding in certain positions on drop handlebars.

Some cyclists prefer mounting the headlight on the left side of the front fork, where it is low enough both to keep it from putting light into the rider's eyes and to make road bumps reveal their presence by casting shadows. Mounting the headlight low may be especially helpful if the roads you ride are rough.

Note: Two headlights are better than one, because the road is still lit even if one bulb burns out, and you don't have to fumble for a spare bulb in the dark.

Many taillights are mounted low on the rear left seat stay. Some cyclists, however, prefer to mount it just under the saddle, so it is more at the level of an automobile taillight and thus more visible to an overtaking motorist.

Circumstances Alter Cases

Technology and model features change so rapidly that any discussion of the details of specific power systems would be outdated in a year or two. There are, however, several established commercial

dual beams may be mounted in front of, above, or below handlebars

white front flasher for extra conspicuity

for bumpy roads, mount headlight low on left fork blade

taillights may be under seat or on the seat stay

add flashers to draw extra attention

Lights and flashers should be mounted in the center or on the left side of the bicycle.

battery-powered lighting systems about which technical comments generally seem to be favorable. Among them are NiteRider, NightSun, and systems by Specialized and Cateye. But less well-known systems, such as those manufactured by the small firm Turbo Cat, have also received praise.

Before investing in an expensive system, read mail-order catalogs, which commonly have comparison tables. Consult issues of *Bicycling* or other magazines for any major evaluation (the December 1996 issue of *Bicycle Guide* had a feature article on lights, including an evaluation of their beam patterns). Post a few consumer-evaluation questions about the latest products on the bike-current@cycling.org listserve: ask about battery life, cost, waterproofness if caught in the rain, bulb life, durability over rough roads, weight, and anything else you might want to know from experienced cyclists who may have already tried the product.

Also, consult the mechanics at local bike shops, stop other bicycle commuters you see with great lights, and talk with members of local bike clubs to find out what they like. Last, please note: What works best for an electrical system may vary with geographical location and the severity or mildness of the local climate. Regional differences in the length of twilight and darkness, the extremes of temperature either hot or cold, and the rarity or frequency of snow, rain, blowing grit, or salt on the roads can also alter the practical performance (for example, durability of wiring and connections) as well as the demands on generators or batteries. Rely on the experience of local riders.

Chapter Ten

RIDING IN FOUL WEATHER

Neither rain nor snow need keep a bicycle commuter from appointed rounds. Note enclosed "winter" helmet.

The Best Intentions Pave the Road to . . .

"Naw, I don't need to read this. I have no intention of riding in the rain."

That's a legitimate resolve. But one evening when you're getting ready to leave work, you'll look out the window and see the pavement is damp. And you'll be faced with three choices: Leave your bicycle at work (which complicates the next day's commute or the weekend plans); bum a ride home for yourself and your bike (don't wear out your friendships); or give it a shot ("It's only a sprinkle; I think I can handle it").

If you develop good techniques for riding in inclement weather, you can greatly increase the number of days you can ride to work. Eventually, you may come to the point—as I did—where you simply enjoy weather, in almost all of its varieties.

Note the "almost." While a few diehard bicycle commuters will ride in any conditions almost as a personal challenge, many others draw a line beyond which they feel that two-wheeled transport is simply too risky or uncomfortable. My line was snow and ice. Even so, my willingness to ride in any other conditions meant that I could ride a bike to work some ten months of the year—even more, if the winter was mild.

Now, however, I am ultraconservative when it comes to riding my daughter to elementary school. Because of her age, I draw the line for riding with her not only at snow and ice, but also at rain, darkness, and extreme heat or cold. Circumstances alter choices.

Riding in inclement weather means you must protect yourself and your stuff from the elements, be visible to motorists, and know how your bicycle handles.

This section assumes that you'll be riding in moderate temperatures (30 to 80 degrees) and in the daytime. For dressing when inclement weather is combined with intense heat or bitter cold, see "Extreme-Season Bicycle Clothing," page 124. For riding at night, see "Riding After Dark," page 81.

Dressing for Rain

Whether you wear bicycle clothes or a business suit on your commute, you want to stay as dry as possible. Allowing yourself to become wet not only rumples your clothing, but also invites a chill and hypothermia—even in moderate temperatures. For maximum comfort after you reach work, exchange at least your top underwear and shirt or blouse for dry clothing. Even if you think you arrived dry, the humidity is high in the rain, and you're likely to be more damp than you realize.

Rain Suits

Rain suits are windbreaker jackets and pants that are also water repellent. Inexpensive rain suits may be made of coated nylon or plain old plastic; they are to be avoided because they do not breathe, and after even the shortest commute you will be drenched in your own sweat. Spring for the price a good rain suit made of Gore-Tex or a similar breathable fabric. Buy one that is of a light color for maximum visibility in the dimness of a rainstorm—yellow is ideal.

The rain suits made for cyclists have jackets that are long in the back (so the water sluicing off your back won't be directed into the waistband of your pants). The yoke is actually a flap over open mesh, so your perspiration can evaporate; there may even be zippers under the arms that can be opened for increased ventilation.

Good rain suits have zippers in the lower pant legs, which provide enough fabric for the rain pants to be pulled on over shoes, yet can be cinched around the ankles to prevent the fabric from being caught in the chain. They have hook-and-loop (Velcro) fasteners in the cuffs to prevent chilly wind from blowing up your arms. The best ones also have detachable hoods large enough to come up over your helmet. And they are trimmed with reflective tape across the yoke and on the pant legs for greater visibility.

Gore-Tex rain and wind suit will keep your clothing dry.

Rain Ponchos or Capes

A poncho or cape acts essentially as an umbrella for a cyclist. Its big advantage is its excellent ventilation, which prevents you from becoming drenched in your own sweat. The ponchos for bicycling have two grommets or loops in the front through which you slip your thumbs to keep the rain-repellent fabric stretched out over your arms and knees instead of blowing up around your shoulders, and an internal waist strap to keep it from blowing off your back. Among other advantages, ponchos are big enough also to cover a backpack or fanny pack and are quicker to don than rain suits. A disadvantage is that, since the invention of rain suits, bicycling ponchos have become harder to locate in sporting-goods stores or mail-order house catalogs.

Be persistent. the camping-goods outfitter Campmor, which also has a mail-order business, sells a cyclist's poncho. With a ponch, note that you'll also have to wear gaiters or spats on your lower legs to keep road spray from drenching your pants.

Plastic Bags

Bicycle commute enough and there will come a time when you're at work with your bike with no one to drive you home and there is a deluge outside that not even the weather forecaster expected. Time to improvise—especially if you rode to work in your best business clothes.

Ask the building janitor for several large garbage bags (the larger the better). Make an 8-inch slit in the center of the bottom of one and two more slits in the sides just up from the bottom. Slip it on upside-down, with your head through the center hole and your arms out the two side holes; the makeshift, sleeveless plastic poncho will protect your shoulders and torso down to your hips or below. Tie plastic grocery bags around your feet to protect your dress shoes. You're now ready to face the elements.

If you have a good supply of bags and some duct tape and a lot of patience (which is directly proportional to the expense of your dress clothes), you can also cut another garbage bag into four strips and tape the long edges to make sleeves for encasing your arms and legs. Make sure to tape, rubber-band, or otherwise fasten the plastic sleeves at your shoulders and hips so they will not slip down en route; leave plenty of room at the rear to accommodate your seated posture on the bicycle. Rubber bands at the wrists and ankles will help keep water out.

Be forewarned, however, using plastic bags for rain gear will make you very hot and steamy. If you're really concerned about your dress clothes, and you think you can tape the bags securely enough for modesty, leave your business clothes safely at work and put the garbage bags over just your underwear. And all the way home, remind yourself to keep an emergency cycling outfit at work so that next time you're better prepared.

95

Equipping the Bicycle

In New York City, I kept two bicycles for commuting: one was a lighter-weight sport-touring bike with thin tires for maximum fun in fair weather, and the other was a fully accessorized city bike with fat tires that I chose for greater traction whenever the chance of rain was 40 percent or greater. In that climate, I ended up using both about half the time year-round.

Fenders, Mud Guards, and Splash Protectors

Riding on roads wet from rain can put a muddy stripe straight up your back. Eliminate that by fitting your bicycle with front and rear fenders or mud guards (fenders that are raised to give more clearance between the guard and the tire). Lightweight plastic ones can be purchased from many bike shops for most mountain bikes.

Some narrow-tire bicycles do not have enough clearance around the brakes to accommodate fenders. Not to worry. Blackburn manufactures a plastic rectangle called a Rack Mate that snaps onto the top of a rear bicycle rack to divert most of the spray away from you and whatever stuff you're carrying (see photo on page 35). A similar plastic splash protector can be snapped onto the down tube to protect your legs from spray from the front wheel.

Fenders are an absolute must for recumbents, because water thrown up from the front wheel is directed straight at your face (water from the rear wheel is directed down the back of your neck).

Rack Mate-style mud guards can be improvised by taping plastic-covered cardboard or thin plywood over the rack with duct tape—just look at urban messenger bikes. Some messengers and commuters extend the length of their front fenders with mud flaps down to within several inches of the pavement to protect their shoes. Cut a triangle-shaped piece out of a plastic half-gallon milk container, soda bottle, or cheap report or book cover, and anchor it just inside the fender with staples or a pop rivet (use a washer inside to keep the plastic from tearing); the fender's curve will also curve the mud flap and keep it stiff. If you ride fairly fast even when the ground is wet and you don't have a rear fender, you also might want to improvise a plastic mud flap that extends half a foot or a foot farther out the back than your rack. Again, whatever works.

In a heavy downpour, give the contents of your attaché case extra protection by wrapping the case in a plastic garbage bag and lashing it onto the top of the rear rack with bungees.

If you use panniers, line them with tall white kitchen garbage bags before inserting your gear. Also, you may wish to purchase pannier rain covers, which are often used on long-distance tours for sealing the outside of the bags as well.

Reflectors, Lights, and Flashers

To be seen in fog, rain, or other conditions of lowered visibility even in daylight, activate your flashers and lights. (See "Riding After Dark," page 81, for a full discussion of reflectors and lights.)

Riding in the Rain

The single biggest risk to riding in the rain is the increase in your braking distance resulting from water on your wheel rims. Even worse, the water might splash motor oil from the pavement up onto your rims, further reducing the friction needed for stopping.

To counteract this reduction in your stopping power, ride much more slowly than you would in dry weather. If possible, leave yourself twice the normal time for your commute—not only for safety on the road, but also for cleaning up once you arrive. And if you know oil was splashed onto your rims, stop right there in the rain and do your best to wipe most of it off (you do have your emergency paper towels and alcohol in a plastic bag, right?).

Light to Moderate Rain

The second greatest risk is the loss of traction between your tires and any kind of metal surface, such as manhole covers, steel bridges, drainage grates, road reflectors, and steel construction plates. Also, remember that painted traffic lines when wet can cause your tires to slide right out from under you. Ride around these hazards rather than over them.

On wet pavement itself, traction between the road surface and your tires remains surprisingly good—especially if your tires are wider than about 1½ inches. But gravel, rocks, and cobblestones can become very slippery.

Also risky are fallen leaves, which when wet are surprisingly slippery; piles of leaves may also obscure a drainage grate or pothole. Similarly, puddles may hide dangers. Even a small puddle might be topped with a thin coating of oil. A larger puddle may hide a pothole of unknown depth and width or—worse yet—a flooded tire-eating drainage grate. Always ride around leaves and puddles rather than through them.

Another significant risk is the behavior of motorists. Anticipate the relative position of yourself and a passing car in areas where you know puddles form; even the most well-meaning driver may not be able to avoid spraying you with a rooster-tail of muddy water when driving through a large puddle.

Heavy Rain

In heavy rain, your ability to see the road may be compromised by water flowing into your eyes or down your glasses. Wearing a visor under your helmet can relieve both.

A rare hazard is the hydroplaning of a passing motor vehicle. A vehicle hydroplanes when its tires momentarily lose contact with the road surface and ride on a thin film of water. At that moment, the driver has as little control of the vehicle as he or she would on ice. Watch the cars

If you use panniers, line them with tall white kitchen garbage bags before inserting your gear.

ahead; if their rear ends seem to be fishtailing a bit—swerving at all sideways with respect to the front of the car—ride through that area with extreme caution or wait for a gap in the traffic before proceeding. You don't want to risk having a car slide into you.

Hydroplaning on pavement is relatively rare; the risk is greatest on curves where the road surface may be steadily washed by a thin, wide, smooth film of water. It is more common on steel construction plates or other exceptionally smooth surfaces.

Thunderstorms

In a thunderstorm, you must contend not only with rain, but also with strong winds and lightning. In a city where narrow streets act like wind tunnels, such winds can be erratic, changing direction abruptly at street corners and threatening to blow you into the path of a motor vehicle. Summer cloudbursts often last only twenty minutes or so, and sometimes the better part of valor simply is to pull under the nearest awning or some other shelter (not a tree—trees can attract lightning) and wait for its greatest fury to pass. Remember, with bicycle commuting, you can't be in a hurry even when you're in a hurry.

Fog

Fog dampens pavement. Thus streets can be as wet in fog as after a light rain—and even slicker, because the motor oils are left in place instead of being washed away. Therefore, fog presents the same hazards of increased braking distance and reduced rolling friction as rain, compounded with reduced visibility.

In a light fog, where visibility is at least one long block, ride with the same caution as you would in rain, and with adequate reflectors and lights.

In heavy fog, where visibility is less than one short block, think hard before you venture out if your commute takes you on heavily traveled shoulderless roads posted with speed limits higher than 25 mph.

Riding in Snow and Ice

As mentioned, I draw the line at bicycle commuting in snow and ice and would not recommend to anyone else something I would not do myself. But there are circumstances in which you may feel you have no choice—especially if you live in a region where it snows a significant fraction of the year. It is useful then to know some basic techniques. Most of this information comes from other commuters, some of whom were kind enough to post long articles kept in the archives of various Internet listserves.

Riding During a Snowstorm

Many snowfalls are episodes of almost unearthly silence and calm; all sounds are muffled and the wind hardly stirs. You almost want to hold your breath. Cars are few and drivers are slow and cautious.

Take care not to be distracted by the falling snow itself—either its beauty or the way it can also waft upward and land on exposed skin. If the air is thick with falling snow, your visibility as well as that of motorists will be impaired.

If there is strong wind, be aware that its direction may suddenly change at street corners, shifting from a headwind or tailwind to a crosswind, just as in a thunderstorm. If wind is significant, the snowstorm may be bordering on a blizzard, and it is unwise to be out.

If the falling snow is wet or is actually sleet or freezing rain, then think twice, thrice, and four times before riding through it. If the ground has been cold before the storm, the wet substance not only will stick, but also will form an extremely hazardous layer of crunchy or slick ice on which it is almost impossible to keep your footing, much less ride a bike.

Be dressed adequately for the cold, taking special care of your fingers and toes (see "Extreme-Season Bicycle Clothing," page 124). Try not to stop for long intervals; keep your body moving and generating body heat until you are safely indoors. Then immediately take a hot bath or shower and change into dry clothes.

Riding on Snow

A light dusting of snow should not stop anyone from commuting. Simply ride slowly and carefully and avoid frozen puddles.

If the snow is dry and only a few inches deep and the air temperature is in the twenties or lower, you may be surprised how much traction your tires have with the road. But all the warnings about puddles and leaves are in full force: You are unlikely to see potholes, drainage grates, steel construction plates, cobblestones, glass, and other hazards—including puddles that have previously frozen into a sheet of ice—under a fluffy blanket of snow. Ride slowly and with extreme caution.

If the dry snow is more than about four inches deep, some cyclists find that the thinner tires of a road bike cut through the powder all the way to the pavement better than the fatter tires of a mountain bike. Riding through unplowed snow may be slow, sweaty labor, because you will be breaking trail. (Past a certain depth, walking to work may be a better choice than riding.)

Side roads might be neither plowed nor salted.

Tire tracks reveal difficulty of riding in a straight line in wet, slippery snow.

Wet snow can jam brakes and fill tread with ice.

If the snow is wet and the air temperature is right around or just below freezing, the snow will be extremely slick. Deep-treaded mountain bike tires are of little use, because the snow will squeeze between the treads, your weight will compact it into ice and you will end up riding on a slippery mass of icy slush. Moreover, this semi-frozen mass may collect under your fenders or brakes, stopping you suddenly and perhaps causing a spill. For this reason, some winter commuters do not like using fenders, at least in wet snow. Mud guards anchored well away from the tires, however, may not allow the snow to collect and will protect you from being

splashed by the freezing, heavy slush.

Winter commuters seem to agree that they find it safest to ride in the tire tracks of vehicles if the snow is just semi-hard-packed or the pavement is exposed. In these conditions, the traction is halfway decent and a cyclist is moving at the same speed as cautious motorists and so can claim the full share of the road. If the hard-packed tire tracks ice up, however, some cyclists prefer the greater traction offered by undisturbed snow on the side of the road—as long as the snow covers a previously clear dry road and they know the locations of pavement defects. But a hidden grate or patch of ice could throw a bike into traffic or into the curb. Other commuters prefer to ride in the icy tire tracks if the road was recently sanded, or if their bikes are equipped with studded snow tires (Yes, such things exist! See below).

Watch also at intersections where you might ride wet, salted pavement onto hard-packed un-salted snow; there is often a patch of slick ice at the transition from one type of surface to the next.

Riding on Ice

Veteran commuter Dennis Coello, experienced in riding through the snows of Salt Lake City and St. Louis, recommends two useful techniques for up-right bicycles. First, round corners not by leaning into them as usual, because on snow or ice that simply invites a sliding fall. Instead, keep the bicy-cle vertical and turn the handlebar almost like a steering wheel; this is a technique that demands that you be riding slowly.

Second, Coello recommends being prepared at a moment's notice to prevent a fall. Ride with the upper inner thigh of one leg braced against the bicycle's top tube. When you feel the wheels begin to slip, immediately free the opposite foot from the pedal and hold it out, pre-pared to touch the ground if neces-sary to keep your balance. The two wheels and your extended foot then form a tripod for stability over treacherous patches.

Commuters who ride recumbents, however, seem uniformly agreed that recumbent bicycles do not handle well on ice or in slick conditions. Juneau, Alaska, commuter John Andersen has hy-pothesized that on an upright, a rider can swing his or her hips and the bike left and right to ac-commodate dicey traction situations, whereas on a recumbent such swinging (or bunny-hopping) is difficult if not impossible. Recumbent tricycles are "the only safe solution," reports Peter Eland, man-aging editor of *Bike Culture Quarterly*, whose own commuting experience indicates trikes handle very well in slippery conditions.

In certain parts of the country, bicycle shops may stock studded snow tires for fat-tire bikes. Such tires are suitable for riding on ice; one com-mon brand is IRC Blizzard. Colorado commuter Michael Leccese affirms that "they really work," al-though they wear quickly, while Maine commuter John Kettlewell remarked that it was astonishing to see one cyclist riding on snow tires on an ice-skating pond "under full control."

For about half the price of commercial studded snow tires, you can make your own. Buy a pair of ATB (all-terrain bicycle) tires with knobby tread and a box of ⅜-inch or ½-inch pan-head or flat-head wood or sheet metal screws. Drill a small pilot hole through every second or third knob on the tread and then insert a screw from the inside of the tire, making sure that they are offset from the cen-terline on each side, and screw them into place (a battery-operated screwdriver eases the task, since you will be inserting some seventy-two screws per tire). Line the tire with a plastic strip, such as a Mr. Tuffy, or part of an old automobile inner tube to protect your bicycle tire's tube from any wear from the screwheads.

Winter commuters agree that stud-ded tires—sometimes aided by re-ducing the tire's air pressure—are the only alternative for riding on ice and are noticeably more stable than non-studded tires on packed snow. They're about the same as non-stud-ded tires on unpacked snow; they are worse on dry pavement, making the bike skittish while corner-ing. They are also very noisy, producing a buzzing sound that one winter commuter likened to mak-ing the bike sound like a big-wheel pickup truck. They also complicate the changing of a flat; the sharp studs can really scratch your skin.

In some areas, bicycle shops may stock studded snow tires.

Riding Days After a Snow

Snow can stick around for weeks or even months if the winter is generally cold. After a few days of brilliant sunshine, however, conditions change. The road surface itself may become clear of snow (although it is still likely to be wet), inviting you to ride again. But there are a few points of caution.

First, after a heavy snowfall (or succession of snowfalls), the plowed snow at the roadsides make the roads half a lane to a lane narrower than usual. Shoulders disappear and two-lane roads may be reduced to one-and-a-half lanes. Thus, there is less clearance between you and the motor vehicles.

If you feel unsafe because of the behavior of vehicles on the main road, alter your route to take advantage of little-traveled back roads. The traveling conditions may be somewhat worse than on main roads, but the traffic is also likely to be much less. In the country, be careful to note the placement of the real edge of the road. Sometimes a road may have been plowed only on one side; don't risk sliding off the pavement or falling into a snow-filled drainage ditch by riding too far off to the right.

Second, both ice and flooding can be significant hazards—even in areas where there usually is no standing water after a rain. In the northeast, winters are famous for temperatures that commonly rise above freezing in the daytime and dip below freezing at night. After a few day-night freeze-thaw cycles, even the fluffiest, driest snow eventually becomes packed and turns to ice—particularly at its base where the melted snow runs off. Also, heavy snow commonly blocks storm drains, giving rise to large puddles in unexpected places, which can freeze overnight.

Third, especially in cities, which tend to be warmer than surrounding suburbs or rural areas, what remains snow in outlying areas may become slush, a semi-frozen slurry mixed with dirt. Slush is also likely to form where roads are salted to prevent ice by lowering the freezing point of water.

Snow gets thrown everywhere on the bicycle—and any salt in it will start to corrode metal.

Slush tends to accumulate at the edges of roadsides and at corners, freezing (despite the salt) on very cold nights and liquifying during the day. At best, riding through slush is vastly unpleasant; at its worst, it combines all the hazards of puddles, mud, and ice.

Last, if traction grit (coarse sand or fine gravel) is sprinkled on snowy roads for traction, that grit will remain on the roads well into the spring, being thrown onto the shoulders by the wheels of passing vehicles. Although it provided traction on snow, as dry sand on pavement, that grit becomes its own slipping hazard to bicycles.

Salt Corrosion

If you commute in an area where roads are salted, each evening you should hose the dirty salt off your bike and chain. Salt is extremely corrosive, and within days will cause exposed metal to rust and moving parts to seize, destroying your bike. To further retard corrosion, pack all bearings with marine or farm-implement grease—even greasing or oiling all the spoke nipples if you want to keep them free enough from rust so the wheels can be trued.

Because roads in Ottawa, Ontario, are so heavily salted, Canadian commuter Pete Hickey regards his winter commuting bicycles as disposable: He picks up ten-speeds for $25 at garage sales (mountain bikes tend to run around $50) and rides them until they dissolve. In his 1991 archival Internet article "Pete's Winter Cycling Tips," which is packed with useful advice, he also advises keeping a ketchup squeeze bottle filled with 90-weight transmission oil to oil the chain, derailleur, and brakes twice a week.

To retard salt corrosion, pack all bearings with marine or farm-implement grease.

Chapter Eleven

SECURING YOUR BICYCLE AGAINST THEFT

A stripped bicycle frame in New York City did not convey its silent lesson on proper locking technique to a later cyclist—who committed precisely the same error.

The Ingenuity of Bicycle Thieves

Probably every New York City bicycle commuter, including myself, has had at least one bicycle stolen—even when correctly locked in a public area at busy hours. Commuter Jim Arth had one stolen when it was *leaning against his hip* as he bent over to pick up his helmet (he was wearing cleated bicycling shoes and could not pursue the agile thief) and had another pinched from a locked office. Commuter John Horgan lost three bicycles—one when a determined thief *took apart the bike rack* to which he had double-locked his steed. Yes, New York City bicycle thieves are world-class professionals, as evidenced by lock companies' offers of reimbursement for bicycles stolen when protected by their locks anywhere, that is, except in Manhattan.

A bicycle has a high monetary value for its size, can be easily hidden or serve as its own noiseless getaway vehicle, and can be fenced for cash. So

deterring theft should be uppermost in your mind whenever you leave your bike in a city, even for the briefest moment. Even if thieves can't walk away with the whole thing, they've been known to strip bicycles of the saddle, the handlebars, the wheels, and even the pedal cranks and chainwheels.

Suburbs tend not to be so rampant with such sidewalk theft, although cautious commuters may want to follow city-level precautions. However, you should secure your steed at home against the occasional rash of nighttime professional garage thefts. One night on my street in suburban New Jersey, all my neighbors who stored bicycles in their detached garages had the garage padlocks clipped and the bikes taken; nothing else was touched. Clearly this was a midnight assembly-line attack by practiced bicycle thieves with a van. The only reason my bikes weren't among the missing, I'm sure, is that

Use two different locks to foil thieves with only one kind of tool—note saddle is secured as well as the rear wheel.

they were kept in my house's finished basement.

Rural areas are probably the least subject to theft, judging from the unlocked kids' bikes left lying about undisturbed overnight. But I still wouldn't present any golden target of opportunity to a wouldbe thief. Remember, an unlocked bike is practically wearing a sign shouting, "Take me, I'm yours."

Locks

Long gone are the days when you can just loop a light cable through one wheel and a concrete block—at least if you live in a city. Urban bicycle commuters must use bulletproof locks.

Locks come in several distinct types: cable locks, rigid locks, and chain locks. Although all are fine for low-crime areas, you'll need the industrial strength models to deter urban thieves. "Deter" is the operative word. Against a determined professional, no lock can withstand an arsenal of Freon spray, sledgehammer, cable-cutters, three-foot-long 4 × 4's, and speedy unobtrusiveness born of much experience. Nonetheless, many bicycle thieves are not of that caliber and will pinch only the easy stuff—even if they can't get the whole bike. It is this more common thief against which a good lock and religious and proper use of it are effective.

Good locks are expensive, running fully 10 percent the cost of a moderately priced bike, if not more. But don't cheap out. Remember not only the value of the asset you are trying to protect, but also the inconvenience and anguish you'll go through if you need to replace it (and its racks and other accessories) for having taken a pound-foolish approach.

The instructions below assume that your commuting bicycle is an upright. Securely locking a recumbent is a challenge, especially if you must leave your bicycle outside for long periods of time, as some designs have no closed-polygon frame members through which a lock can be run.

Cable Locks

Cable locks are coils of braided or twisted hardened steel wire. At the low end, a cable lock is a ⅛-inch-thick token deterrent perhaps two feet long that you attach with an ordinary hardware-store padlock just to remind people that the bike belongs to someone. At the high end, a cable lock is ½-inch-thick coils that can stretch out to six feet and is secured with a pick-resistant key or combination lock. Cable locks are usually encased in vinyl or Kevlar, both to protect the coils from rust and to keep them from scratching the bicycle's frame.

A heavy-duty cable lock is all I've found to be necessary for running errands in the suburbs, where I might leave the bike for less than an hour. Its six-foot length is convenient; it can be slipped through both wheels and through the frame without taking off the wheels. A long cable lock can also be threaded through the frame of a child's trailer cycle without separating it from the adult bike.

One clever light-duty cable lock, which could be useful for running a quick errand on a rural commute, is called Officer Frank. Instead of occupying valuable space on the frame when not in use, it is stored inside the tube of your handlebar. Removal or replacement takes only a minute "if you're really slow," notes the literature.

Rigid Locks

The rigid U-, C-, O-, and J-locks—so named because of their shapes resemble those letters of the alphabet—are high-security locks especially intended for urban use. Common brands include Citadel and Kryptonite. Also popular is the Bike Club, from the maker of The Club for automobiles. All are heavy locks of half-inch hardened steel bars sheathed in vinyl and secured with keyed, pick-resistant cylinders of various designs.

U-locks consist of a U-shaped bar whose open ends insert into a fatter solid steel crosspiece and are secured with a key. Depending on the design, the ends of the U may or may not project through the crosspiece. This crosspiece may be anywhere from ¾-inch to 1¼-inch thick; go with the thicker one if you're an urban commuter.

To secure a road bicycle, you'll want the standard sized lock, whose U is a bit less than a foot long and 4 to 5 inches wide. Remove the front wheel (easily done by loosening the quick-release lever) and place it parallel to the rear wheel. Then pass the U part of the lock around both rims, the bicycle's seat tube, and the pole or other object to which you are locking the bike. Securely replace the crosspiece over the open ends of the U; turn the key to lock the cylinder. Then tug on the crosspiece to make sure the lock is secure (sometimes it is possible to lock the cylinder without properly engaging both ends of the U). If possible, lock the bike so the keyhole of the lock points down toward the pavement—not only to prevent rain from entering the lock, but also to make it harder for a thief to pick it.

A mountain bicycle with its fatter tubing and wider rims and tires may be too tight to fit inside a standard U-lock. ATB U-locks for mountain bikes have a U that is another inch wider. Another possibility is a motorcycle U-lock, which has a longer U. But buy the smallest U-lock that works: You don't want to leave any spare room inside the U that a thief can use to leverage tools.

Unlike two-piece U-locks, O-locks are one hinged or articulated piece of metal, with one end slipping securely into the other. The bicycle's wheels, frame, and pole are secured in the same way as with a U-lock.

If you don't like disassembling your bike each time you stop, or if your bike is an oldie-but-goodie with standard nut-and-bolt axles instead of quick-release skewers (or if you've replaced your quick release skewers with nuts and bolts for extra security), try using two locks. Anchor the rear wheel and seat tube to the pole with a standard U-lock or O-lock, but also buy a miniature

U-lock—the size for a BMX bike—for separately anchoring the front wheel to the down tube. Vetta also makes a small triangular lock for this purpose. You'll have to deal with two locks each time you stop, but you won't have to hassle with removing wheels.

C-locks and J-locks have one open jaw for anchoring the rear wheel to a pole or to the bicycle's frame. In spite of the open jaw, they are as effective as a boot on an automobile tire in immobilizing the vehicle. You'll need a separate lock for securing the front wheel to the down tube—or you'll need to carry the front wheel inside your workplace.

When you're riding, rigid locks can be carried on your bicycle either in a pannier or in a mounting bracket designed for the lock bolted to the seat tube. Looping a lock around the handlebar or seatpost is not satisfactory; the thing is heavy and tends to swing as you ride and can interfere with pedaling.

Chain Locks

Chain locks are three- or four-foot lengths of hardened steel chain—sometimes vinyl-covered—that can be wound through the frame and wheels much like a cable, and then secured with a padlock. Some chains consist of ½-inch-thick steel rods linked by hefty hinges; others are 1½-inch chain links whose open ends are welded closed. They can be purchased at bicycle shops, motorcycle outfitters, or dealers in industrial wares.

Make sure that the padlock itself is not the weak link in the system. There is no point in having an industrial-strength chain secured by a $2.59 locker-room combination lock that can be readily clipped with long metal-cutting shears. Get a beefy heavy-duty padlock that is itself almost a tiny U-lock.

Chain locks are usually carried on the bicycle by wrapping them around the seatpost. They are, however, among the heaviest of security devices. If your bicycle is always parked outdoors in the same place and you almost never do errands en route, you might consider leaving the chain and lock around the

> *There is no point in having an industrial-strength chain secured by a $2.59 locker-room combination lock.*

pole semi-permanently to spare yourself lugging around the extra five-plus pounds. You might also want to encase the chain in an old piece of inner tube to prevent it from scratching your frame.

Saddle Locks

When New York City commuter Caroline Bliss secured her bicycle outdoors near Wall Street, she returned in the afternoon to find her new Avocet saddle missing. "Riding five miles home up Broadway without a seat was quite a trick, especially at stoplights," she recalled.

If you must regularly park your bike outdoors in a city, you might follow the lead of bicycle messengers. Some anchor the seat post into the seat tube with a quick-release mechanism, similar to the one on the wheel hubs. Any time the rider leaves the bike, he or she takes the saddle along. Of course, you must always remember to do this, as any passer-by can simply flip the quick release lever and make off with the saddle.

Other messengers permanently secure the rails of the saddle to the top of the rear triangle by a length of bicycle chain that has been wrapped with handlebar tape to avoid scratching the frame. Removing a bicycle chain requires a rivet tool (or exceptionally heavy-duty metal cutters); casual thieves may consider it too time-consuming a procedure for such a small trophy as a saddle. Make sure the chain is long enough to accommodate the proper leg extension of the tallest person likely to ride the bike; also, check whether the presence of the chain might interfere with a large tool wedge.

Wheel Locks

Some quick-release skewers are designed with a built-in lock. One well-known brand is Cyclox. (One caution: The skewer itself may be slightly thinner than a non-locking skewer and can be bent; see "Bonehead Maintenance" about quick-release skewer failure.)

A poor man's improvisation is simply to install a small padlock through the front fork or rear

triangle near the hub in such a position that the rear quick-release lever cannot be raised without first undoing the padlock.

Either device might keep a rear wheel from being pinched if you lock only the front wheel and frame to a pole to duck into a store for a quick errand on a suburban or rural commute, but I would not trust my rear wheel to such a weak expedient in a city.

Lock Assistants

Some security devices are not locks themselves but add strength to locks by reducing a thief's leverage.

One such item is Bad Bones by Vetta, which consists of a couple of flat steel rods that slide onto the U part of a U-lock. If your bicycle frame, wheels, and the pole to which you are locking them do not completely fill the U-lock, slide on one or two Bad Bones to take up the rest of the space.

Another item that will strengthen the crosspiece of a U-lock is simply a plumbing T, a low-budget item available at any decent hardware store. Slide the top crossbar of the T onto the lock's crosspiece so

A plumbing T can be used as a lock assistant on a U-lock.

that the upright part of the T is centered on the hole into which you insert the straight end of the U part.

Burglar Alarms

Some home-center stores market bicycle burglar alarms that, when disturbed, will emit a piercing tone or even speak the words "Take your hands off me!" The ones I've seen do not seem as reliable or as strong as would be needed in a city, but a bike burglar alarm is just novel enough that maybe it could have some value in chasing away nosy potential thieves. If used in conjunction with more secure devices, a burglar alarm could alert you to a potential theft—if your office is near enough to the bike to let you hear the alarm. But beware of becoming like automobile owners who routinely ignore the alarm because it is so often set off by the wind or by other users of the parking lot.

Future Locks

Suburban and rural commuters can likely buy one lock and keep using it for the lifetime of the bike.

Urban commuters, however, are advised to keep abreast of technology. The best bicycle thieves are always doing their research to break every security device invented by humans, and so the lock companies keep changing and evolving their merchandise to keep ahead of the thieves. Read articles in the bicycling magazines, talk with the owners of bike shops, and chat with an occasional bicycle messenger to learn the scoop on which types of locks seem to be becoming more vulnerable to theft. Plan to spend $50 or even $75 every year or two upgrading to the best lock available—by bicycle commuting, you've undoubtedly saved much more than that just in gasoline or bus fare, right?

How and Where to Lock a Bike

Deterring theft is a matter not only of good equipment, but also of good practice and good psychology—especially if you must park the bike outdoors. A prospective thief might move on to another target if he or she suspects your bicycle's security measures will be too time-consuming to defeat, or the theft would be too visible, or the bicycle would be too difficult to remove.

Also, a good number of thieves are just amateurs interested only in a quick, uncomplicated snatch. Although nothing will deter a real professional, much can be done to discourage amateurs.

Urban Locking Strategies

Make sure your lock passes through the bicycle's frame, which is the most expensive part of the bike. Make sure it also passes through both wheels. Don't get lazy about this. That was strikingly demonstrated for me one weekday afternoon near Saks Fifth Avenue when I stopped for an errand. The only nearby sign pole was already occupied by

another bike; but its U-lock passed through only its front wheel and frame, leaving the rear wheel unsecured. Half an hour later, my bicycle, which was secured to the pole with the U-lock through both wheels as well as the frame, was untouched, but the rear wheel of the other bike was gone, the chain left dangling onto the pavement. Same pole, same type of lock, proper versus lazy use. Effective object lesson.

Also make sure that the object to which you're locking your bike is as sturdy as the lock itself. The best choice is a bike rack designed to allow the frame to be locked—preferably one made of three-inch pipe without bolts. A good standard alternative is a sign pole of three-inch pipe. Bad choices include parking meters (whose tops can be removed), saplings (which can be cut down even with the wood saw blade on a Swiss army knife), old-fashioned bolted metal bike racks (which can be disassembled), and chain-link fences (which can be clipped with wire cutters). If something seems too flimsy, it is.

Hang a bicycle up high to make a potential theft more obvious to passers-by.

If you leave your bicycle in an office building overnight, lock it to something as securely as if you were leaving it outdoors. Don't tempt the most honest janitorial staff with the opportunity for a casual "lift"—and "inside job" thefts do happen. Even locking your bike to a desk chair would make an attempted theft obvious to the night watchman. The same is true any time you leave your bicycle untended in a hotel room while you are out.

For added safety in a high-risk area, double-lock your bike using two locks of different types to discourage thieves that carry tools for picking only one type of lock. For example, use both a U-lock and a heavy cable lock. For extra security, run the cable lock through the chainwheels as well as through the wheels and frame to discourage

removal of your bottom bracket assembly.

Whenever your bicycle is unlocked—even on the subway or in a park—keep one hand on it at all times. Alternatively, loop your leg through the frame. Once again, I've heard of intermodal commuters losing their bikes or accessories to stealthy thieves when they had dozed off or were engaged in lively conversation.

As paranoid as this may sound, lock your bike at night even if you store it in your own garage. Especially if you have a detached garage, as is common in older suburbs, you're unlikely to hear an intruder quietly snipping the garage-door padlock. Also, store it in a place where it cannot be seen by anyone looking through a garage window. Don't make it easy for a bicycle thief to case out your $750 bicycle and roll it out the door.

This bicycle is properly locked with an O-lock — but that sapling could be cut in minutes with a Swiss Army knife's wood saw.

This bicycle is properly locked with an O-lock to a rack of the most secure design.

Protect Components and Accessories

Remove all accessories (light, odometer, seatcover, pump, etc.) to discourage petty stripping. If you commute in a high-theft area, organize your valuables and tools into one bag that can be readily removed from the bike and carried with you whenever you stop for an errand. You'll be less likely to forget a pump or other item that is normally attached to the bike, and you'll save yourself a lot of time if you must make several stops.

To further discourage stripping, some cyclists apply Loctite, Vibra Tite, or some other brand of thread locker (a solvent-resistant solution that is applied to screw threads to secure fasteners against vibration) to screws holding on racks, seat bolt binders, handlebars, derailleur bolts, and other screw-fastened components. Loctite, one of the best known, comes in various grades ranging from purple (the mildest, suitable for small fasteners under moderate vibration, which can be loosened with normal tools) to green (the strongest, which has almost the strength of a steel weld). Obviously, care must be exercised so that you don't immobilize a screw you really may need to loosen.

Other cyclists use a silicone sealer/adhesive to fill in the screwdriver slots or Allen bolt recesses into which the thief must insert a tool to remove such parts. You can still pry out the plugs when you need to overhaul the bike, but the unexpected resistance might represent enough of a delay to deter a thief.

Be ingenious about locking the frame of your bicycle if the only rack available is not designed for frame-locking.

Deception and Trickery

If you've ridden to an event with a set time (such as to church or the theater), do not park directly in front of the place. You don't want to advertise the fact that a thief has a whole hour to work on your bike.

Instead, park the bike in front of a restaurant's plate-glass window. The thief might think you're inside keeping a eye on the bike, even if you're not; and a patron might report suspicious activity just as a good citizen (you might also foil an attempted theft against some other cyclist someday).

If you have ridden to a restaurant, ask for a table near the window where you can keep an eye on the bike. Failing that, check on it every ten or fifteen minutes.

If you park somewhere regularly, make friends with a doorman or security guard (that is, tip him) to keep an eye on your locked bike. Make sure to tell him when you've returned and are going to remove the bike—not only to thank him, but also to let him know it was removed by its owner.

Do things to the parked bike that would make it difficult for it to be used as a get-away vehicle: remove the front wheel or saddle, deflate the remaining rear tire, or drop off or remove the chain.

Ride a clunker, or make an expensive bike look like a clunker—thereby diminishing its fenced

value—by giving it a crummy spray-paint job or by wrapping the frame in handlebar or electrical tape (I could never bring myself to do this).

Always park your bicycle in some highly visible area, not off in a dark corner near the dumpster where a thief can work in privacy. In my experience, the prize for the most visible parking goes to the New York City messenger who climbed up onto the base of a traffic light on East 42nd Street to lock his bicycle onto the WALK-WAIT sign ten feet above the ground. Such a high position would have also bollixed up a thief's leverage.

Follow your gut. If your gut tells you that there is something no good about the place you were thinking of parking or riding through, move on. Who knows what prehistoric instincts of self-preservation still exist in our lower brains?

Last, don't be discouraged or overly scared by all this advice. It works, and it soon becomes second nature. In my view, my having just one bicycle stolen in five years as a 1,500-mile-per-year commuter in the city that never sleeps is not a bad average for an urban commuter. With fares saved, I was ahead of the game financially as long as the theft rate was lower than one bicycle a year.

By the same token, don't get careless about observing good practice after a year or two of hanging onto your bike. Good practice is probably why you still have it.

> ■
> *As paranoid as this may sound, lock your bike at night if you store it in a detached garage.*
> ■

Part Three

PRACTICALITIES

Chapter Twelve

CLOTHING AND LOGISTICS

With a bit of planning, it's easy to freshen up at work.

The Secret to Being Fresh for Work

Possibly the most frequently heard objection to bicycle commuting, particularly from the white-collar set, is, "For my job I have to look nice, and I don't want to arrive at work all sweaty and hassled."

The surprising truth is, depending on the weather and the nature of your commute, you may not arrive at work all sweaty and hassled. And even if you do arrive sweaty, with a bit of planning you can freshen up quickly and completely.

Aside from that, thinking "bicycle commuting equals sweaty" and "not bicycle commuting equals not sweaty" is misleading. After all, even without bicycling, how many times do you already arrive at work sweaty and hassled after having been crammed into a subway car in the summer humidity or having run to catch a bus or train or having your car stuck in rush-hour traffic? For all that perspiration, you may as well feel good about having ridden your bike—and be prepared for freshening up!

Best Tip: Leave Early

Perhaps the single most important tip for being fresh at work after bicycle commuting is, leave home early. I mean really early—if possible, an hour earlier than you think you might need. Early morning riding allows you to enjoy the freshest air of the day with the least traffic. You will arrive at work with plenty of time to wash up, cool down, calm your heart rate, have coffee, apply makeup, and in general get in the right frame of mind for your job.

Arriving early could also give you additional bonuses. You might find you have the freedom to take your bicycle up to your office in an empty elevator instead of one crowded with co-workers objecting to sharing the space with your greasy bike. You might find that, once at work, your productivity is increased (it's amazing how much you can get done in a solitary hour before the phones start ringing). And, possibly, arriving early might allow you to leave early in the afternoon to beat rush-hour traffic on the commute home.

Aside from that universal tip, the options are many. This section will help you decide which ones make sense for you.

What's Right for You?

In previous chapters you analyzed the needs of your commute and your desires in cycling to help you select a good bicycle. A similar kind of analysis will pay off for your choice of clothing and logistics for dealing with what you need both on the bike and on the job.

- How must you be dressed for work? (Affects the logistics of the clothes you need, where you keep them, and how you transport them)
- Is your bicycle commute easy or arduous? (Affects whether you have the option of wearing work clothes on the bike or must change when you arrive)
- What provision is there at work for freshening up? (Does your company offer showers or just a sink in a public rest room? Do you have access to a closet?)
- Once on the job, must you drive to other sites? (If so, do you have access to a company car or truck once your arrive, thus allowing you to bicycle to the main site? Or can you schedule all your visits to other sites on just one or two days of the week, leaving you free to bicycle-commute the others?)
- What flexibility do you have with your work day's starting and ending times? (May give you access to your building's facilities early or late and allow you to choose the best times for riding)

Sartorial Logistics

People in some professions—such as those in which one only occasionally meets the public or other people one must impress—have great flexibility of dress. If their commute is not very strenuous, they might even wear business clothes while bicycling. In New York City, which is geographically small and relatively flat, it is quite common to see bicycle commuters wearing dress suits or skirts.

People in other professions—such as doctors, nurses, sales representatives, accountants, lawyers, and plumbers—must appear crisp in uniforms or three-piece suits (another type of uniform) or must visit clients on their premises. They will likely prefer to wear athletic clothes on the bicycle and change once they arrive at work—especially if their commute is at all strenuous.

The only way you can tell which choice is right for you is to experiment with both. You may find that you actually prefer a combination of both (a solution I favored in New York City), commuting in business clothes on pleasant days but wearing athletic clothes on very hot days and changing at work.

If you choose to wear athletic clothes on the commute, the big question is how to get your business clothes to and from work. Different commuters like different solutions.

One solution is to pack a work outfit and fresh underwear for the day and strap it onto the bike (see the section on bicycle bags, "Carrying Load with the Bicycle," page 45).

Another solution is to drive a car to work once a week to drop off the next week's clean clothes and pick up the current week's dirty laundry. You might want to set a regular day of the week to do this—say, Friday (which, for some reason, seems to be a day that motorists drive particularly fast and heedlessly). Alternatively, you might wish to maximize your time on the bike by driving only on a day you would not commute by bicycle anyway (because of rain, heat, a special function at work for which you must be well-dressed, plans after work, or the like).

A third solution is to leave several suits, uniforms, dresses, shirts, and blouses at work permanently. This option is worth exploring particularly if you have access to a closet and if your commute is very long and strenuous or if you must be very well dressed at work all the time. To minimize the logistics of toting dirty laundry—and the chance of running out of clean clothes—look for a dry cleaner and hand laundry near your job.

A fourth approach is to vary your routine, depending on the weather, your needs for local travel on the job, your after-work plans, and other factors. A bit of experimentation will reveal which choices you like best and under what conditions.

Freshening Up at Work

Some people have all the breaks, including access to a shower at work. Or maybe they have access to a shower within a block or two of work, such as at a nearby YMCA, YWCA, or health club. If you're one of these, your life as a bicycle commuter is a ready-made dream.

Many others—including myself for five years—must make do with the workplace's employee rest room, equipped only with toilet stalls and sinks. Don't despair. A thorough "sponge bath" and clean, dry underwear will make you feel amazingly fresh.

When I arrived a good half hour or more before the rest of my colleagues, I took my "sponge bath" at the sink: stripping my torso down to my skin, washing well under my arms with that industrial-strength institutional antibacterial soap, and blotting off with paper towels. A real sponge or a terry washcloth and towel kept at work might have been more civilized, but I never bothered: I'd have had to find a place to hang them to dry and they'd have been be two more items to launder. Some bicycle commuters don't even bother with soap and water: They just do the job with cotton and a bottle of witch hazel or alcohol, pre-moistened hemorrhoidal pads (which are just witch hazel on cotton fabric), or baby wipes.

On very hot and humid summer days, I'd wet

and soap up some paper towels and retire into a stall to wash, rinse, and dry the ischial tuberosities as well as my upper body. Theoretically, because most employee bathrooms are single-sex, one need not preserve one's modesty. In practice, however, employees are not accustomed to walking into a bathroom to find a fellow employee washing genitalia, and you might not be an employee for long if someone took it wrong that you were exposing yourself. If I arrived at work "late," that is, around the same time as everyone else, I also observed this precaution for the upper body. Moreover, greater modesty should be observed in a rest room intended for the general public as well as for employees.

Last, for your own good, go out of your way to be scrupulous about basic courtesies. It's weird enough (in many people's minds) that you want to commute by bike. For your own sake, don't risk alienating your colleagues who must also share the bathroom by being a slob as well. If you splash water or soap onto the mirror, sink, or floor, take an extra few seconds to dry and shine them up. Don't occupy more than one sink, and don't hang smelly clothes all around. Throw out the used paper towels, clear the sink of dropped whiskers and strands of hair. Turn off the water and check that the toilet has been flushed. In short, when you leave the rest room, no one should even suspect that a bicycle commuter had just bathed, shaved, put on makeup, washed underwear, or blow-dried hair.

Help for "Helmet Hair"

Helmet hair, as any semi-serious cyclist knows, is what is left of your hairdo after riding while wearing your helmet, especially if you sweat. In my case, the top of my hair gets squashed down against my skull and the ends of my hair flip up like a 'do from the 1950s or early 1960s.

My take is that most guys don't care about helmet hair and maybe don't even notice it; helmet hair for them is nothing that a little water or a little nonchalance can't handle. For some women, however, the risk of messing up Pierre's $150 styling job is the trashing of a major investment and one not easily reclaimed in a moment or two (as one female friend observed, natural beauty is a lot of work). Helmet hair even may be enough to keep some appearance-conscious women from bicycle commuting altogether.

My solution, as a woman, was to be open with my hairdresser: I told her I was a cyclist and I wanted a no-work, no-set style that looked reasonably good after a workout. The result was a short cut that was deliberately styled to be a study in randomness following my hair's own natural wave. If the helmet made it just a bit more random, the whole effect was not ruined (it wasn't improved, but it wasn't ruined). If after my commute I really detested what I saw in the mirror, I simply washed my hair in the employee rest room sink, toweled it damp, and let it air-dry in the better position of the cut. If I had to be really dressed up, I used a portable blow-dryer.

Another solution, which I tried for about a year, was to get a curly perm. That worked exceptionally well, and helmet hair was easily eliminated with a damp comb and a shake (don't ever blow-dry a perm). The major disadvantage is that a good permanent is even more expensive than Pierre.

Women, or men, with hair longer than shoulder length, be it straight or wavy, are well-advised to bind it so it does not fly out behind while riding. Those tresses dramatically flowing in the breeze will be filled with wicked knots. Breaking of those knots day after day could result in each individual hair being split an inch or more up the shaft. And regrettably, the only reliable cure for split ends is to have the hair cut well above the splits.

A simple band at the nape of the neck and a second band at the ends of the hair will prevent knots and make combing it out after a ride much more humane. (Observe this mercy also for any long-haired child you convey to and from school on your bike.) You can also try spraying the ends with a detangler—one brand is Johnson &

Johnson's No More Tangles, found with the hair products in any drugstore—before combing. Always remove knots with a comb, preferably one with wide teeth or one with staggered teeth designed for combing wet hair; use a brush only for styling after the comb has done the real work.

To Makeup or Not To Makeup?

For a short, essentially flat commute of three to five miles, it seemed to make no difference whether I applied makeup before or after the ride. It was handy to know this if I was riding to an early-morning breakfast meeting, where I had to arrive looking terrific.

For a long commute involving working up a sweat on steep climbs, or for hot, humid days, makeup is probably better applied after arriving at work. It's not that makeup runs or smears (many mascaras are excellent about not running—I particularly recommend Clinique's Naturally Glossy Mascara for bulletproof confidence); it's just that after you arrive, you might want to have the option of washing your face.

If you absolutely do not want to be seen by anyone in your work building without some enhancement of natural beauty, try putting on only mascara and lipstick before leaving the house; once at work, you can still daub your face and eyelids with a damp washcloth before completing the makeup job with foundation, blusher, and eyeshadow.

By the way, many brands of foundation or pre-makeup moisturizer have some sun protection, ranging from SPF 2 to SPF 15. In the summer, it might be worth applying the foundation before your ride just for the sunscreen.

Bicycle Commuting in Business Clothes

Here are some helpful tips for wearing business clothes on the bike without either ruining the clothes or creating a safety hazard.

Long Pants

With dress pants or trousers, you want to avoid catching the fabric in the greasy bicycle chain. Wrap the bottom of the right pant leg above your ankle and secure it with a rubber band, a clip, or a strap with hook-and-loop closures. Actually, for complete security, you may wish to use rubber bands or straps in two or three positions from the ankle to just below the knee. Let the fabric balloon a bit above the fastenings like knickers to give your right knee enough room to bend while pedaling. If the pant legs are loose, you may also want to bind the left leg as well. Special reflective clips and straps for just this purpose can be purchased from bike shops or mail-order houses.

Avoid wearing jeans while on a bicycle; many denims are stiff and heavy and tend to chafe, especially when wet.

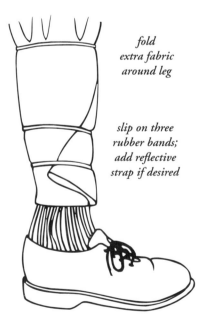

fold extra fabric around leg

slip on three rubber bands; add reflective strap if desired

Three rubber bands will keep the fabric of trousers away from the bicycle chain without wrinkling; allow enough "give" to bend your knee while pedaling.

Shirts, Blouses, and Underwear

For a short commute on cool or low-humidity days, a dress shirt or blouse will work fine on the ride if the fabric is a cotton-polyester blend. For complete freshness and comfort at work, you may still want to sponge off and change into dry underwear (it's amazing how clammy even a slightly damp T-shirt or bra can be once you've cooled down), even if you wear the same top.

On warm days, you may want to compromise between business and bike clothes when it comes to your torso. Wear dress pants or a skirt topped by a polypropylene bicycling jersey or T-shirt. Once at work, remove the damp bike shirt and underwear, sponge yourself off, and don dry underwear and your dress shirt or blouse.

Even if the day on which you ride is cool, definitely plan to change if you want to wear pressed cotton, silk, or rayon at work. Pressed cotton is guaranteed to be wrinkled after the ride, silk is too expensive to ruin with perspiration, and rayon is notable for holding onto odors.

Hang up the duds you wore on the ride to dry and air out for the trip home.

Socks and Stockings

Dress socks, tights, nylon stockings, and panty hose may all be worn on a bike with success and without special preparation.

Chain grease on nylon stockings or panty hose may be washed off easily with soap, even without undressing, just as if the stockings were part of your leg. The nylon dries fast, especially if blotted first with paper towels. Chain grease on socks or tights must be removed by applying some extra-strength laundry preparation such as Shout before laundering.

Skirts

With a skirt, your main concerns are having enough room to pedal, preserving modesty, and preventing the fabric from catching in the rear wheel or brake.

Knee-length culottes or split skirts can be worn without modification. Long split skirts should be restrained like long pants.

An A-line skirt that comes just below the knee—particularly if made from chambray, twill, or some other relatively heavy fabric—is ready-made for

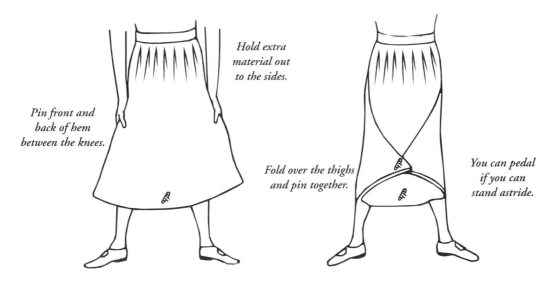

Hold extra material out to the sides.

Pin front and back of hem between the knees.

Fold over the thighs and pin together.

You can pedal if you can stand astride.

A fuller skirt of lightweight fabric can be sewed for bicycle commuting with two safety pins.

biking; the hem usually will be held together by the fabric's lying over the bike's top tube, giving you just enough room to pedal comfortably. If the fabric is lightweight (such as silk or a rayon blend), pin the front and back of the hem together between the knees to form instant culottes.

Straight short skirts tend to ride high up your thighs; for modesty and comfort, you must wear bike shorts underneath. Expect catcalls nonetheless.

A full skirt, particularly of lightweight fabric, tends to billow in the breeze and poses some risk of being caught between your rear brakes and tire, which can rip and stain the fabric and may even cause an accident (voice of experience here). Pin the front and back of the hem together through the knees as for an A-line skirt; in addition, hold the excess material out to the sides and fold it over the top of your legs to be pinned in the middle as well. You'll have instant culottes.

A wraparound skirt must be pinned several places along the open flap from waist to hem. If you don't, you may find yourself pedaling along with your underpants exposed as your skirt sails out behind you, attached to you only at the waistband.

Tip: 1½-inch or 2-inch safety pins will grab more material and hold more securely than the smaller sizes, and will be less inclined to snap open en route. Make sure they're really sharp, so they don't leave holes. With lightweight material, weave the pins through the fabric twice—as if sewing with a needle—so they don't pull out a chunk of cloth.

Dress Shoes

Even if you wear business clothes on the bike, you may want to make an exception for shoes on a long commute. Dress shoes can get scuffed by toe clips, splashed by the water in a pothole, damp inside from perspiration, or dusty from dirt on the side of the road. On the commute, you might prefer to

wear walking shoes, bike shoes, or light hiking shoes and keep dress shoes at the office or in your bike bag.

Sneakers may also be worn on the bike, although on a longer commute the feel of the pedal against the ball of the foot may become uncomfortable, and people with larger feet may find the soles too flexible for efficient pedaling.

- Double-knot long laces so they do not get caught in the chainwheels or chain.
- Orthopedic shoes are longer and have a higher toe box than ordinary shoes of the same size. To wear orthopedic shoes while riding with toe clips, you may have to install the next size larger clips.

To wear orthopedic shoes while riding with toe clips, you may have to install the next size larger clips.

Do not wear sandals on a bike. Injuries (including ripped-off toenails) have occurred because of the slick leather soles and open toes.

Women should not wear high heels on a bike. They do not give needed support, the longer heel can pose a hazard at the bottom of the pedal stroke, and your ankle may turn when you put your foot down to stop.

Suit Jackets and Sweaters

If you wish to wear a suit jacket on your commute, remember that your forward-leaning posture on the bike is very different from that of sitting at a desk and is not a posture for which most suits are designed. You'll be most comfortable if the jacket is of a loose cut.

With a fitted jacket, leaning forward to reach the brakes may cause a back or shoulder seam to split. Before you ride, test how much room and give there is across the shoulders and upper arms: Stretch your arms straight out to the front and then cross them as far as you can over your chest. If your hands can grab behind the opposite shoulders with ease, the jacket is fine. If you cannot cross your arms all the way or if the fabric is pulled uncomfortably tight, you'd best carry the jacket with you and put it on only when you arrive.

Sweaters, on the other hand, are infinitely forgiving. They don't wrinkle, they stretch, and the right sweater can look quite dashing and formal on the job. Most sweaters also can be machine-washed in cold water on the delicate cycle and laid flat to dry, making them far easier and cheaper to clean than jackets. For my three-mile New York City commute, I became such a sweater enthusiast that my usual spring and fall business uniform became a pullover sweater or sweater-vest, a cotton-polyester blouse, and an A-line skirt.

Wool for sweaters while bicycling is wonderful, especially in winter, because it remains warm and insulating even when damp. Wool-cotton or wool-polyester blends are great on those in-between fall and spring days when you need less warmth. Silk-cotton blends are so lightweight you scarcely notice them, with the same warmth as wool blends; they also do not retain odors. Silk-wool blends give

extra warmth on cold days. Stay away from pure cotton sweaters, though, because they have both less warmth and less give than the others, and a cotton sweater becomes a heavy clammy nuisance when wet.

Business Outerwear

Forget trying to wear a trench coat or long winter coat on the bike; it's too bunglesome for both comfort and safety. It is possible, however, to wear a hip-length coat (such as a pea jacket) with some success, although it may feel tight across the shoulders when you lean forward. Remember, however, you're generating heat while pedaling on the bike, even if your commute is very short and the weather is very cold. Chances are, you'll be roasting in a coat by the time you get to work. You'd be better off leaving a dress coat at work for use after you arrive.

Commuting in Bicycling Clothes

Athletic attire designed for cycling may be more comfortable than business clothes for a longer commute. For those who don't like the look of cyclists' "bumblebee suits," I've also included some tips for duplicating some of the specialized features in ordinary sport clothes.

Shorts and Padding

Padded cycling shorts minimize saddle soreness. The most effective padding is made of genuine or artificial chamois. Although polypropylene padding wicks away moisture, I've never found it effective for protecting against saddle soreness. In some makes of shorts, the padding is cut differently to maximize comfort for the male and female anatomy (women: Once you try shorts with padding designed for you, you'll throw out the others).

Cycling shorts extend well down toward the knee to protect the skin of your inner thighs against chafing against the saddle. Lycra shorts are skin tight to prevent chafing of skin against the

raised seam of ordinary shorts or long pants while pedaling. They are cut in a sitting position, so the rear waistband comes high to cover your lower back. Although cycling shorts are available in many colors, black is always good because you can wipe bicycle chain grease on black shorts without producing stains.

If you don't like the looks of skintight Lycra, note that some bike shops and mail-order bicycle merchandise companies sell padded cycling underwear, which may be worn under any clothing you prefer. Just be sure that the padding is some form of chamois and the legs are close-fitting and long enough to prevent chafing. There are also some novelty Lycra shorts patterned to look like faded cut-off jeans. Quite realistic from a distance.

Jerseys

Bicycling jerseys serve several practical purposes. Solid—not patterned—light colors increase your visibility (neon yellow and neon green are especially

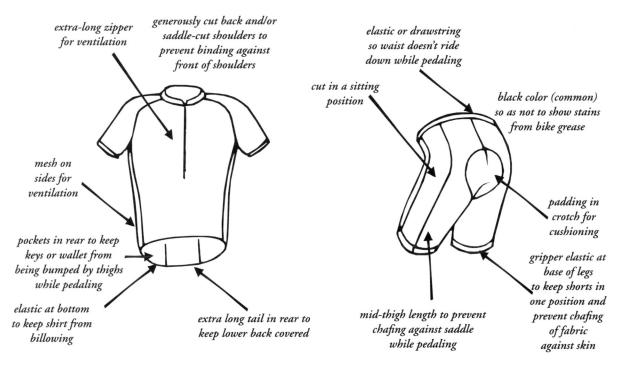

extra-long zipper
for ventilation

generously cut back and/or
saddle-cut shoulders to
prevent binding against
front of shoulders

elastic or drawstring
so waist doesn't ride
down while pedaling

cut in a sitting
position

black color (common)
so as not to show stains
from bike grease

mesh on
sides for
ventilation

pockets in rear to keep
keys or wallet from
being bumped by thighs
while pedaling

elastic at bottom
to keep shirt from
billowing

extra long tail in rear to
keep lower back covered

mid-thigh length to prevent
chafing against saddle
while pedaling

padding in
crotch for
cushioning

gripper elastic at
base of legs
to keep shorts in
one position and
prevent chafing
of fabric
against skin

Athletic clothing designed for bicycling offers many advantages on a long commute.

effective). Their polypropylene or wool fabric increases the wicking of perspiration to keep you dry. Their longer cut in the rear shields your lower back from the sun and wind. Their rear pockets allow you to carry a wallet and keys without your legs hitting them at the top of every pedal stroke (although rear pockets may not work well for recumbent riders). And their elasticized hems prevent the cloth from flapping around in the wind.

Cycling jerseys come in different weights and cuts, ranging from sleeveless nothings for summer to heavy long-sleeved woolens for winter. Most have zippers that go either part or all the way down the front. Many have mesh under the arms and down the sides of the torso to provide extra ventilation. Some winter jerseys have a windproof material just over the chest and the front of the arms to minimize the chilling effects of riding into a winter wind while still providing ventilation off the back.

An all-cotton T-shirt is not a good choice for a long ride. Cotton becomes clammy with sweat and can chill you on a cool day when you stop. And it becomes abrasive when wet, rubbing the skin raw at friction points, such as the front of the shoulders near the underarms. The abrasion can be minimized by wearing cotton blends, although they're not absorbent. And most T-shirts, unless cut very long and tucked into your shorts, will flap all around your back and even ride up toward your shoulders in a wind, possibly interfering with your ability to hear and see traffic approaching from behind.

Foundation Garments

On a long ride, especially over bumpy roads, there's a surprising amount of vibration that can be transmitted to tender organs. Depending on your anatomic build, men may want to consider a jock strap and women may want to consider a sports bra. Try your commute both with and without and go with whatever gives you the most comfort.

Socks designed for bicycling are ankle height and are often made from polypropylene for wicking away perspiration. Some designs have the fabric made in two thin layers to minimize chafing in the shoes. Commonly they are white, but some are neon yellow or some other eye-catching color for visibility.

Bicycling Shoes

Some cyclists swear by hard soled cycling shoes, saying they deliver full power to each pedal stroke. There are a wide variety available designed for either toe clips or clipless systems. In appearance, some of these are almost indistinguishable from ordinary sneakers or loafers—appealing to commuters who don't want their garb to shout "Cyclist! Cyclist!" the moment they walk into a building. On the other hand, if you relish the macho duck walk of Tour de France pro racers trying to walk on cleats, go for the traditional cleated cycling shoes.

Some commuters dislike cycling shoes because the stiff soles make their feet feel as if they've stood on a hard floor all day. Women, and some men with small feet, may find comfortable walking shoes or orthopedic oxfords are just fine. Men whose feet are so long that the soles of walking shoes flex too much may prefer the stiffer soles of lightweight hiking shoes.

■

An all-cotton T-shirt is not a good choice for a long commute.

■

Windbreaker Jacket

A nylon windbreaker stuffs up small and can be crammed into a pocket, tied around a seatpost, or wedged into a tool kit. In California, where the early mornings and the evenings tend to be cool all year round, a windbreaker might be welcome if you find yourself working later than expected. In other places, it might be just enough to keep off an unexpected drizzle. If the windbreaker is particularly bright and reflective, you might wear it at dawn and dusk just to increase your visibility. Chances are, you'll use it so often you might even consider keeping it with the bike.

Untreated nylon is not waterproof, and a windbreaker made of it will soak through in the lightest drizzle. But coated nylon is worse, because it doesn't breathe at all and you'll be drenched with your own sweat even when you're sitting still. Gore-Tex or a similar fabric, which is designed to breathe even though it is water repellent, is slightly heavier than nylon, but it will keep you relatively dry if you should get caught in a light rain. As with your shirt, opt for light or bright colors such as neon yellow.

The windbreakers intended for cyclists often are longer in the back to cover the lower back when you're bent forward. For ventilation they may have mesh under the arms and under the yoke in the back and may be trimmed with reflective tape.

A Gore-Tex windbreaker worn over a wool sweater or a down vest can keep you quite comfortable even when the outdoor temperature is below freezing.

Chapter Thirteen

EXTREME-SEASON BICYCLE CLOTHING

Dennis Coello

It's possible to commute when the temperature is below 30 degrees Fahrenheit, or above 80.

The Four Seasonal Extremes

Even people who normally commute in business clothes in the spring or fall may find it more practical to wear athletic attire in the frigid depths of winter or in the proverbial dog days of summer.

Winters and summers differ crucially in different parts of the nation. As their residents well know, winters are rainy and chilly in California and the Southwest, while summers are (depending on the area) warm to hot and very dry. In Florida, winters are pleasantly mild (attracting retirees and tourists), and summers are beastly hot and muggy with a cloudburst scheduled each day at precisely 4:00 PM. In the Midwest and the East Coast, winters can feature high winds, rain, slush, snow, and ice, or clear frosty days of humidity so low that static electricity becomes annoying on carpeting; summers alternate with pleasant sunny temperatures and moderate humidity to killing waves of sultry heat. In Colorado and the Rocky Mountain areas, winters feature powdery dry snow that in the cities often evaporates quickly in the dry air and brilliant sunlight; summers are hot and dry—but in all seasons, a cyclist must be prepared for rapid and dramatic changes in the weather.

Each of the four seasonal extremes of temperature and humidity—cold and wet, cold and dry, hot and wet, and hot and dry—has its own hazards and requires its own strategy for dress. The advice in this chapter is for the extremes: commuting when the mercury plunges below 30 degrees Fahrenheit or soars above 80 degrees.

Dressing for Winter

Many fabrics do not insulate when wet, so most of their warmth-giving characteristics disappear in high humidity or drenching rain. Water is a conductor, so all your body heat is conducted right out to the outside air. In a cold and wet winter, prolonged chilling by this mechanism can cause hypothermia.

Long-Sleeved Jerseys

Some of the new miracle synthetic fabrics—such as Polartec—are better about insulating while wet than they once were. For the most reliable performance, however, my preference is still to stick with the old standby, wool. The softness of many wool weaves designed for bicycling are so improved that they can be worn right next to the skin. For bitter cold, layer a lighter-weight wool jersey under a heavier one.

Covering the wool garments with an outer breathable windbreaker, such as one made of Gore-Tex, will allow your sweat to pass to the outside air while reducing the wind's ability to transport away your body heat. Look especially for a windbreaker that has zippers under the arms to increase the venting of moisture.

Tights and Warmers

Leg and arm warmers are great for in-between days because they can be rolled down or stripped off at will without compromising your modesty. Such warmers are tubes of wool or polypropylene fabric with stretchy cuffs—essentially individual sleeves for your arms or legs. They are available at many bike shops and sporting goods stores or from mail-order catalogs. (Get leg warmers with some kind of gripper or elastic band at the thigh end, so they don't work their way off your upper leg as you pedal.)

Cycling tights of wool or polypropylene can be worn over cycling shorts, but some commuters find the extra material at the crotch too binding (hence the popularity of legwarmers). Cycling tights do not have feet, so you must wear socks.

Women (or daring men) will find surprising warmth just from ordinary pantyhose, winter-weight hose, or dress tights. For much East-Coast winter commuting, pantyhose under cycling shorts and leg warmers are sufficient. Pantyhose and dress tights have feet, adding warmth to socks.

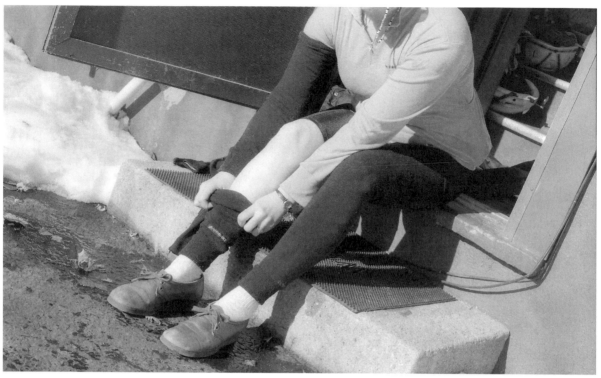

Arm and leg warmers are essentially tubes for the individual limbs.

Long Underwear

On the bitterest of winter mornings, wear long underwear of silk instead of traditional bulky cotton or wool. Silk is a superb insulator, is exceptionally lightweight, is far more durable than its reputation for delicacy suggests, has great stretch and little bulk, dries quickly, and does not chafe—all admirable characteristics for winter bicycle commuting. Top the silk off with wool layers and a Gore-Tex windbreaker and you'll have a combination unbeatable for warmth.

For temperatures below zero degrees Fahrenheit, an important clothing item for men is a third sock, notes Ottawa, Ontario, winter commuter Pete Hickey. "You put it in your pants. No, not to increase the bulge to impress the girls, but for insulation . . . [F]rostbite on the penis is not funny. I speak from experience! Twice, no less!"

Vests

In winter, you want to keep your core temperature up. If your torso and head are warm, your extremities will also be warm (except on the most bitter of days). A vest, be it of wool, down, or some synthetic, will give you almost as much warmth as a long-sleeved jacket and will give you much more mobility. Make sure it zips in the front, because you want to be able to unzip it for ventilation as your exercise also warms you. Even in air as cold as the high twenties, a vest under a good windbreaker is sufficient for warmth.

Head and Face Warmers

Bands of acrylic, wool, or neoprene (the same stuff of which scuba-diving wet suits are made) can be worn under your helmet to shield your forehead and ears from winter's cutting winds. Some cycling jerseys also have hoods that cover the ears and head under the helmet. I also have a helmet I wear only in winter because it has smaller ventilation holes and comes down farther around my head.

Some cyclists wear knitted balaclavas that cover the ears, forehead, cheeks, nose, and chin. Others cover their nose and mouth with a breath-warmer—a mask of fabric overlaying a thin layer of rubber foam perforated by a half-inch hole (one brand is Spense). Both options are indeed warming, but they direct warm moist breath up toward glasses, steaming the lenses and impairing vision. Perhaps you can get the best of both worlds by wearing glasses with fog-proof lenses.

> ■
>
> *Wear silk or polypropylene liners under ordinary bike gloves, and then encase the hands in windproof mittens or neoprene handwarmers.*
>
> ■

Eye Protection

Bitter cold air on the eyeballs is enormously uncomfortable; among other things, it causes your eyes to water, and sometimes the tears can partially freeze on your eyelashes. High winds—including those generated by descending a hill fast—have been known to blow contact lenses out of a person's eyes.

Even if you have 20-20 uncorrected vision, wear some kind of goggles or glasses as eye protection. To protect my contact lenses from dust and grit when I'm outdoors, at all times I wear large-frame nonprescription glasses with photochromic lenses that darken with exposure to sun or lighten in the dark; these are great for both night and day. Other cyclists prefer wraparound sport goggles of the type used by skiers, where the single frame comes with several colors of plastic lenses that can be interchanged depending on sun and snow conditions.

Gloves and Hand-Warmers

Winter cycling gloves with both padding and long fingers are available, but if you suffer from that ail-ment where your outer two fingers are always icy (as I do), no winter gloves are ever satisfactory for warmth. Off the bike, mittens are the only answer. On the bike, I wear silk or polypropylene liners under ordinary bike gloves, and then encase my hands in windproof mittens or neoprene handwarmers to keep in the toasty air. Other riders swear by "lobster claws" or "Vulcan mittens" by Pearl Izumi, Performance, or Specialized—a cross between gloves and mittens where the index finger and middle finger are in one "finger" of the mitten and the ring finger and pinky are in the other; these allow you to keep your outer two fingers curled around the handlebar while the inner two operate the brake levers. They can be a trick to locate, although some mail-order houses have offered them.

Foot-Warmers

Foot-warmers are booties of neoprene or Gore-Tex that fit over the outside of your shoes (and toe clips) to block the wind and allow warm air to insulate your toes. They are most welcome when the temperature drops below the low twenties and the wind is cutting.

Canadian and far northern cyclists who commute in extreme cold speak words of praise for various models of Sorel boots. Note: Sorel boots won't fit in toe clips or on clipless pedals.

For one-time use on a rare bitter day, try one of those chemical heat warmers. Shaped like a tiny pillow that you shake or squeeze to activate, some are small enough to be inserted into your shoe near your toes. Sold for about a dollar apiece from serious sporting-goods stores, they last for several hours; keep extras in your panniers for emergencies. For those who regularly commute in bitter cold, you might invest in battery-powered heated insoles, such as those made by Hotronics; two C-cells last anywhere from one to eight hours, depending on the heat setting used.

Dressing for Summer

In dry summer heat you can dress to take full advantage of the body's mechanism of evaporative cooling. Humid summers, however, pose the risk of heat prostration, because the wetness of the air defeats the body's natural mechanism of sweating to reduce core temperature by evaporative cooling.

Hot and Dry

There is a lot you can do to relieve dry heat. Wear a highly ventilated cycling jersey and helmet. I find that a relatively loose jersey is cooler than a skin-tight one; it will billow a bit when you're coasting downhill, allowing the dry breeze to enter the garment and circulate around your torso to cool and dry the sweat off your back. This air current (which feels delightful) flows especially well if the jersey's zipper is long enough to be pulled halfway down your torso.

You can cool yourself even further by wearing long sleeves to protect your skin from being heated by the direct rays of the sun. As much as wearing long sleeves in desert sun befuddles common sense, it really does work. One vacation when I was bicycling the length of arid Baja California, I found that the fair skin on my arms was still being burned after several days' exposure to the high sun, even after I applied SPF 15 sunblock. To shield my arms from the sun's burning ultraviolet rays, I donned a long-sleeved yellow jersey, expecting (from my experience with East Coast summer humidity) to swelter. To my shock, I discovered that I felt significantly cooler than I had with short-sleeved jerseys, because the fabric also blocked the thermal infrared rays.

The key, of course, is that the long-sleeved fabric (and your helmet) must be a light color to reflect the rays (you will roast in black or in a black helmet) and it must be breathable to allow the full benefit of evaporative cooling. The dryer the air, the more dramatic the benefit. Even if you're skeptical, try it to see if it works with the humidity level in your area.

Hot and Humid

There are a few things you can wear to try to counter humid heat, but only a few. Wear exceptionally well-ventilated clothing and a well-ventilated helmet—and again, make sure your helmet is white to reflect rather than absorb sunlight. Tie a package of reusable "blue ice" in a lightweight cloth or mesh dishtowel and pin the towel around your neck so the cooling package hangs over your back. (The reusable blue ice will not drip like regular ice, and it can be put into the freezer at work to be chilled again for the trip home.) Try one of those ties or scarves filled with crystals that you soak in water for five minutes before tying it around your neck; the scarf or tie will feel cold for an hour or so.

Unfortunately, there's not a lot you can do to shield your skin from the direct rays of the sun. Long sleeves—unless made of a very gauzy light-colored material—will make you unbearably hot.

Face it, on a humid hot day, you will arrive at work drenched and in need of bathing and a complete change of clothes and underwear. But you probably would be in the same condition if you walked, took a subway, or drove.

Health in the Heat

In dry heat, you might not even notice you are perspiring. In fact, in a truly arid climate, your clothes may not even smell after a workout. That is because your perspiration has evaporated so fast the odor-producing bacteria have not had a chance to grow and multiply.

Therefore, your biggest risk—especially on a long commute—is dehydration. Don't rely on thirst to tell you when you need to drink; thirst is a lagging indicator. The rule of thumb is, drink before you are thirsty, at least one full bottle of water per hour. Two would be even better.

When the humidity is low, the midday temperature

- *Tie a package of reusable "blue ice" in a lightweight cloth or mesh dishtowel and pin the towel around your neck.*

may peak at more than 100 degrees Fahrenheit, but it also tends to plunge as the sun goes down, and a breeze may kick up. Avoid bicycling around lunchtime, when the air is hot and still. By late afternoon, though, the temperature may be quite reasonable, and by the evening you might even need your windbreaker.

In humid heat, even if your commute is under five miles, take a full bottle of water or an electrolyte-replacement drink such as Gatorade. Ride very slowly, stop often, and drink all the fluid in the bottle en route. Your sweat glands are working overtime, and it is imperative that you keep hydrated. If you normally don't put much salt on your food, it may also be advisable to eat a salty, low-fat snack such as pretzels. One symptom of needing salt is that no matter how much you drink, you're still thirsty; one confirmation is that when you first eat some salt, it doesn't taste salty.

When the humidity is high, the lowering of the sun brings little relief from the heat. Even worse, the air tends to be stagnant and holds all the pollutants of the day. Thus, the afternoon is the most brutal and has the worst air quality. When the temperature-humidity index (the meteorological "misery index" that calculates the joint effects of heat and humidity) is predicted to top 100, don't risk your health by being hard-line about bicycle commuting. Ride only in the early morning and make other arrangements for your afternoon return—preferably arrangements that involve air conditioning.

Sunscreen

In the summer, sunscreen should be considered as much a part of your wardrobe as underwear: Put it on every morning, especially if you have fair skin

If your skin cannot tolerate sunscreen, you have no choice but to physically block some of the sun's rays by wearing a light, breathable fabric.

or a long commute. Not only is sunburn uncomfortable, but many years of accumulated sun damage can lead to premature aging of the skin and even skin cancers. Prevention of burning is the best remedy, even for people who tan.

The higher the sun protection factor (SPF) number, the better. The SPF number tells you how much longer you can stay in the sun before beginning to burn than you could if unprotected. As a redhead, in the height of summer at noon, my unprotected skin begins to burn in 20 minutes. Using SPF 15 sunscreen means I can stay out five hours without burning—and it really works.

Be forewarned, though: Everyone's body chemistry is different and not all brands of sunscreen work with all skin types, nor are they all equally effective (voice of experience here). If you find that one brand gives you a rash (more common with sunscreens containing PABA), switch to another brand—preferably one advertised to be good for children or persons with sensitive skin. Moreover, if you are very fair skinned, you may find that you burn even with a brand having a high SPF number. Switch brands again—and do so until you find one that works. Then stock up and stick with the winner.

If your skin cannot tolerate sunscreen, then you have no choice but to physically block some of the sun's rays by wearing a light, breathable fabric such as gauzy cotton or thin nylon. You might also want to look into getting a long-sleeved jersey of some high-tech sun-reflecting fabric such as Aloft by Pearl Izumi. Wear a visor under your helmet to shade your nose—or protect your nose skin with zinc oxide cream. And make a practice of riding to work early and leaving late, when the sun is low and its rays are relatively harmless.

Chapter Fourteen

HEALTH AND PERSONAL SAFETY

Bicycle commuting in Chicago, Illinois, can be lovely along the bicycle path that edges Lake Michigan.

Health and Street Crime Precautions

When I was in my thirties, I wondered what the big deal was about aging. Every day, every year, I felt physically better than the previous day or year. At my peak at age 36, I swam a mile several times a week (once swam three miles nonstop for the Leukemia Fund) and one New Year's Eve day on a bicycle tour the length of Baja California, I rode seventy-five miles and then danced until midnight. I never stretched before riding on tour or commute, I seldom worried about falling or bicycling home late from a night class or party through a questionable neighborhood, and I thought everyone should be on a bike. I felt immortal and invincible.

Now that I am old enough theoretically to have kids in their thirties (well, very young thirties), my perspective and wisdom have changed. Even in youth, not everyone is so physically blessed—or dumb-lucky—as I happened to have been. Moreover, some of the chances I took were so foolhardy that I now feel grateful that I merely survived.

Also, now with a child and other major responsibilities I did not have then, I no longer have twenty hours a week of disposable free time for strength and endurance training—nor do most other professionals with young children. As physical condition suffers, basics such as stretching before a ride become more important.

Medical Precautions for Special Conditions

If you haven't ridden for more than a year or if you have back or heart problems or some other special medical condition—including pregnancy—it would be wise to check with a physician before beginning any appreciable bicycle commute.

Be prepared, though, that unless your general practitioner or specialist also happens to be an avid cyclist, he or she may be unacquainted with special equipment or techniques that could aid your commute. In fact, for some medical conditions, he or she may simply advise against all bicycling out of the prudent conservatism all too common in this age of malpractice litigation. If you get a flat "No,"

definitely don't stop there—ask for a recommendation to a sports physician for a second (and more informed) opinion.

Street Sense

In urban areas, bicycle commuters occasionally are asked, "But aren't you afraid of being out alone on your bicycle at night? What with street crime and all, don't you feel vulnerable?"

The answer generally is, "No. As a matter of fact, I feel safer on my bicycle than I do on foot." Still, there is no sense in taking foolish chances. Since forewarned is forearmed, what precautions should you take if your commute calls for an unavoidable brief stint of riding through a questionable neighborhood? Good practice can benefit both male and female commuters.

Common sense, not fear, is the rule of the day when bicycle commuting.

Preventive Health

You certainly don't want bicycle commuting to aggravate some pre-existing condition, such as inflamed tendons, arthritis, or asthma. Therefore, assuming your physician gives you the okay, here are a few extra precautions.

Stretch Before You Ride

Stretching exercises can prevent injury, especially for middle-aged riders with a long and strenuous commute. Stretching is particularly important if you tend to have tight ligaments or tendons, if you are out of shape, if you have arthritis, and if the weather is cold. Think of it as warming up for a Saturday recreational day ride.

A few basic stretches need not take more than a couple of minutes—about the same length of time as the basic safety check of your bicycle.

Air filters

If you're commuting through a city where buses belch diesel exhaust into your face or if you suffer from asthma or some other respiratory condition, you may want to consider a face mask to filter out air pollution. Such masks can make breathing somewhat more labored and can be hot in the summer, but some bicycle messengers swear by them.

The simplest mask is the disposable kind used to filter out dust and pollen. These can be found at many drugstores or hardware or paint stores and come half a dozen to a box. Such dust and pollen masks basically consist of a concave filter paper that covers your mouth and nose that is held on by an elastic band around your head and a small adjustable nose clip.

A more elaborate mask is the type worn by professional construction workers while stripping paint or gutting plaster. It consists of a pair of circular metal frames that hold replaceable charcoal filters and is fastened around the head with an adjustable strap. Such filters are effective enough to be approved by the Occupational Safety and Health Administration (OSHA).

Bicycle Commuting While Sick

I'm a big believer in preventive medicine. At the very first signs of a cold—that initial scratchy throat and punk, wiped-out feeling long before any show of overt symptoms—I call in sick. Then I stay in bed, sleep, drink plenty of warm orange juice and herb tea, and mentally concentrate on staying well. At least 80 percent of the time, I literally can head off a cold within one or two days, and the result is far less absenteeism and greater productivity at work, not to mention less physical misery. Why the early bed rest? Because for my body, a cold is a major siege: If allowed to develop, a typical cold will lay me low for a week or 10 days, followed by two weeks of incessant coughing and possibly laryngitis.

So my first advice is, if you're catching a cold, don't commute. Fight a cold at the outset before you are really sick, to give your immune system a chance to prevent the cold from developing. Don't tough it out and persist in going to work until you are blowing and sneezing, because then there's no question of winning, just of mopping up. And that's altogether too many days off the bike.

Actually, bicycle commuting may help reduce the incidence and severity of colds in the first place. A person at peak physical fitness will get sick less often, and sicknesses are shrugged off more quickly.

Bicycle Commuting with Hay Fever

Hay fever is an allergy, not an illness. Once again, you must consult with your physician about the amount of aerobic exercise you should do with your respiratory condition. On days when the pollen or mold-spore counts are high, outdoor physical exercise may be completely inadvisable for people with severe hay fever or asthma.

For mild hay fever, lasting perhaps only the months of April and May—peak tree-pollen season in much of

If you're catching a cold, don't commute.

the United States—the biggest "danger" to bicycle commuting is sneezing your head off and having your eyes blinded by tears. Sneezing can cause you to jerk the handlebars and keep you from hearing approaching cars, while tears can prevent you from seeing hazards. Because whiffs of pollen come unpredictably, you may be riding along in perfect comfort and then suddenly be seized by a paroxysm so severe you must stop until it passes.

My spring hay fever is so mild that it is fully eradicated by the regular twice-daily use of a prescription topical steroid nasal spray such as Nasalide.

Some people also benefit from prescription antihistamines such as Hismanal, Seldane, or Allegra, which are far superior to over-the-counter preparations in that they do not induce drowsiness or apathy.

Knee Pain

Painful twinges just behind the kneecaps are very common in cyclists, especially early in the riding season. The pain is generally experienced in the early spring and often means that you've ridden too hard too soon. If your commute is longer than five miles one way, you've been off the bike most of the winter, and your joints seem to be creaking more than you remember, take it easy. Work up to more miles gently and gradually.

Knee pain may also mean you're pedaling in a gear that is too high. Gear down on all terrain so you're spinning easily at least 60 to 80 rpm, especially early in the season if you've not been riding much over the winter. Take your time on your first rides to work. You may, in general, also benefit from shorter crank arms on both sides; your leverage is reduced, which keeps your legs spinning and reduces stress on your knees.

Knee pain may also signify that something is incorrectly positioned at the ankle or foot. On an upright bicycle, a saddle that is positioned too low

Knee pain may mean you're pedaling in a gear that is too high.

will actually cause knee problems because the knee is excessively bent at the top of the stroke. Make sure your saddle is high enough that your knee is almost—but not quite—completely straight when the pedal is at its lowest position. If that doesn't solve the problem, experiment with adjusting your cleat position on the shoe or your foot position in the toe clips and straps, your saddle height, the fore/aft position of the saddle, saddle tilt, and the relative position of the handlebars to the saddle.

Knee pain may also indicate that your legs may be of unequal length. Consult an orthopedist if no adjustment gives you relief. If the difference in length is less than a quarter of an inch, you can correct for it by putting a spacer under the cleat or sole of the foot on the shorter leg. If the difference is greater than about half an inch, experiment with using a shorter crank arm on the short-leg side, if your bicycle shoes are not equipped with lifts.

For severe or persistent knee pain, however, enough with the self-diagnostics. See a qualified medical professional.

Saddle Soreness

If you hurt where you sit, you'll find excuses not to ride. The good news is, there are many causes and many remedies: help is on the way. If your ischial tuberosities ("sit bones" at the base of your pelvis) ache after a while, perhaps a saddle slightly wider in the rear or a padded or gel seat cover would help.

Before altering anything, however, take your bicycle to a reputable bicycle shop and make sure that it actually fits you properly. On an upright bicycle, too long of a reach can cause pressure on the genital area at the front of the saddle (as well as pain in the shoulder muscles). Also, make sure the seat post is not raised so high that your hips rock back and forth as you pedal.

Try tilting the saddle's nose a millimeter or two up or down, to shift your weight back toward your pelvis or forward toward your arms (but not so far forward that you risk pinching nerves in your wrists). Adjusting the length of your handlebar stem also alters the tilt of your pelvis, perhaps enough to relieve pressure on genitalia or even on a pinched nerve that could be causing a leg or foot to go numb. Many riders have also reported relief of saddle soreness by installing a shock-absorbing seatpost in the bicycle's seat tube: well-known brands are Tamer and USE.

If your build is at all asymmetrical—as might happen, for example, with scoliosis—you may obtain relief of genital pressure by slightly rotating the nose of the saddle a millimeter or two in a direction *away* from the side suffering pressure.

Experiment with different types and thicknesses of padding in your shorts: gel, genuine chamois, artificial chamois, and polypropylene. Bicycle shorts that are most comfortable for the female anatomy have a "baseball-stitch" pattern with no central seam, either in the Lycra or the padding. Many cyclists recommend that for best comfort padded bike shorts should be worn without underwear—although I find the idea rather unsanitary, and sanitation is essential in preventing skin infection. Keep real or synthetic chamois soft by rubbing it liberally with a good chamois cream before riding. If your skin is susceptible to chafing or infections, apply Desitin, the preparation used to prevent diaper-rash in infants.

For Men Only

Speaking of saddle soreness, one issue that has come to public awareness in recent years is an apparent link between bicycling and some cases of male impotency. In an August 1997 article in *Bicycling,* Irwin Goldstein, a urologist at Boston University Medical Center, is quoted as saying that the culprit is compression of the main penile artery.

Most commonly, Goldstein has seen compression and blockages within the penile artery resulting from trauma—a fall onto the top tube, for example. But he also speculates that chronic vibration from regular riding can also play a role. While nature intended humans to sit on their pelvic bones (as you do when seated on a low curb), a

Dennis Coello

bicycle seat supports a good share of body weight on soft tissues *between* those bones.

"I cannot say that sitting on a bicycle seat causes impotence," Goldstein said in the *Bicycling* article, "but I can go on record with supporting data to show that sitting on a bicycle seat compresses the artery."

What might any of this mean to male bicycle commuters?

First, if you have an accident that includes falling onto the top tube, or if you experience numbness or pain in the genital region while, or after, riding your bicycle, wisdom is the better part of valor: get a medical checkup.

Second, if everything is fine (including your sex life), you might want to take a few precautions to ensure it stays that way. Take a tip from BMX riders and pad the top tube to prevent trauma in a fall. When you ride, stand up every 10 minutes or so to encourage blood flow. Try tipping the nose of the saddle downward a little to relieve pressure on the genitals. And minimize time on aero bars, as the aerodynamic position encourages riding on the saddle's nose.

Consider a wider, padded saddle, especially if you ride now on a narrow, unpadded saddle set very high. If your legs are fully extended at the bottom of the pedal stroke, lower the saddle a smidge so your knees are a little flexed—that will allow your legs to support more of your weight when pedaling in a seated position. Or try one of the anatomical saddles with a hole or with a flexible nose (see the section on saddles in "Selecting Bicycle Components," page 19). And if you're already tempted by a recumbent, maybe this is one more factor to help justify the purchase.

Other medical professionals do not share Goldstein's views that saddle compression alone can cause impotency, or that cessation of bicycling is the sole solution. Diabetes, smoking, arteriosclerosis, hypertension, aging, and many other factors may also play a role. "There's no doubt there's a real issue here," declared Harin Padma-Nathan, a urologist and the director of The Male Clinic in Santa Monica, California, and a former student of Goldstein's. "But bicycling is an important form of cardiovascular exercise. Rather than terminate it, I would recommend tailoring this information to your own bicycling and body type."

For Women Only

Let's get down to nitty-gritty basics here: just how *do* you handle the mess of your monthly menstrual cycle, especially if you have heavy periods or cramps? And is it advisable to continue bicycle commuting if you're pregnant?

Bicycling While Menstruating

Here are a few techniques to prevent menstrual accidents while commuting that have worked for me.

It's handy to know when your period is about to start so you can carry or wear the necessary accouterments a day in advance. Even a woman with highly irregular periods can predict their onset if she can learn when she ovulates. Why? *Because virtually all the irregularities in a woman's cycle alter the time of ovulation—yet the time from ovulation to the shedding of the uterine lining remains consistent at about two weeks.*

Many women can feel ovulation in a sensation well-known enough to have a name: mittelschmerz, or mid-cycle pain. The irritation feels like a sharp stitch in the left or right lower abdomen, a couple or three inches in from either hip bone. This stitch lasts about three to six hours, then fades away; the woman also may—but not always—feel a bit low-energy, chilled, or slightly flu-y, symptoms that disappear altogether with a good night's rest.

Even if a woman cannot feel herself ovulate, she can still tell when ovulation happens by plotting her waking temperature at the same time every morning and noting the date it jumps a degree or

Dennis Coello

two and remains high (buy an ovulation thermometer from a good pharmacy and follow the instructions in the box).

Once a woman feels the stitch or sees her waking temperature jump, all she needs to do is mark the calendar for two weeks later, and she should hit her period's start date within a day.

What if your flow is heavy? Menstruation naturally tends to suspend itself temporarily during exercise or sleep. The event for which you want to be prepared is the rush of flow when changing position—getting off the bike to walk into the building.

For most women, the heaviest day is the second day of the period. So even if your period actually starts mid-commute, the amount of flow is unlikely to flood your clothes before you can get matters under control. For extra confidence on the two or three days of heaviest flow, wear *both* a super-size tampon and a super-size pad.

The ultra-thin style of super pad is the most comfortable when sitting on a bicycle saddle. But don't rely on the pad's adhesive strips for sticking to the crotch of your panties while

If you were athletic and a regular cyclist before your pregnancy, you can probably safely continue at your pre-pregnancy level of activity even into your ninth month.

pedaling, especially if the undies are damp with perspiration. Instead, pin both ends of the pad to the fabric of the panties. A panty-girdle or Lycra bike shorts under your skirt also helps keep the whole assembly centered. (Note: tampons and pads can also double as bandages for road rash.)

For mild cramps—generalized pain in the lower abdomen, lower back ache, discomfort in the upper thighs, and swelling from water retention—bicycling slowly and gently can be therapeutic and soothing, sometimes moreso than any of the over-the-counter menstrual analgesics and diuretics. Keep the abdomen and lower back warm. If your commute requires you to grind up a steep hill, however, experiment to see whether attacking the hill eases or aggravates mild to moderate cramps.

Truly severe cramps could prevent a woman from riding altogether, however, as the waves of pain are so great they might endanger her concentration in traffic. If you regularly suffer from debilitating cramps—the type requiring you to lie down for several hours cradling a hot water bottle on your abdomen —or if your period lasts longer than seven days, check with your gynecologist to see whether you may have some condition (fibroid tumors, polyps, etc.) needing medical attention.

Bicycling While Pregnant

Nothing I am about to say should supersede any instructions from your OB/GYN regarding your own specific pregnancy. In general, however, a healthy woman enjoying a normal pregnancy should be able to continue her bicycle commuting until her size makes her feel uncomfortable about her balance or weight.

The following seems to be the consensus of the opinions and experiences posted on a number of the touring listserves on the Internet, as well as the advice of Seattle gynecologist and tandem rider Al Truscott:

If you were athletic and a regular cyclist—commuter or otherwise—before your pregnancy, you can probably safely continue at your present level even into your ninth month of pregnancy (a number of fit women have reported riding 40 or more miles even up to within a day or two of delivery). Unless you have some special medical condition, there is no need to reduce physical exercise during pregnancy for fear of depriving the fetus of oxygen; your own tolerance will stop you from overdoing anything long before the baby could notice an effect. But pregnancy is also not the time for setting new personal-best records for distance or speed.

The extra weight of the growing fetus and amniotic fluid places extra stress on the body's support structures—abdominal muscles, back muscles, hip and upper thigh muscles, and the associated bones, tendons, and ligaments. Also, ligaments in the pelvis (and other places) stretch during pregnancy in preparation for giving birth. All these changes make joints more susceptible to injury. Stop if something is hurting. Keeping the

back arched like a cat's can help. This might also be the time to try a suspended seatpost to absorb more road shock.

Late in the term, some women reported gaining relief to the lower back by raising their handlebars; others reported that sitting more upright killed their lower back and was uncomfortable on the saddle. Some reported needing to sit more upright to avoid hitting their legs on the bulge while pedaling. Experiment to see what works for you. Some women also reported needing to urinate more often—in the last month, as often as every five miles (planning bathroom stops thus may be something to consider if your commute is long).

As your waistline grows, you'll have to get creative about what to wear. Even if bike shorts still fit, their elasticized waistband may be uncomfortable. Instead, try drawstring sweat pants or jogging bottoms—perhaps with suspenders. Large, baggy T-shirts are soft and comfortable, as might be a rain cape during inclement weather.

In general, the earliest one might want to resume bicycling after vaginal delivery is probably two weeks—four weeks if you had a C-section. Of course, all this experience of others pertains to you only if you have a trouble-free pregnancy. Circumstances alter cases. For your own individual case, rely first and foremost on your own personal medical professional.

Combatting Yeast Infections

Saddles with a central hole in the nose intended to relieve pressure on female genitalia also reportedly help if a woman has problems with yeast infections while cycling. Yeast infections start and thrive in damp, warm, air-tight darkness, which is why women susceptible to yeast infections are advised against wearing pantyhose. A hole in the saddle's nose allows significant air circulation.

Street Crime and Uncertain Neighborhoods

In a large urban center such as New York City, a significant concern—especially of solitary women—is avoiding obvious circumstances where one might be mugged.

Bicycle commuting can actually reduce your risk of being a victim of certain street crimes. For example, your position in the street, your speed relative to pedestrians, and the zippering and lashing of your possessions onto the bike together reduce your risk of a grab-and-run purse snatching—that is, as long as your purse or briefcase isn't sitting loose in a wire basket, shouting "Take me!" while you are stopped for a red light. Similarly, your removal from the rush-hour throngs on the sidewalk makes you an unlikely target for a pickpocketing, which is commonly staged in a crowd with accomplices creating a distraction. In isolated areas after dark, your speed and position in the street also removes you from a pedestrian's risk of being accosted by an ill-intentioned person lurking in a shadowy doorway.

All these factors led me, as a solitary female bicycle commuter in New York City in the 1980s, to ride solo later at night than I would ever walk or take a subway alone. And in five years of commuting almost daily, even over the Brooklyn Bridge and through Central Park, Spanish Harlem, and the heart of downtown Newark, New Jersey, I never was accosted—even as late as between midnight and 5:00 AM. To be sure, sometimes I was nervous, so I made a practice of timing the lights to stay in constant motion and of listening acutely for footsteps or voices. But I did not feel the same level of exposure or vulnerability that I would have on foot, because I had speed and agility on my side.

Nor am I alone in this feeling of reduced risk. New Jersey bicycle commuter John King—the person who first made me aware of bicycle commuting around 1982—rode from his refrigeratorless single-room occupancy through the bombed-out sections of Passaic to his job in Saddle Brook. (Actually, for

him, bicycle commuting was also an act of social defiance: "I don't want anyone actin' tough, tellin' me where I can go or can't go at any time, day or night.")

Precautions for Questionable Neighborhoods

No sane bicycle commuter would ride through neighborhoods known to be unsafe, but it may be helpful to examine what it is you consider "safe"—whether you're going by actual crime statistics for an area or you are also including areas that simply give you the willies (such as industrial areas after hours).

If you have a "bad feeling" about riding through a certain place, who knows what primordial instinct for self-preservation is warning you? Heed it.

But maybe you're caught out late somewhere and simply have no choice about where you need to ride to get home. Or the bike may make you inclined to broaden your range and hours of travel beyond what you would attempt on foot—even through "questionable" areas. Here are a few tips for maximizing your safety.

If speed is to be an ally through an abandoned area, avoid going where your speed is reduced to that of a pedestrian.

If speed is to be an ally through an abandoned area, avoid going where your speed is reduced to that of a pedestrian: over cobblestones, for example, or over a long series of railroad tracks diagonal to your direction of travel, requiring you to dismount. Also avoid long, steep climbs or narrow bridges in an area where a couple of thieves could be waiting to leap out and steal your bike: There was a series of such bike-snatchings at the crest of the Brooklyn Bridge, where cyclists were compelled to ride slowly or dismount to weave around the bridge's support structures.

Also, make sure your equipment is in top condition. Industrial areas and other lonely stretches may be littered with broken glass. A flat tire would temporarily immobilize you, rendering you even more vulnerable than a pedestrian if you choose to fix your bike rather than abandon it.

Keep in mind that the character of some areas may completely change from winter to summer. Certain urban residential neighborhoods that are isolated on February's cold evenings may in July's heat be thronging with street merchants, stoop-sitters, and groups of boisterous residents. While you may be glad for the company, keep an ear out for the tenor of the voices. Are any raised in alcoholic belligerence? Is there a domestic quarrel on the sidewalk about to spill out into the street? Listen also for barking dogs, especially if the area has no leash law—you may have a few Dobermans or pit bulls racing at your heels.

For such a route, I strongly recommend that both male or female commuters avoid wearing black Lycra bike shorts and form-fitting jerseys. Certain groups view Lycra-clad men as being effeminate and women as being brazenly provocative and will deliver verbal abuse to that effect. Cyclists differ in their recommended responses to catcalls—do you just keep blithely riding as though you heard nothing or do you give a jolly grin and a wave as if the extended middle finger meant "You're number one!"? Responding in a nasty manner is generally not advisable, because antagonism just ups the ante, and these strangers may look to get back at you on your next ride through.

Instead, wear regular pants over the bike shorts to minimize the attention you'll draw. Women might feel more comfortable dressing in a full Gore-Tex rain suit to disguise their sex. Once again, whatever works.

No cyclist ever likes to contemplate getting into real trouble. But sometimes trouble comes looking for you. One Saturday afternoon, as I was at the northern end of my exercise circuit around Central Park, a boy of about 9 or 10 years old, who was threatening a younger sibling with a baseball bat, saw me and abruptly raised the bat against me as he looked me directly in the eye. I fixed him with my best no-nonsense-mom "You wouldn't dare" look; but once out of sight, I wilted and rode home, wondering if escape would have been so easy had he been a bit older.

Another cyclist some years ago reported being harassed by a group of several teens, who spread out across the street, ready to try to grab the bike as he rode between them. The quick-thinking cyclist put on a burst of speed and instead rode directly *at* one of the youths, who instinctively jumped aside at the last moment to avoid being mowed down—allowing the cyclist's escape. The cyclist also suggested looking out for a would-be attacker carrying a stick, which could be thrust or thrown through your spokes, causing you to pitch over the handlebars (although the force of the stick ramming against the frame breaks spokes and thus ruins the wheel, thereby ruining the bike's usability if theft of the bike is the aim of the attack). If you find yourself being pursued by persons in a car, deliberately violate every "Effective Cycling" mandate and make maneuvers impossible to follow in a motor vehicle: Turn in the street and ride back against traffic, bunny-hop onto the curb and weave through pedestrians, run a red light—whatever.

Don't court this kind of trouble, however. If on the bike you use the same prudence about safe times and places that works for you off the bicycle, you should be just fine.

If you find yourself being pursued by persons in a car, make maneuvers impossible in a motor vehicle.

Chapter Fifteen

BONEHEAD MAINTENANCE

Checking the bottom bracket should be a routine part of a weekly "Two-Minute Bike Check."

Prevent Problems from Arising

Mechanical problems, like dental problems, never go away by themselves; at best they stay the same, and usually they grow worse. Don't ignore a small problem; fix it before it becomes a big (i.e., expensive) one.

The best form of maintenance is preventive. Become aware of your bicycle's normal feel and sounds—preferably after the bicycle has been overhauled at a shop so you get used to it at its best. Then when you feel or hear something abnormal, you can detect problems early, while they are still quick and easy (i.e., inexpensive) to repair, and you can talk informatively with your shop's mechanic. For example, do you feel some extra rolling resistance while riding? Check to see if a tire is soft or a brake pad is rubbing. Does your chain keep jumping to a higher gear? Check the tension and adjustment of your rear derailleur. Is there a clicking or slight wiggle in the headset or bottom bracket? Insist that it be checked and tightened appropriately.

Second, the biggest and easiest favor you can do yourself is to store your bicycle indoors. Dampness is the greatest enemy of metal and rubber. A bicycle stored outdoors—or even in a detached garage or under a plastic sheet on a screened-in porch—can be turned from an expensive precision machine into junk in the course of one wet winter, especially if there is salt in the air (from the ocean or from streets being salted after snow is plowed).

A steel frame will begin to pit and rust through tiny nicks in the paint. Ditto for any moving part not completely lubricated. The chain will rust and seize, wearing down the teeth of the chainwheels and freewheels. Tiny brown spots of rust on the rims of the wheels will impede braking. The rubber of the tires will begin to stiffen and crack. Mildew can form on the handlebar bag.

It is truly a crime. And how much money do you intend to spend each year on replacement bikes?

On the other hand, a bicycle stored indoors—in an attached garage, a basement, or on a porch that is dry and somewhat heated—can keep you on the road for ten, fifteen, or twenty years or more. (Make sure the bike is easily accessible, though; if you have to always climb up a ladder to get it down from hooks above a doorway, you won't use it.) Some people even store their bicycles in their living rooms—I did when I lived in a one-bedroom apartment, and later I put my bikes in my heated finished basement. Fifteen years later, my original two commuter bicycles are still serving me well.

Two-Minute Bicycle Check

In addition to a general awareness, get into the habit of regularly giving the bicycle a quick overall exam. The League of American Bicyclists recommends what it calls the "ABC Quick Check" before each ride: the *a*ir pressure of the tires, the *b*rakes, the pedal *c*rank arms (bottom bracket), the *quick* releases, and the general ride-worthiness of the bike.

That's a good reflexive habit to get into when the bike is maintained in generally good shape. To get it into good shape, however, I prefer the more thorough exam dubbed the "Two-Minute Bike Check" by the American Youth Hostels and various commercial tour groups. Once you get the routine down pat, it really does take only two minutes to determine the mechanical health of your steed. Make a practice of doing the Two-Minute Bike Check at least once a week—say, every Friday night—so that if you do discover a problem, you can get it fixed over the weekend before Monday's commute.

A variation on the Two-Minute Bike Check is also useful for evaluating the condition of a second-hand bicycle you may be considering purchasing (see "Rehabilitating a Second-Hand Bicycle," page 23).

Below, I have prefaced each section with a brief explanation of why each aspect of the check is so important for your safety. When you know, you'll have motivation for maintenance.

Note: In the descriptions below, a slash (/) means check first one and then the other, not both at once. In general, the check starts at the front of the bicycle and works its way to the rear.

Front/Rear Wheels

There are four weekly tests for wheels: the air pressure of the tires, the trueness of the wheels, the soundness of the hub bearings, and the tension of the spokes.

Air Pressure of Tires

For many bicycles, the tires are the bike's only suspension system and shock absorbers. Riding with too little air in the tires can dent the metal rims of the wheels at the first bump or pothole; it can also increase the chance of pinching the inner tube and getting a snakebite flat (so named for the characteristic twin punctures). Moreover, riding with properly inflated tires means less work for you. If the tires are squishy, your weight on the bike will compress them further so a larger surface area of rubber contacts the road; that translates

into greater rolling resistance and more effort in pedaling, as if you were always dragging a brake.

Test the tire pressure by pressing directly down on the middle of the tire; it should feel hard.

Remedy: If the tires feel soft, or if it has been more than a week since you last filled the tires, pump them up to the manufacturer's recommended pressure (usually stamped into the tire's sidewall). Many floor pumps come with an accurate pressure gauge.

Trueness of the Wheels

A bicycle's wheels are enormously strong for their weight, and the source of that strength is the tension exerted by the spokes on the metal rim. But a wheel is strong only if it is both radially true (perfectly circular) and laterally true (in one plane).

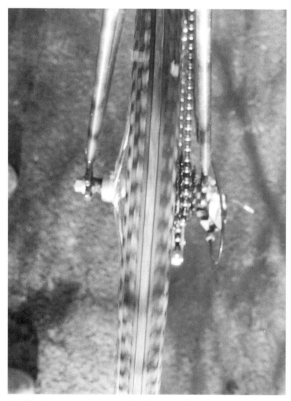

Sight down a spinning wheel to make sure it is laterally true (rotating in one plane).

Check air pressure of tires—the tire should feel hard.

The rims are also your braking surface, and an untrue wheel will pull away from the brakes each rotation, jeopardizing your stopping power.

Lift the front end of the bike and spin the wheel. When you sight directly down from the tire to the hub, the wheel should appear to rotate in exactly one plane. If it appears to wobble, or has an obviously potato-chip shape, or if a brake rubs in just one spot, it is no longer laterally true. Also, if there is an annoying bump with each rotation of the wheel that increases in frequency with increasing speed as you coast downhill or pedal, the wheel may be out of round.

Remedy: Tighten the appropriate spokes to true the wheel (if you know how) or take it to a shop to have it trued. Do not ride on wheels out of true. Riding on untrued wheels can break spokes and bend the rims beyond repair, and even cheap replacement wheels start at $50 each. This is a perfect example of a cheap, quick fix staving off a costly replacement.

Tightness of the Spokes

The spokes are the thin rods of metal that hold the wheel's rim under tension. Most standard road and mountain bicycle wheels have thirty-six spokes.

Grasp them in pairs with both hands and gently but firmly squeeze them to release uneven tensions; work your way all around each wheel. You'll hear all kinds of marvelous sounds as they readjust themselves. If one or two spokes appear to be under no tension at all, or if one happens to be broken, immediately take the bike to a shop for a check-up and repair. Do not ride with a broken spoke—you are only asking for a ruined wheel.

Tightness of the Hubs

The hubs are where the rotating wheels contact the frame. The hubs take a pounding, and occasionally the ball bearings break or wear through the metal of their confining rounded cones. With such wear comes increased internal friction and

> *Riding with a loose headset can strip the threads of the front fork—which is second only to the frame in replacement cost.*

possibly even a broken wheel. With the bike resting on the ground, push against the top of the front/rear rim perpendicular to the plane of the wheel. You should not feel any movement or hear any clicks in the hub bearings.

Remedy: If there is a slight movement, tighten the hub cones with a cone wrench, taking care not to overtighten them. If you are uncertain, or if you have ridden the bicycle for a number of years, take it to a shop to see if the hubs need to be repacked with grease, need new ball bearings, or even if the cones need to be replaced.

Handlebars and Headset

The handlebars and headset are two vital parts that are overlooked by the ABC Quick Check and need regular monitoring.

Tightness of the Handlebars

The handlebars are the communication link between your hands and the front wheel. If the handlebars are loose, turning them will have no effect on the front wheel— and in an emergency could cause a fall or worse.

Stand in front of the bicycle with the front wheel gripped between your knees. Try to twist the handlebars from side to side while holding the wheel still. They should not move. Also, the handlebars should be perpendicular to the front wheel.

Remedy: If the handlebars are loose, tighten the bolt on top of the handlebar stem.

Tightness of Headset

The headset is the set of bearings in the head tube through which the handlebars attach to the front wheel's fork. If the headset becomes loose, there is a permanent, unsafe wobble in the handlebars.

Continue standing in front of the bicycle with the front wheel gripped between your knees. Try to lift the handlebars straight up out of the frame. There should be no slight movement or click.

Remedy: If there is a slight but perceptible click, gently tighten the headset with a headset wrench, taking care not to overtighten it; you want the headset to be able to turn freely under its own weight when the front end of the bicycle is lifted. Do not ignore a loose headset. Riding on a loose headset can strip the threads of the front fork, which is second only to the frame in cost ($100 or more for replacement). This is another example of free maintenance that prevents an expensive replacement.

Front/Rear Brakes

The brakes are possibly the most important part of the bike, because they are responsible for stopping you. There are two checks: one for the cables and one for the pads.

Brake Levers and Cables

A stretched brake cable will, at best, increase your braking time and, at worst, may not let you brake as hard as you need to stop in an emergency.

With the bike stationary, squeeze the left/right brake lever as if you were braking hard. At its lowest point, there should be close to an inch of clearance separating the lever from the handlebar grip.

Remedy: If there is less than half an inch, tighten

When the brake lever is squeezed, there should be an inch of clearance to the handlebar grip.

the front/rear brake cable. If you don't know how, take the bike to a shop; tightening is so quick that the mechanic may do it right in front of you and charge only a couple of bucks. Worth it, since with brakes your life is literally in your hands.

Brake Pads

With the front/rear brake lever squeezed, note the position of the rubber pads pressing against the appropriate rim. Their entire braking surface should contact the metal of the rim, not partly on the rubber tire or partly in the air below the rim.

Remedy: Adjust the position of the screw that hold the brake pads in the brakes.

While moving the bike forward, grip both brake levers hard. The bike should stop securely, with no slipping of the brake pads and with no squealing of the brakes.

Remedy: Replace worn pads; pads are worn if there is only $\frac{1}{8}$ inch of rubber left. Pads are cheap—a couple of dollars a pair. To eliminate squealing, adjust the angle of the brake pads so that the leading edge touches the rim a little before the trailing edge. Also, make sure the rims and pads are completely clean by rubbing them with a lint-free cloth soaked in rubbing alcohol. If one pad persists in rubbing one side of the rim, adjust the tension springs on the proper side of the brakes. This adjustment can be an exercise in frustration, but it is easily and cheaply done in a shop.

Bottom Bracket

The bottom bracket is the link between your feet and the bike in providing the forward motion. There are two things to be checked: the bottom bracket where the pedal crank arms enter the frame, and the pedals.

Tightness of the Bottom Bracket

Grasp the pedal crank arms with your hands and try to move the cranks in and out perpendicular to the plane of the frame of the bike, that is, perpendicular to the plane in which the chainwheels spin. The pedal cranks should not move or click.

The entire braking surface of a brake pad should contact the metal wheel rim when the brake lever is squeezed.

Remedy: If you sense any slight movement or perceptible click, tighten the bottom bracket. Really crank it down; it should be the tightest thing on the bike. If the bracket really cannot be tightened, then take the bike to a shop to have it checked for a broken spindle or stripped threads.

Pedals

Spin the pedals on the ends of their crank arms. They should spin freely, unless they are designed to stop in certain positions.

Remedy: If they resist movement, they may need to be repacked with grease. This repair is not very common.

Drive Train

The drive train consists of the chainwheels (front sprockets), freewheel (rear cogs or sprockets), and the chain in between; it is what conveys your pedaling motion back to the rear wheel.

Wear of Gears

Look at the chainwheels and freewheel cogs for broken or worn teeth. A broken tooth is usually obvious. Worn teeth are asymmetrical: One side of each tooth is concave while the other is straight. (If in doubt, compare the shape of the teeth of the gears you use the most with the shape of the gears you use the least.)

Broken or worn teeth cause the chain to jump annoyingly so it will not shift properly or stay in one particular gear. Worse, broken or worn teeth cause excessive wear of the chain, which in turn wears other gears. If left unattended, eventually all the gears will be ruined.

Remedy: If there are broken or worn teeth on a gear, it must be replaced— a moderately expensive repair. Because both sets of sprockets are stacked in layers, the replacement of one gear does not necessarily mean the replacement of all. If properly cleaned and lubricated, sprockets should last tens of thousands of miles.

Wear of Chain

A bicycle chain stretches and wears, and when it is worn, it slowly grinds down the teeth of your chainwheel and freewheel sprockets. This wear will be accelerated if the chain is dirty (sand is very abrasive) or dry. A stretched chain also does not shift well.

Remedy: Develop the habit, after each ride, of brushing off the worst of the dirt with a toothbrush or soft cotton rag (not paper towels—they shred and leave little bits of paper on the chain). If the chain is positively encrusted, especially with sand or sandy dirt, then remove the chain with a chain tool or rivet extractor and soak it in alcohol, kerosene (use rubber gloves), or other grease-cutter. Reinstall the chain, making sure that you replace it in the same orientation (guaranteed if you always push the rivet out toward you away from the frame when you remove the chain and reinstall it by pushing the loosened rivet toward the frame). Put a tiny drop of motor oil or sewing-machine oil in each link.

To preserve your gears (which are expensive), often replace the chain (which is cheap)—kind of

On an older bike with unseated bearings, drip motor oil into a spinning freewheel to quiet bearings.

like getting frequent oil changes in a car. A chain should be replaced routinely every 1,000 to 2,000 miles, that is, at least every spring if you commute year-round more than three miles each way and don't do much other riding.

Squeaking Drive Train

If the drive train squeaks while you pedal, put a drop of oil onto each joint in the chain and the axles of the pulleys on the derailleur.

Also, if yours is an older bike without sealed freewheel bearings, oil the freewheel. Lay the bicycle on its left side. Have a companion support the frame to raise the rear end just enough so you can rotate the pedals while dripping oil into the center of the freewheel in the circular slit near the rear axle. You may need twenty or thirty drops of oil. Listen carefully as the centrifugal force throws the oil into the freewheel: the clicking of the ball bearings dramatically quiets.

Use motor oil, tenacious oil, sewing-machine oil, or a light oil designed for machinery. Do not use 3-in-1 oil or some other vegetable-based oil, which will gunk up the works.

Derailleurs

The derailleurs literally derail the chain—pushing it left or right lateral to the frame of the bicycle to allow you to shift gears. This check covers the derailleurs themselves and their cables.

Rear Derailleur

Check that all the nuts and bolts attaching the rear derailleur are secure. Shift the rear derailleur into lowest gear—that is, onto the largest cog in the back. Make sure the derailleur arm does not hit the spokes or ride on the sprocket. While turning the pedals, shift through all the gears with the rear derailleur to make sure all are accessible without the chain jumping off the largest cog into the spokes or off the smallest cog onto the axle.

Remedy: The derailleur's range of travel is controlled by twin stop screws, usually Phillips head, which are located on the body of the rear derailleur. Sometimes the screws are helpfully marked "L" (for low gear) and "H" (for high). If the chain jumps off in the lowest gear (largest cog) or highest gear (smallest cog), tighten the appropriate rear derailleur stop screw a quarter turn and try it again. If the chain cannot reach all the cog, loosen the appropriate stop screw a quarter turn.

If the rear derailleur rests on the cog, the spring holding the arm may be worn and weak and impede proper shifting; the cost of a new derailleur is moderate.

Front Derailleur

Repeat the shifting exercise with the front derailleur to make sure the chain can make all transitions without jamming, rubbing, or falling off. Remedy: Adjust the front derailleur stop screws and adjust the angle of the derailleur. (See photo, page 148.)

Shift Levers

If the derailleurs and gears seems to be in good shape but the shifting is really sloppy—especially if you get stuck in high gear when trying to downshift at the base of a hill—see how far you must push the gearshift lever to make the chain shift. If the

Two stop screws on the rear derailleur can be loosened or tightened a quarter-turn to allow the chain to reach all freewheel gears without jumping off.

distance seems excessive before you get a response, the cable may be stretched or the cable housing may be too long. If the lever pulls the cable with no response at all or there seems to be some obstruction, the cable may be broken or frayed.

Remedy: Shorten the cable housing or replace the cables (grease them well with white lithium bicycle grease before inserting them into the housing). This is a relatively inexpensive repair at a shop and will make your riding life infinitely happier.

Saddle

Few things are more annoying than a saddle that is too loose, unexpectedly rotating or tilting.

Try to move the saddle up and down in the seat tube; try to rotate it, push its nose up and down, and slide it backward and forward on its rails. The saddle should remain firm.

Remedy: If it moves, tighten the appropriate bolts. If the bolts won't tighten, replace the appropriate parts, which may be worn.

Accessories

Check to see that your reflectors are still firmly attached to the front and rear and on the spokes.

Lift the bike a few inches and drop it. If nothing falls off, you're ready to roll.

The Bicycle's Annual Physical Exam

Give your bicycle a thorough physical examination once a year, or more often if your commute is long and rough, if you weigh more than 200 pounds, if you haul a lot of heavy stuff, if you use your bicycle for loaded touring, or if the bike has been in an accident. Some developing problems will give you plenty of warning. Others may not. Some failures can be catastrophic, causing great injury. Remember, prevent problems from arising.

If you don't have much knowledge about bicycles or don't have some of the special equipment needed for some disassembly, take your bike to a good shop. If you can get the head mechanic to walk you through this inspection, so much the better (some of the tips below are suggestions from the frame-builder Keith Bontrager on an Internet archive post).

Welds

Carefully inspect all the welds on the bike's frame for thin hairline cracks, especially if your bicycle is aluminum (which is not as strong as steel). Look at the place where the top tube and the down tube join the head tube, especially the underneath sides of the welds. Inspect the weld at the base of the seat tube near the bottom bracket shell and near the slot for the seat binder clamp.

Also inspect the dropouts on the front fork and the rear triangle where the wheel axles fit. Scrutinize the welds where the chainstays meet the bottom bracket shell and are joined at the bridge just in front of the rear tire. Look also where the seat-stays join the top of the seat tube.

Bottom Bracket and Cranks

Look for cracks near the tapered ends of the bottom bracket assembly where the crank fits. Scrutinize the bottom-bracket spindle, especially if the crank somehow "feels funny" when you pedal or if the crank comes loose unexpectedly. If your bicycle has a cartridge bottom bracket that allows you to change the bearings, replace the bearings with new ones as a routine part of this annual maintenance.

Look for hairline fractures or other weaknesses all over the right crank arm where the arm leaves the spider and also near the pedal threads.

Seat Post and Saddle

Pull out the seatpost and sight down it. Any deformation or ripple where the post is clamped into the frame signals an incipient failure. Replace the post. Also, if you have to crank the fasteners down extra tightly to keep the seatpost from slipping, put in a new set of high-strength fasteners as a routine part of this annual maintenance.

Inspect the rails and the tilting mechanisms that support the saddle. Some cheaper designs have a

Front derailleur's position is also adjusted by stop screws if the chain cannot reach all chainwheels. See page 146.

kind of ratcheting tilt mechanism that really wears. Replace it, especially if once it's tightened, a good yank can still change the saddle's position.

Wheels

Inch by inch, inspect the wheel rims for places where spokes may be pulling out, where sidewalls may be wearing through (from grit lodged in the brake pads), or for other deformities. Look carefully at the hubs for places where the metal flanges may be pulling away from the hub body—a rare problem for commuters on quality bicycles, but you never know.

Quick-Release Skewers

Pull out the quick-release skewers from your front and rear wheels and inspect them for wear. Even when used properly, skewers can wear out—especially alloy, aluminum, or titanium skewers (steel seems to hold up better). The skewers are subject to stress each time a wheel is removed and replaced, each time the temperature changes quickly, or each time the wheel is subject to unusual trauma. If one breaks while you are riding at high speed, the result can hospitalize you (skewers are

Even when used properly, quick-release skewers can wear out.

the bicycle's equivalent of the "Jesus nut" holding the rotor on a helicopter).

Look for signs of stripping of the threads on the nut. Check that the cam end (with the closing handle) seems intact, and make sure the skewer itself is still completely straight. Skewers are relatively cheap; if you see signs of wear, replace that skewer.

Whenever you replace the wheel, make sure that the skewers are installed properly. Slide the skewer itself with the first conical spring through the wheel's axle, slide the second conical spring onto the projecting threaded tip (make sure the wide ends of both springs are pointing away from the frame), and then screw the nut onto the threaded end a few rotations. Experiment with closing the handle. If the handle closes easily, tighten the nut a rotation or two, and try again. The tension is correct when you begin to feel resistance when the handle is half closed (at a 45-degree angle to the frame) and you must apply firm pressure to close it all the way. Keep the handle aligned either upward (parallel to the fork blade) or backward, so that when you're riding no stick or other foreign object can get wedged inside the handle and flip it open.

Chapter Sixteen

EMERGENCY ROADSIDE REPAIRS

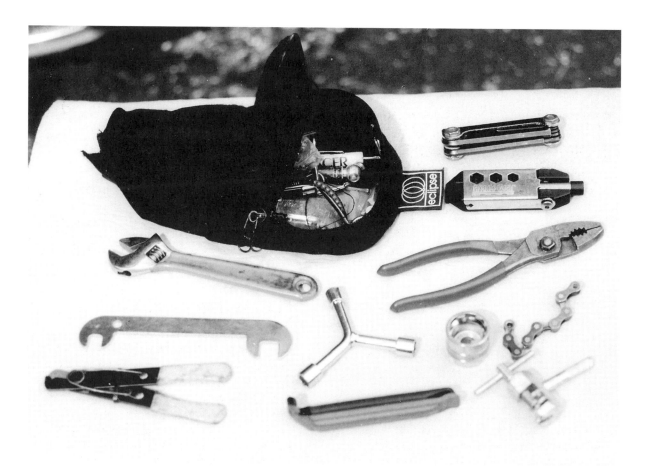

A surprising number of tools for roadside emergencies can fit into a medium-size tool wedge (kit).

Tools for Peace of Mind

Even if your commute is only a couple of miles, you don't want a simple mechanical problem to force you to walk your loaded bike halfway to work when you're wearing dress clothes.

You don't need to know everything about fixing bicycles—just enough not to be stranded by a common mishap. How much is "enough" depends on your commute: If work is a mile away and you pass two bicycle shops en route, you can afford to carry fewer tools and to know less about the bike than if you have a fifteen-mile run each way through forests and fields.

It's also important to distinguish between mechanical failures that will stop you dead in your tracks and those that will simply make riding harder or awkward or delicate. You definitely want to know how to fix a problem that will immobilize you and how to gin up a temporary solution that will at least get you to or from work until you can take the bike to a shop.

There are many excellent guidebooks describing bicycle tools and step-by-step repairs (see Appendix II, "Additional Resources," page 162). Better yet, take a basic bicycle maintenance and repair course offered by a local bike club, YMCA, American Youth Hostels chapter, or adult education center. In about five class hours plus practice, you will learn how to repair a flat tire, adjust a rubbing brake, adjust the front or rear derailleurs to allow the chain to reach all the gears without falling off, jerry-rig a broken spoke until you can reach a shop, and rejoin a broken chain—enough to get yourself to work or to the repair shop.

The best benefit from taking such a course, however, is that you'll feel more confident about relying on your bicycle for basic transportation if you're comfortable knowing that you can get yourself rolling again after a minor breakdown.

This brief section is meant to be only a primer on the necessities for a first-time commuter or a refresher checklist for what an experienced cyclist already knows.

Bare-Bones Tool Kit for the Road

Your biggest priority is to avoid being immobilized mid-commute.

A flat tire—probably the most common mishap—will stop you dead. There is no way you can ride on the metal rim even if you didn't care that you would ruin the rim, tire, and tube; it's hard merely to push a bike with a rear flat while walking alongside it (for a front, you can hoist the bike up onto the rear tire and wheel it upright down the road). The punctured tube must be repaired or replaced before you can continue your commute.

Likewise, a broken chain—a rare mishap (it's happened to me only once in fifteen years of riding)—will also stop you dead. The chain must be rejoined before you can continue riding, unless the rest of your route is completely downhill.

A broken spoke does not need to be replaced on the road, but you must immediately distribute the lost tension among the neighboring spokes to avoid turning the wheel into a metal pretzel.

Therefore, at the least, you should carry tire levers (or a Quick Stick), a patch kit, a frame-mounted air pump, a spare inner tube, a spoke wrench, and—for a long or isolated commute—a chain tool and spare links for the type of chain on your bike.

Tire Levers or Quick Stick

The tires on most road bikes and all mountain and hybrid bikes are called clinchers (also sometimes called wired-on or beaded tires). Although I have seen strong young men use only their bare hands to leverage a clincher's wire bead over the slightly larger edge of the wheel rim, tire levers make the job easier. (Actual instructions for fixing a flat follow in the section "How to Repair a Flat Tire," page 154).

One end of each tire lever is rounded for slipping it between the tire bead and the rim, and the other end is hooked for anchoring the lever to a spoke. They usually come in sets of three.

The lightest tire levers are made of durable, high-impact plastic and can be snapped together for easy storage. Although less common, metal ones also exist, but they are heavier and I find that the angle of the bend of some makes is wrong to allow their hooked end to clip onto a spoke.

A clincher tire also can be removed with a Quick Stick: a notched hard plastic rod with a handle. The Quick Stick does not hook to the spokes; instead, you lever it under the bead and then slide the notch along the edge of the rim until the tire pops off. The Quick Stick requires more hand strength than tire levers and so I find it harder to use, but some people swear by its simplicity.

Patch Kit

The patch kit has the necessary ingredients for patching a puncture in an inner tube. The traditional patch kit is a little hinged box containing a half-dozen black rubber patches (often with tapered, scalloped, red-colored edges) of different sizes and shapes, a square of sandpaper, a small tube of glue,

Patch kits contain materials for glued patches (left) or glueless patches (right); tire levers (bottom) are also helpful.

and some instructions in tiny mouse-sized type. As small as the box is, there is still room for tucking a quarter, a dollar bill, a pencil stub or piece of mechanical pencil lead, and any adapters you might need for Schrader or Presta valves for your pump (assuming you carry the same tool kit on two or more bikes having tires of different types).

There also exist glueless patches; they come in a container the size of a quarter that holds several plastic patches and (depending on the type) perhaps an alcohol wipe. Glueless patches are significantly quicker to apply than traditional patches because there is no glue to dry. They also work for both butyl and latex rubber tubes. I've heard some cyclists complain, however, that they find the inflexible patch does not form as airtight a seal, particularly if the patch must go over the inner tube's raised seam.

Try both and see which type you prefer.

Frame Pump

A frame pump is an air pump designed to attach to a bicycle's frame. Usually the pump is hung below the top tube—about the only place it can fit on a small to medium-sized frame if a second water bottle is on the front of the seat tube. On a bicycle frame large enough to have a couple of inches of clearance between the seat tube and the rear tire, the pump can also be attached behind the seat tube. Pumps have also been designed to be hidden inside the seat tube.

A standard frame pump is about fifteen inches long and pumps air into the tire only with the inward stroke. Mini-pumps are about half that length, and many of those are double stroke: Air is pumped with both the inward and the outward strokes. Although mini-pumps take up less room (they can be put into a fanny pack) and are lighter in weight, they also require more strokes to fill a tire—and more upper-body strength to reach the high pressure required for a thin road tire, which should be inflated to more than 100 psi. (I personally find it hard to reach even 90 psi with a standard frame pump.)

Most frame pumps come with adapters that readily convert them from Presta to Shrader valves.

One annoyance about hanging a frame pump from the top tube is that it is easily hit with your thigh when you dismount at a stop, and it can interfere with shifting if the shift levers are on the down tube. I've had my pump fall off on a downhill run. That stopped when Florida commuter Jim Arth showed me how to wrap a hook-and-loop (Velcro) pant-leg strap around the pump and top tube, giving the strap a half-twist to make the Velcro surfaces meet. End of problem—even if the pump becomes loosened, it remains attached to the bike. Some new frame pumps now come with their own retaining straps.

Some high-end frame pumps come with a pressure gauge, and some even have a folding foothold and handle, so they can be operated like a floor pump for greater leverage. If your commute is long, your upper-body strength not the greatest, and your budget allows, you may appreciate these niceties on the road.

Some people prefer to use a system that relies on carbon dioxide cartridges, because the cartridges are no larger than a set of plastic tire levers. But many inflation systems using carbon dioxide cartridges are one-shot: Once the seal is punctured, all the gas comes out at once. On the one-shot systems, you have no way of experimentally inflating the inner tube to low pressure to make sure the patch is holding or that there are no other leaks. Also, I've heard at least some cyclists complain about some of the cartridge inflation devices ruining Presta valve stems. If you're a real freak for carrying absolutely the minimum weight, experiment with the cartridges first before relying on them.

Spare Inner Tube

Even if you carry a patch kit, it is wise also to carry a spare inner tube. Some leaks cannot be patched—for example, the inch-long rupture from a blowout or the loosening of a defective valve stem (both of which I have suffered). Or you may not want to take the time right then to find a very tiny hole or to wait for glue to dry. Just replace the whole inner tube, and patch the leaky one later at your leisure. Do take the time, however, to examine the tire casing for the cause of the puncture so the new tube is not punctured as well.

Although standard butyl rubber tubes are rated by size, they expand under pressure. Thus, in a pinch, you can use one a size smaller than the rating.

Some cyclists prefer the lighter weight of latex rubber, whose greater elasticity supposedly lessens road shock to hands and saddle. Latex stretches so much that it is also more puncture-resistant than butyl rubber—but it is also more porous, so it does not hold air under pressure quite as long. One company, Air-B, has sought to combine the best of both worlds by offering butylized latex tubes, which are advertised to reduce all types of punctures by a factor of 1 to 10.

Floor pump with gauge is for the shop at home while frame pump (foreground) can be carried on your commute.

153

Chain Tool and Extra Links

A chain tool (also called a rivet extractor), used to disassemble most ³⁄₃₂-inch-wide bicycle chains of derailleur bicycles, has two sets of grooves and a movable rod-shaped punch that is cranked in and out by turning a handle. (The measurement of ³⁄₃₂ inch refers to the thickness of the gear teeth on the bicycle.) It is not common for a bicycle chain to break, but it does happen, and it happened to me once in a very isolated spot. At the time, I was glad that I'd followed the advice of Les Welch, bicycle mechanic instructor at the East Coast Bicycle Academy of Harrisonburg, Virginia, to carry a small chain tool and a few extra chain links.

Extra links usually come along with any new replacement chain for a derailleur bike. New chains are usually one to three inches too long for any given bike to allow leeway for the longest possible chainstays and the most chain-eating combination of gears. Whenever you install a new chain, throw the extra links into your tool wedge (or ask the mechanic to give them to you, if the chain is being installed at a shop).

By the way, get a really good portable chain tool. The metal of some cheapie ones is softer than the chain itself, and I've had the groove walls bend

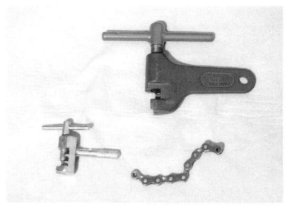

Shop and portable versions of chain rivet extractors are shown with extra links of chain.

and break off after a certain number of uses. Also, the small handle can be really hard to turn, especially if you have arthritis or some other problem with your fingers.

(The ⅛-inch chains for non-derailleur bicycles—most BMX bicycles, one-speed cruisers, and three-speed bicycles—are of a fixed length and are disassembled by pushing open a spring clip of a master link. A chain tool is not needed for normal disassembly. If the chain breaks—an exceptionally rare occurrence—the whole thing must be replaced.)

How to Repair a Flat Tire

Since punctures are so common, I am including detailed instructions for this repair. But this book on bicycle commuting is not intended to be an exhaustive repair manual. For other repairs, you'll find excellent step-by-step instructions in classic maintenance-and-repair reference books (see Appendix II on page 162 for some full citations).

Repairing a flat is easy. Some people have mastered the art so well that they can literally remove a tire, replace the tube, and reinstall the wheel in two minutes—and they don't even seem to be in a hurry. A large number can do it in under five minutes; I have timed them myself. Beginners may take half an hour, but that time will decrease radically

with experience. My time is about fifteen minutes, but only because I don't like being hurried and I am methodical and meticulous by nature. Repairing a puncture takes much longer (because of the glue-drying time) than installing a spare tube. In short, don't be daunted by the length of the instructions below; they thoroughly cover every blessed detail and reason why. Fixing a flat is simple, and everyone should know how, just for peace of mind.

Note: If the brake cables loop up above the handlebars (as most do), do *not* turn the bicycle upside down to rest it on its seat and handlebars to remove the wheels. You may well bend or break the cables or housings near their attachment points, giving yourself even more mechanical headaches.

Anatomy of a Clincher Tire

First, an anatomy lesson is helpful so you'll understand what you'll be doing. A clincher tire itself is U-shaped in cross section for holding the inner tube, with the open sides pointing inward toward the hub. The wheel rim, in turn, is generally U-shaped in cross section with the U pointing outward away from the hub. Embedded in the rubber along each open edge of the tire is a spring-steel wire called a bead, which is slightly smaller in circumference than the edge of the rim. Once the inner tube is pumped up, the tire is held in place inside the rim both by air pressure and by the two nonexpanding wire beads.

Removing the Wheel from the Frame

Flip up the quick-release lever or loosen the nuts on the bolts at the wheel's hub. If your side-pull or center-pull brakes have a quick-release lever, loosen it. Cantilever brakes can be loosened by squeezing the brake pads together and then flipping the loose end of the cable out of its stay.

For the front wheel, lift the bicycle with one hand while grasping the wheel around the tire and rim with the other. Then give the wheel a quick jerk to pull the wheel down out of the drop outs on the front fork. On some later-model bicycles you may also need to release an additional little safety catch at the hub (a "lawyer tab" intended to prevent the wheel from separating from the frame while riding, even if the quick-release is loose).

For the rear wheel, you must also deal with the chain and derailleur. Shift the gears so the chain is on the smallest chainwheel and the smallest rear cog—that is, cross-chaining—to make it as loose as possible. Then, hold up the back end of the bike while jerking the rear wheel down out of the drop outs. Lay the bicycle down on its left side so it does not rest on the derailleur.

Removing the Tire from the Rim

To remove the tire from the metal wheel rim, the inner tube must be completely deflated, which it probably already is after a puncture. If the tire has been mounted on the wheel for a long time, use your fingers and thumb to squeeze the tire together along the bead to break any sticky seal between the rubber and the metal rim.

As you squeeze the tire, examine it carefully to see if you can find the nail, staple, or piece of glass wedged into the rubber—or at least some kind of hole. Also look between the treads for any otherwise invisible slits. If you do find the culprit, remove it and then mark the outside of the tire casing with a pencil lead (you have stashed one in your patch kit, right?).

Wedge the smooth, curved end of the first lever under the tire's wire bead and then clip the hooked end onto a spoke; this will take a bit of force. Slide the curved end of a second tire lever under the raised portion of the bead along the rim as far as it will go (several inches), and then clip it onto another spoke, thereby levering out even more of the bead. Last, push the curved end of the third tire lever even further along the rim under the raised bead—and the tire bead will pop completely out of the rim, exposing the tube.

Alternatively, lever a Quick Stick under the wire bead and slide it along the edge of the rim in one strong motion until the bead pops out of the rim.

Never use a screwdriver to lever a tire from a bicycle wheel; you risk both nicking the rim and further puncturing the tube.

Finding the Puncture

To fix a butyl rubber inner tube with traditional patches, find the puncture. If you've already located the culprit on the tire, you'll need to pull only that section of inner tube from the tire; chances are, the corresponding hole in the tube will probably be large and obvious.

Other times, however, you won't see anything on the outside of the tire. In this case, you'll need to pull the entire tube out of the tire (be careful; it may stick).

Once the tube is free, inflate it and then rotate it axially and move it slowly along its length while holding it close to the sensitive skin of your cheek or lips to try to feel the telltale delicate jet of cool air. Start near the valve so you'll know when you've been once around. If you're patient, this technique will allow you to detect most medium-sized or small punctures.

Mark the a big X over the hole with your pencil lead.

If you absolutely cannot find the puncture and yet it is clear that the tube is not holding air, use your extra inner tube so you needn't bother with fixing the leak immediately (gee, you did bring an extra tube along, didn't you?). Some holes are too tiny to be seen or even detected by the jet of cool air. (Or the flat may have occurred in the rain or the dark, or you simply may be in too much of a hurry to bother with patching the tube right then.)

The way to find an invisible leak is to take the tube home and put it under water in the sink or bathtub; the puncture will make itself immediately obvious with a trail of tiny bubbles.

Patching the Puncture

Once you have located and marked the site of the puncture, use the sandpaper to rough up the surface of the inner tube for a full inch or so around the hole.

Then liberally apply some of the glue over the roughened area. Spread it well beyond the edges of the anticipated patch.

Peel the backing off an appropriate size patch, leaving intact the clear cellophane on the top of the patch. You may also want to apply glue liberally to the underside of the patch (opinions differ about whether or not this step is really necessary; some people swear by it, but I've had good luck not doing it).

Now, wait for five to ten minutes while the glue dries. You'll know it's dry when it is dull instead of shiny and is not wet or tacky to the touch.

Finding the Cause of the Puncture

While the glue is drying, use the time to inspect the inside of the tire casing to locate the cause of the puncture—especially if you did not find the culprit from the initial external examination.

If you don't see anything, then very carefully and with a light pressure, feel along the inside of the tire with your fingers. Be careful! you don't want to cut yourself on a tiny shard of glass. To help with the tactile inspection, put a bit of facial tissue over your fingers—the tissue will snag on the point of a glass sliver or staple.

Usually you will find the cause of the puncture. The few times I haven't have made me feel insecure, and rightfully so. One time I had repeated flats on a mountain bike tire until I found that a *one-inch threshold nail* had wedged itself nearly horizontally through the tread with just the bare tip of the point inside the tire; I had to remove it with pliers.

Especially if the tire is old, examine the sidewalls for holes. You may also find that the tire appears to be slit, as if cut by a razor blade. You can ride on a tire with a hole or slit if you insert a "boot" or internal patch between the tire and the tube; the boot prevents the tube, which is under high internal air pressure, from squeezing through the hole or slit. A boot is readily improvised from a folded dollar bill, a piece of an energy-bar wrapper, a piece of thin plastic cut from the side of a soft-drink bottle (which you may find lying by the side of the road), or even a nylon clothing tag from a shirt. The boot can easily get you to and from work and may carry you many miles until you have the time to buy and install a new tire.

If the puncture had an odd rubbed appearance and was on the *inside* circumference of the tube, it was probably caused by rubbing from the raised head of one of the spoke nipples. Examine the rim of the wheel. All the spoke nipple heads should be almost flush with the surface of the rim and covered by a rim strip. If one spoke-nipple head is not lying flush with the rim or if a spoke is protruding through the nipple head, the puncture will eventually recur.

Rim strips are commonly made of butyl rubber and look like a half-inch-wide giant black rubber band; some, however, are made of cotton fabric that is backed with an adhesive, or of plastic, or a combination of latex rubber and Kevlar. (Serious cyclists seem to like Velox woven cloth tape best for sheer durability; plastic rim strips tend to split and cause the flat that they are supposedly intended to prevent.) The theory behind all rim strips is the same: keeping the tube away from the nipple heads and spoke ends.

If one nipple head or spoke tip has worn through the rim strip, install a new strip—in fact, that's always a nice preventive step, especially if an extra rim strip happens to be included in the box with a new inner tube. Buy the widest tape that covers the floor of the rim without coming up the sides. You may have to widen the rim strips valve-stem hole a bit to get the stem to seat properly.

If the puncture consisted of two holes a quarter of an inch apart that looked like a snakebite, it means that the tube was improperly installed and was caught between the tire's wire bead and the rim wall. We'll guard against another such pinch flat this time around.

Applying the Patch

Back to the repair. When the glue on the tube is dry to the touch, press the patch over the puncture (it is now that you will appreciate your penciled X, because the roughening and the application of the glue will likely have obscured the tiny hole).

Then take the curved edge of a tire lever and rub, rub, rub the patch, burnishing it from center to edge as thoroughly as possible. Rub, rub, rub to remove air bubbles and to make as tight a seal as possible. Rub until the thin cellophane over the patch starts to lift. Then remove the cellophane.

Pump a little air into the tube and hold the patch near your lips or cheek; if you do not feel a tiny jet of air, it is a sign the patch is holding. Then squeeze the tube in several places and wait a few seconds to see whether it continues to hold air or whether it slowly deflates from a second

leak elsewhere in the tube (this does happen).

If the tube seems sound, lightly coat the whole thing with a bit of talc (baby powder works fine) to reduce stickiness between the tube and the inside of the tire casing to minimize pinch flats. Deflate the tube and insert it into the tire, smoothing it out as much as possible. Helpful hint: Place the valve stem of the inner tube through the valve-stem hole in the wheel and then orient the tire so the recommended inflation pressure label on the outside of the tire falls right next to the valve stem for convenient reference.

Reinstalling the Tire onto the Rim

Reinstall the tire onto the rim with just your hands. Hold the wheel horizontally with the valve stem closest to your body at the 6 o'clock position. Keep the valve stem always pointing radially in toward the hub, and start from there so as to exert the least force possible on that delicate device (another nicety: orient the reflector in your spokes on the side diametrically opposite to the valve stem to balance the wheel's weight). Make sure the bead of the tire on the underside of the wheel is completely inside the edge of the rim. Then use the outer edges of your thumbs of both hands to push the tire bead on the upper side of the wheel into the rim, simultaneously working your hands from 6 o'clock up to and past 3 o'clock and 9 o'clock.

You will encounter progressively more resistance as your hands reach the 11 o'clock and 1 o'clock positions. At this point, switch from using your thumbs to using a rolling motion of the heels of your hands. Also, for greater leverage, squat on your heels, using your elbows to hold the wheel steady on your knees and against your abdomen (another effective trick courtesy of the East Coast Bicycle Academy's Les Welch). Between the heels of your hands and the leverage allowed by the squat, exert a last bit of effort and the bead should pop into place inside the rim.

Only if the tire's fit is extremely tight in the rim or if you lack sufficient strength in your hands should you try to use a Quick Stick or the curved end of a tire lever to lever the last bit of bead into the rim; with any tool, there is some risk of puncture or of undoing your installation work so far. Never use a screwdriver.

Inflating the Tire

Now you'll take steps to avoid another pinch flat. Once the tire is completely inside the rim, squeeze it all around its circumference to make sure no bit of the tube is caught between the bead and the rim; also, look down into the rim to make sure you do not see any bit of tube.

Pump the tire up to low pressure, deflate it again, and squeeze the tire all around its circumference yet again. Then pump the tire up to its rated pressure. (If you have no bicycle tire pressure gauge, pump the tire up to a pressure that feels on the hard side of normal—unless you're Superman, it's doubtful you'll overinflate the tire with a frame pump.)

Reinstall the wheel into the frame (Note: You may need to partially deflate the tire to squeeze it between the brake pads if the clearance is narrow). Cinch down the hub quick-releases or bolts. Close the brake quick-release or reinstall the cable on the cantilever brakes. Pack up your tools, and you're on your way.

Helps for Preventing Flat Tires

If you live in an area with many potholes, shards of glass, thorns, or other sharp hazards on your commute—and especially if you and your bike top out at heavier than 200 pounds—you can minimize the incidence of flat tires by installing Kevlar-belted tires, expedition-weight tires, extra-thick inner tubes, latex inner tubes, or a plastic tube protector between the tire casing and the tube (the most well-known brand is Mr. Tuffy). All these measures dramatically reduce the incidence of flats. Hint: Some commuting cyclists report that the plastic flat-prevention strips themselves cause flats by rubbing the tube where the two ends meet; that problem apparently can be solved by smoothing any sharp plastic edges with a file.

Some cyclists recommend such products as Slime or its competitors. Essentially they are antifreeze with fibers or little spheres that you squeeze into an inner tube (only through Shrader valves) that will plug punctures up to $\frac{3}{16}$th of an inch. You can also buy puncture-resistant tubes with Slime already inside. Some cyclists swear *at* these products for making the ride feel more slushy and for making it difficult to repair a high-pressure tube that has "green snot" dripping all over everything. Others, however, swear *by* these products because of the peace of mind of knowing the stuff protects them from being thrown by a front-tire blowout on a high-speed downhill and knowing that the air will bleed out slowly enough that they can reach home, eliminating the urgency for a roadside repair. Experiment and see what works best for you.

How to Repair a Broken Chain

A bicycle chain consists of pairs of parallel plates joined by bushings through which pins are wedged. To disassemble a chain, you want to push the pin out far enough to allow the plates to be slid apart—but not so far as to let the pin fall out altogether, because it's essentially impossible to replace it.

Therefore, experiment on an extra piece of the type of chain that is on your bike to find out how far out is just far enough.

Disassembling the Chain

To remove a broken link, turn the handle of the chain tool to back out the punch (central rod) far enough for a chain link to be slipped into the slot provided for it. Position one link into the slot of the chain tool. Turn the handle clockwise until the tip of the punch is touching the center of the pin in the chain, making sure that both are aligned. Then continue to turn the handle clockwise to start driving the pin out, counting each half-revolution as you turn it. If the pin falls out on, say, the thirteenth half-revolution, then you know you should turn the chain tool's handle only eleven half-revolutions to disassemble that chain—which will also leave just enough (about 1/32 inch) of the pin sticking into the inner plate to help with alignment. Write that number down and put it in your tool wedge.

Try it again on another link the lesser number of revolutions. The pin should stay in the bushing. But when you remove the chain, you should also be able to pull the links apart—leaving the pin in place—by gently squeezing or working the plates back and forth.

Chain links are joined in pairs, alternating inner and outer plates. So replacing an injured or broken link means replacing a complete pair (outer plates cannot be joined to outer plates; they must be joined to inner plates). If the outer plates ruptured, remove the broken half of the outer plates from their inner plates from one end of the chain; then remove the other half of the broken outer plates plus their inner plates from the other end. Then use the chain tool to separate a new pair of links from the extra length of chain you're carrying in your bag.

Reassembling the Chain

Reassembling the chain is the reverse of the disassembly procedure, the object being to drive the protruding pin back into the chain. Ease the plates together; you may feel the inner plate snap into position over the raised edge of the slightly exposed pin. Turn the handle of the chain tool to back out the punch. Slip the chain into the slot of the chain tool with the protruding chain pin pointing toward the punch. Begin turning the handle of the chain tool until the punch touches the center of the chain pin. Now, continue rotating the handle clockwise while counting the half-revolutions until you reach the proper number, then give one-quarter turn more.

Remove the chain from the tool, turn the tool around, and apply one-quarter revolution to push the pin back just a hair. This reversal will keep the inner and outer metal plates from binding and usually loosens any stiffness in the link. Flex the links back and forth by hand to make sure there is no more resistance than in any other link in the chain.

Thread the chain through the derailleur on the bicycle. You may find it convenient to place it on the smallest freewheel cog in the back and the granny gear or smallest chainwheel in the front so it is under the least tension. Rejoin the last link. Add a drop of motor oil or mineral oil to both links for lubrication.

Chains wear in a preferential direction. Therefore, for smoothest shifting, you want to replace the chain so that it is facing the same direction it was before removal. How? Always remove a pin by pushing it *outward* from the bike frame toward you. When putting the chain back onto the bike, turn the chain tool around so that you push the protruding pin *in* toward the bicycle frame away from you. Not only will the chain be reinstalled in the same direction, but you'll also ease the reassembly, which is trickier under tension, by eliminating the awkwardness of wedging both your hand and the chain tool between the chain and the frame.

Working Around a Broken Spoke

A broken spoke, which is less common than a flat tire unless you and your gear weigh 200 pounds or more, is something you can work around if you catch it right away. The problem is, if the spoke snaps when you're traveling at high speed or you simply do not hear the telltale audible "sproing,"

you may not notice anything until your brakes start rubbing erratically; by that time your wheel may already be bent—especially if the broken spoke is in the rear wheel, which bears most of your weight.

Once the wheel is severely bent, the rim may have weakened to the point where you have no choice but to invest in a new wheel. The object of this one-minute work-around is to prevent that from happening while still getting you back onto the road.

At the first suggestion of a semi-musical sound that could be a spoke breaking, stop immediately. Carefully squeeze pairs of spokes as described in the "Two-Minute Bike Check" and visually inspect them to see whether all are intact. If a spoke has snapped in two, either tape the two ends together, or snip off the excess pieces to prevent them from puncturing your tire or falling into your freewheel, or wind the parts of the spokes around neighboring spokes.

Then use a spoke wrench to tighten the nipples of the two adjacent spokes (the nipple is the threaded tube that fits through the rim to accept the threaded end of the spoke) to take up the lost tension. The only trick is to remember that the proper direction for tightening a spoke nipple, when viewed from the hub, is *counterclockwise*—which is, of course, clockwise when viewed from outside the rim. To avoid rounding the delicate edges of the nipples, use a wrench of the proper size: It should fit snugly around the nipple with no play.

Then ride slowly and carefully for the rest of the commute, being especially cautious over bumps and potholes, until you can get the bike to a shop or can replace the spoke yourself—a repair outside the purview of this book.

A Word About Tools for Home

Some bicycle commuters have only a floor pump with a gauge (an air pump that stands on the floor and is pumped vertically—much easier than using a frame pump). And you can get by with that, although you'll either be frequenting your favorite bike shop even for small problems or will be tempted to "get by" until they become bigger and thus more expensive. But, hey, that's how most people today are with their automobiles. Schedule maintenance regularly (say, every 1,000 miles or so unless your bike mechanic advises you differently) and you'll do fine.

Other bicycle commuters have a full shop in their basement or garage, complete with a stand for holding the bicycle at eye level and tools for such high-tech activities as removing bottom brackets and freewheels, repacking hubs, and truing wheels. This is nice if repairing bikes is truly a hobby you love. But it is not necessary, despite what some macho gearheads may imply about "real" he-man prowess.

I fall somewhere in between. I have tools for rehabilitating second-hand bikes already in fairly decent shape and for routine maintenance and repairs, such as tightening headsets, adjusting brakes, and cutting cable housings. Yet despite the fact that I'm a certified bike mechanic, the really high-tech stuff (such as installing new gears or derailleurs or a headset) I leave for a shop. I'm glad I know enough about bicycle mechanics to diagnose and jury-rig a solution to just about any common mechanical mishap on the road, to discuss mechanical problems in an educated way, and to save myself some time and bucks in routine maintenance. Past a certain level of complexity, level of investment for specialized tools, and level of time commitment, however, I prefer to leave my bike's problems in the hands of professional with thousands of hours of experience.

Everyone's choice is different. But let me add that the more you come to know about your bicycle's workings, the more relaxed and adventuresome you will be with your bike—and the more you will appreciate and delight in its extraordinary simplicity and efficiency as a machine. As you learn through classes and books and hands-on experience, your tool kit will grow accordingly and appropriately. And eventually you may arrive at the point where for all practical transportation you reach for the keys to your bike lock first, instead of the keys to your car.

Tailwinds!

THE UNIFORM VEHICLE CODE

The Uniform Vehicle Code (UVC) is a model set of motor vehicle and traffic laws designed and advanced as a national comprehensive guide or standard. Listed below are greatly simplified selected sections from the UVC.* To obtain a complete listing of the bicycle-related portions of the UVC, write to the League of American Bicyclists, 1612 K Street NW, Suite 401, Washington, D.C. 20006.

- Traffic laws apply to persons on bicycles and other human-powered vehicles.
- No bicycle can be used to carry more people at one time than the number for which it is designed or equipped.
- No person riding on a bicycle, coaster, roller skates, sled or toy vehicle can attach the vehicle or himself to any other vehicle on a roadway.
- Anyone operating a bicycle on a roadway at less than the normal speed of traffic must ride as close as practicable to the right-hand curb or edge of the roadway, except:
  a. when overtaking and passing another bicycle or vehicle proceeding in the same direction.
  b. when preparing for a left turn at an intersection or into a private road or driveway.
  c. when reasonably necessary to avoid conditions, such as a sub-standard width lane, that make it unsafe to continue along the right hand curb or edge.
- People riding bicycles on a roadway must not ride more than two abreast except on paths or parts of roadways set aside for the exclusive use of bicycles.
- A person operating a bicycle must keep at least one hand on the handlebars at all times.
- Left turns:
  a. A person riding a bicycle must use the turn in the extreme left-hand lane lawfully available to traffic for that purpose.
  b. Or, a person riding a bicycle must approach the turn as close as practicable to the right curb or

edge of the roadway. After proceeding across the intersection to the far corner, the bicyclist must stop out of the way of traffic. The bicyclist must yield to any traffic and obey all traffic control devices before proceeding in the new direction.

- A right or left turn signal must be given not less than the last 100 feet traveled before turning, and must be given while the bicyclist is stopped waiting to turn.
- A person using a bicycle on a sidewalk or in a crosswalk must yield the right of way to any pedestrian, and must give an audible signal before overtaking and passing any pedestrians.
- Every vehicle on a highway from a half hour after sunset to a half hour before sunrise must emit a white light visible from a distance of at least 500 feet to the front. A red rear reflector must be visible for 600 feet to the rear.
- Every bicycle must be equipped with reflective material to be visible from both sides for 600 feet.
- A person must not drive a bicycle with earplugs in both ears or while wearing a headset covering both ears.
- Every bicycle must be equipped with a brake or brakes which will enable its driver to stop the bicycle within 25 feet from a speed of 10 miles per hour on dry, level, clean pavement.
- A bicycle must not be equipped with any siren or whistle. Bicyclists must not use sirens or whistles.
- If conditions warrant, a uniformed police officer may require the cyclist to stop and submit the bicycle to an inspection.
- When two vehicles approach or enter an intersection from different highways at approximately the same time, the driver of the vehicle on the left must yield the right of way to the vehicle on the right.

*Courtesy of Outdoor Empire Publishing, Inc., Seattle, Washington. Reprinted with permission.

Appendix II

ADDITIONAL RESOURCES FOR BICYCLE COMMUTERS

Bicycle commuting can be completely laid-back and timeless. If you have a twenty-five-year-old ten-speed and no wish to do anything beyond enjoying riding to work, then all you really need is a thorough grounding in sharing the road with traffic. For that, all you need is John Forester's classic work *Effective Cycling* (6th edition, MIT Press, Cambridge, Massachusetts, 1992), which has several detailed chapters devoted to commuting in the context of good, all-around, safe, lawful, and efficient bicycling. Forester's book is the fundamental text for the Effective Cycling instruction program offered by the League of American Bicyclists.

On the other hand, for a gadget-lover, bicycle commuting can be as high-tech as racing. If you're keen to stay current with changes in technology and people's experiences with new developments, consult magazines and resources available electronically: subscribe to one or more Internet listserves (ongoing e-mail discussions among people of similar interest) or point your browser to sites on the World Wide Web to locate a wealth of information on current products and in electronic archives. A good primer giving step-by-step instructions on how to access electronic references for bicyclists is *Cycling in Cyberspace* by Michelle Kienholz and Robert Pawlak (Motorbooks International, Osceola, Wisconsin, 1996).

General References on Bicycle Commuting

If you wish to compare my advice with that of other authors, check out one or more of the references below (some of the older ones you may find only in a library or second-hand book shop).

Urban Bikers' Tricks & Tips: Low-Tech and No-Tech Ways to Find, Ride, and Keep a Bicycle by Dave Glowacz (Wordspace Press, Chicago, 1997) advises commuters on how to "get through traffic, avoid theft, deal with assailants, bring their bikes on buses, trains, and planes, choose a bike and equipment, and dress for cycling." It has many nice illustrations, but some of its tips for riding in traffic are completely contrary to the vehicular principles espoused by John Forester and Effective Cycling training.

Bicycle Commuting Made Easy by the editors of *Bicycling Magazine* (Rodale Press, Emmaus, Pennsylvania, 1992), is based on articles that have been published in *Bicycling* from 1986 to 1991. It has a lot of good tips, but because of its heterogeneous background is a little bit of a hodgepodge and its depth is spotty. It is written in *Bicycling*'s trademark punchy, chatty, somewhat macho style with a lot of first-person anecdotes.

The Bicycle Commuting Book by Rob Van der Plas (Bicycle Books, San Francisco, 1989), despite its name, is largely devoted to effective cycling techniques valid in all uses of the bike. It includes great detail on all the mechanical aspects of a bike. Only Part III "Bike Commuting as a Way of Life" (chapters 12 through 15) address the specific needs of bicycle commuters. It is, however, an excellent book.

The Complete Bicycle Commuter by Hal Zina Bennett (Sierra Club Books, San Francisco, 1982) is comprehensive in its discussion of traffic techniques but is very dated in its discussion of bicycles and accessories and in its limited discussion (five pages total) on what to wear, how to plan a commuting route, and how to park and lock the bike.

See also Encycleopedia, a 148-page color yearbook with an emphasis on cycling as practical transportation, published by the same people who produce Bike Culture Quarterly, called the "National Geographic of the cycling press."

The century-old League of American Bicyclists (called until 1994 the League of American Wheelmen) is a national, nonprofit bicycle-advocacy organization serving the interests of utilitarian (commuting), touring, and club cyclists. It has local chapters for local activists as well as a full-time government-relations advocate, who represents the League's concerns with legislation and other activities to gain for cyclists greater legal rights and safer access to roads. It publishes the magazine Bicycle USA eight times a year for members, including the annual TourFinder and Almanac issues, which also contain sources of maps and other materials relevant to commuters. It also develops and coordinates the Effective Cycling courses. (League of American Bicyclists, 1612 K Street NW, Suite 401, Washington, D.C. 20006, 202-822-1333; fax 202-822-1334; http://www.bikeleague.org.)

The Adventure Cycling Association, whose annual Cyclists' Yellow Pages contains information about riding the interstate highways, can be contacted at P.O. Box 8308, Missoula, MT 59807, 406-721-1776; fax 406-721-8754; http://www.adv-cycling.org.

For ongoing discussions on general questions of interest to bicycle commuters, to which you yourself may post questions or answers, subscribe to the commute-logistics@cycling.org listserve maintained by VeloNet. (Subscription is free. All you need is access to e-mail. Send a message addressed to majordomo@cycling.org. In the body of the message type "SUBSCRIBE COMMUTE-LOGISTICS@CYCLING.ORG" without the quotation marks. That very day, you'll start receiving half a dozen or so e-mail messages a day.)

Bicycles, Components, Apparel, and Accessories

The best way to stay current with advances in equipment is to subscribe to a bicycling magazine.

Bicycling magazine is the biggest newstand publication and has occasional articles relevant to bicycle commuting and many equipment reviews (such as portable bicycles). (Bicycling Magazine, 33 East Minor Street, Emmaus, PA 18098, 610-967-5171.)

The only source of information in the U.S. on commercially available recumbent bicycles is Recumbent Cyclist News. Started in 1990, it is the only publication in the world devoted exclusively to recumbent cycling. Send $5 for a sample issue and information packet. (Recumbent Cyclist News, P.O. Box 58755, Renton, WA 98058-1755, info line: 253-630-7200, office phone/ fax: 253-631-5728; e-mail: DrRecumbnt@aol.com; Web sites: http://diskspace.com/rcn/ and http:www.bikeroute.com/RCN.htm.)

Another source of some information about recumbents is Human Power magazine and HPV News, which actually cover all types of human-powered transportation (including aircraft and watercraft). You can find plenty of good advice on recumbents and tricycles at http://www.ihpva.org. (International Human Powered Vehicle Association, 1308 Broad Street #72, San Luis Obispo, CA 93401.)

If you want to know what other experienced users think of certain bicycles or components before you shell out a major investment, post a query to the VeloNet listserve marketplace@-cycling.org. If you're interested in discussions about electric bicycles, subscribe to the VeloNet listserve power-assist@cycling.org (see the information above in "General References on Bicycle Commuting" for how to subscribe to a listserve).

Bicycling components, apparel, and accessories—including reflective tape and foul-weather gear and some bicycles—may be puchased through a number of reputable mail-order houses, which also have retail stores.

Intermodal Bicycle Commuting

One of the few books to address intermodal access (bicycles on other forms of transportation as part of the commute) is the wonderfully complete and quirky book *Bike Cult: The Ultimate Guide to Human-Powered Vehicles* by David B. Perry (Four Walls Eight Windows, New York & London, 1995), which devotes almost 10 percent of its 570 pages to bicycles as transportation—including bikes on trains, buses, planes, boats, and vans. It also has a lot of historical and political information not available from most sources.

Current information about carrying your bicycle on public transportation can be obtained by subscribing to the VeloNet listserve bikes-n-transit@cycling.org. Information about bicycle commuter centers at transit stations can be obtained by subscribing to the VeloNet listserve bike-station@cycling.org (see the information above in "General References on Bicycle Commuting" for how to subscribe to a listserve).

Foul-Weather and Low-Visibility Commuting

The December 1996 issue of *Bicycle Guide* magazine had a major article on lighting systems, including an evaluation of beam patterns.

Campmor is one of the few mail-order houses from which one can obtain a cyclist's rain poncho or cape. (Note: They run small if you intend to cover a backpack.)

More information about ScotchLite reflective products is on the home page for the 3M Coorporation: http://www.mmm.com/market/safety/scotch/sports.html

Fifty-foot rolls of amber reflective tape are available from American Science & Surplus, 3605 West Howard Street, Skokie, IL 60077, phone: 847-982-0874; fax: 800-934-0722; http://www.sciplus.com/

Pressure-sensitive retroreflective sheeting is also available from barricade or highway sign companies in red, orange, yellow, green, blue, brown, and white. See the Manual of Traffic Signs Web page of Richard C. Moeur (practicing traffic engineer, Phoenix, Arizona) at http://members.aol.com/rxmoeur/sgnsheet.html

The highly informative article "Winter Cycling According to Pete," dated October 9, 1991, by Pete Hickey of the University of Ottawa in Ontario,

Canada, is available through the archives of rec.bicycles newsgroups, as the file called "wintertips." An excellent companion article is "Tips for Enjoying Long Winter Rides," by Pamela Blalock, written in 1994; the file is called "wintertips.pam." Point your browser to http://draco.acs.uci.edu/rbfaq/rbfiles.html

Without Web access, you can download copies of these and other files in the archives via plain old e-mail. To obtain a help file with information on how to use the ftpmail ("ftp" stands for "file transfer protocol") server, send an e-mail message to ftpmail@gatekeeper.dec.com and write the word "help" (without quote marks) in the body of the message. Also, if you want an annotated index of the files in the archives, send a message to ftpmail@gatekeeper.dec.com and write the following in the body of the message:

> connect draco.acs.uci.edu
> chdir pub/rec.bicycles
> get README

For either Hickey's or Blalock's articles, substitute WINTERTIPS or WINTERTIPS.PAM for "README"

Electrically savvy bicycle commuters who may wish to build their own lighting systems more cheaply than the ones commercially available can get lots of hints by subscribing to the VeloNet listserve bikecurrent@cycling.org. Those who don't intend to be stopped by snow and ice can learn a great deal from the winter-commuting experiences offered by the subscribers to the VeloNet listserve icebike@cycling.org (see the information above in "General References on Bicycle Commuting" for how to subscribe to a listserve).

Health and Women's Concerns

To my knowledge, only two books have been published on issues of unique concern to female cyclists. Both are concerned with bicycling in general—racing or touring—rather than commuting.

The Woman Cyclist by Race Across America champion Elaine Mariolle, along with Michael Shermer (Contemporary Books, Chicago, 1988), is 378 pages of information that includes inspiring photos of female cyclists as well as detailed content. Although somewhat outdated (for example, the equipment discussion focuses on a ten-speed bicycle), it has a short chapter on bicycling for transportation and a detailed discussion on the feminine physique.

A Woman's Guide to Cycling by Susan Weaver (Ten Speed Press, Berkeley, California, 1991), a former managing editor of *Bicycling*, focuses its 256 pages primarily on recreational riding, touring, and racing, but it has an entire chapter devoted to cycling while pregnant and another on "other feminine matters" (menstruation and menopause).

Keep On Pedaling: The Complete Guide to Adult Bicycling by Norman Ford (The Countryman Press, Woodstock, Vermont, 1990) is focused on cycling after age 50, primarily for touring and racing. Despite its title, one glaring omission is the major concern of women after age 50—menopause!—and its potential changes in the bones and in the tender tissues in contact with the saddle. However, it does have an entire chapter devoted to knee problems and other common ailments of older cyclists.

Bicycles designed specifically for women—as well as clothing and accessories—can be obtained from Terry Precision Cycling for Women, 1704 Wayneport Road, Macedon, NY 14502, 1-800-289-8379; fax 315-986-2104; http://www.terrybicycles.com

Maintenance and Repairs

There are many excellent books on bicycle maintenance and repairs. There are also a number of classics that are updated every few years as technology changes. Three of them are in large format with superb step-by-step close-up photography guiding you through the anatomy of a bicycle and its repairs:

Richard Ballantine and Richard Grant, *Richards' Ultimate Bicycle Book* (Dorling Kindersley, New York, 1992) is a physically beautiful, four-color glossy book that would be at home as much on a coffee table as on the basement workbench. Only a third of it devoted to maintenance and repair; the rest is on bicycles in general, including city bikes and recumbents.

Bicycling Magazine's Complete Guide to Bicycle Maintenance and Repair (Rodale Press, Emmaus, Pennsylvania, 1994) is the real nitty-gritty, with many helpful photos.

Clarence W. Coles, Harold T. Glenn, and John S. Allen, *Glenn's New Complete Bicycle Manual* (Crown Publishers Inc., New York, 1987). The revision of a work published in 1973 at the height of the bike boom, this book has much of relevance in repairing and maintaining older bicycles. You might obtain it secondhand.

Index